THE
IRON
CAGE

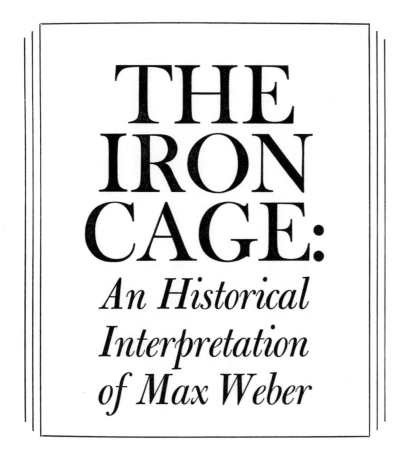

THE IRON CAGE:

An Historical Interpretation of Max Weber

Arthur Mitzman

19  70

Alfred A. Knopf NEW YORK

THIS IS A BORZOI BOOK
PUBLISHED BY ALFRED A. KNOPF, INC.

First Edition
Copyright © 1969 by Arthur Mitzman
All rights reserved under International and Pan-American
Copyright Conventions. Published in the United States
by Alfred A. Knopf, Inc., New York, and simultaneously
in Canada by Random House of Canada Limited,
Toronto. Distributed by Random House, Inc., New York.
Library of Congress Catalog Card Number: 79-79339
Manufactured in the United States of America

PREFACE

It is now almost fifty years after Max Weber's death. Since then it has become indisputable that he is the towering figure in modern sociology, although only a few among his contemporaries fully realized it during his lifetime. Equaled in stature only perhaps by Émile Durkheim, Weber's impact on modern social science is similar to that of Lord Keynes on modern economics. Like the work of Keynes, the work of Weber is a landmark. There is a pre-Weberian and a post-Weberian sociology.

Weber's writings are still in the center of most discussions of the methodology of the social sciences. His contributions to the sociology of religion have continued to bear fruit among scores of investigators trying to unravel the complicated threads that link sacred practices and beliefs to profane and quotidian interests, be they economic or political. Similarly, it is hard to imagine contemporary political sociology without the impetus of Weber's writings. Certain Weberian terms, such as the notion of charisma or of the Protestant Ethic have become part of everyday language. No diagnosis of our times can afford to by-pass Weber's powerful analysis of bureaucratization and rationalization in the course of modern Western history. His pessimistic and despairing vision of the future as an "iron cage" increasingly has come to replace images of the coming of a Golden Age and of the perfectibility of man to which most social thought tended to cling ever since the Enlightenment. The shadow of Weber's work lies over most serious attempts to come to terms with the fundamental issues of our day.

Much has been written on Weber's work. Detailed critical expositions and analyses of his over-all approach and of his specific contributions are now available. But perhaps because of the sense of awe that Max Weber inspires, and because of a displaced sense of diffidence, previous work on Weber in English, and largely also in German, has shied away from close scrutiny of his personality. There has been little attempt to bring together the work and the man, to show the ways in which Weber's cognitive intentions, his choice of problems, were linked with the details of his personal biography. Arthur Mitzman fills this gap brilliantly. Most writers on Weber, even when they have noted his tormented personality, have tended to neglect it when focusing on the development of his ideas. Mitzman shows the intimate relation between Weber's private troubles and the public record of his scholarly contributions. He makes it vividly apparent that Weber's stand on some key issues in historical and sociological evaluation, and in political orientation as well, were rooted in his existential conditioning. Weber's work did not emerge from some antiseptic psychological and social vacuum. It is, as it were, a highly creative response to social and psychological pressures that might have dampened and even extinguished all creativity in a less resilient man.

Mitzman uses the resources of cultural history as well as of psychoanalysis to account for Weber's heroic struggle to rid himself of the incubus of the repressive and authoritarian "cultural superego" of Wilhelmian Germany. This cultural repressiveness was mediated in Weber's case by a father who was, in many respects, the perfect exemplar of the authoritarian and self-satisfied upper middle class which had helped found and sustain Bismarckian and Wilhelmian Germany. Mitzman's attempt to draw parallels between Weber's relations with his domineering father and his attempts to escape from the suffocating structure of German politics is extremely suggestive—even though it may not be fully convincing in all its details.

Mitzman has thrown a new light on the dualistic aspects of Max Weber's thought by pointing in significant detail to his dual identification with the hardness of his free-thinking and authoritarian father and the soft though stern religiosity of his pious mother. Such an interpretation allows one better to understand the contradictions in a man who as an adolescent was sickly, shy, and withdrawn and yet, during his student days, joined a fraternity and became as active in dueling as in drinking bouts. It accounts for the fact that a man who stated that he was "tone deaf" when it came to religious matters spent a major part of his scholarly career in concentrated and passionate investigations of religious orientations. It helps explain why the deeply and passionately political man who was drawn almost by a kind of tropism into the political arena also proclaimed that the scholar's vocation enjoined a strict neutrality in the sphere of values. It makes clear why the committed German nationalist and *Realpolitiker* could refer to the realm of power as the domain of the devil. Above all, it throws light on the fact that this scion of a bourgeois age ceased to believe in its traditional justifying ideologies while remaining unable to propose a positive counterimage.

Max Weber saw himself in a role similar to that of Old Testament prophets, those harbingers of disaster and doom who castigated their contemporaries for the errors of their ways. But, unlike these prophets, he could not bring himself to promise his people a better future were they to change their course. What the future held in stock for Western man, Weber believed, was a new ice age where the supreme mastery of a rationalized and bureaucratized way of life would lead to the "parceling out of the soul." Only occasionally did he allow himself a vague hope that some new charismatic leader, endowed with heroic virtues, might possibly arise to lead his people out of the "cage of the future." This despairing and disenchanted view, as Mitzman documents convincingly, is rooted in Weber's sense of imprisonment in his own family constellation and in the German empire as well. The lucidity of Weber's vision, Mitzman shows, was achieved only at the price of a never-ending battle with demons which assailed him over and over again. He snatched his work from their hands at a high psychic price. This work was the product of continual torments that rent his psyche.

Mr. Mitzman's book will enjoy a privileged position among the interpretations of Max Weber. It is likely to bring forth high praise as well as scholarly dissent, but it cannot be ignored or by-passed. Together with its forthcoming companion volume on Sombart, Michels, and Tönnies, it will provide a perspective on the intellectual history of Bismarckian and Wilhelmian Germany that is as novel as it is exciting. Mitzman's is a new voice in intellectual history. I am sure that I am not mistaken when I say that it will be heard.

Lewis A. Coser
State University of New York
Stony Brook, New York

ACKNOWLEDGMENTS

T HIS BOOK, written between the summers of 1966 and 1968, was begun as an addition to another work, a study of Tönnies, Sombart, and Michels. In size and perspective, the material on Weber outgrew its originally intended, more modest role: with the editorial assistance and encouragement of Ashbel Green, managing editor of Alfred A. Knopf, Inc., it appears here in its own right. In earlier stages, another of Knopf's efficient editors, Ellen Fertig, read, annotated, and encouraged the author's efforts.

The intellectual debts accumulated in the writing of this work are finite but heavy. Eduard Baumgarten has been a priceless source of information on Weber's last decade and gave the entire manuscript his close scrutiny. Else Jaffé, who should by now have caused renewed speculation among philosophers on the immortality of the soul, discussed freely her friendship with Max and Marianne Weber and read carefully the closing chapters on Weber's retreat from Puritanism. Several colleagues at the University of Rochester read and discussed with the author part or all of his work. Hayden White's reading of the first half of the manuscript helped tighten the structure and spared the world of scholarship at least one impossible metaphor. Dr. Otto Thaler gave the benefit of a psychiatrist's wisdom and took the trouble to write an extensive running commentary on the psychological portrait of the early Weber. R. J. Kaufmann brought to the entire work his sympathy, his knowledge and, where necessary, the scalpel of a master stylist. Loren Baritz's critical comments on the chapters he read were most useful.

Finally, it is difficult to conceive of this work attaining its present form without Lewis A. Coser's generous donation of critical intelligence and moral support. He is in no way responsible for the conclusions and general approach of the work; yet by fully engaging himself, by willingly serving as a sounding board for the ideas in it when their formulation was still primitive, he enabled the author to grow in confidence and to challenge much more directly than might otherwise have been the case the accepted images of his subject.

Grants for summer research from the American Philosophical Society, the American Council of Learned Societies, and the University of Rochester significantly lessened the amount of red ink in the author's domestic budget during the years of his labor.

CONTENTS

INTRODUCTION

Max Weber's shadow falls long over the intellectual life of our era. His insistence that a value-free methodology is indispensable to the scientific analysis of society dominates contemporary sociology, often paralyzing the scholar's human commitment and justifying his remoteness and irrelevance. Further, the Weberian vision of modern society as subject to an inexorable rationalization of human activity, and of the modern mind as necessarily disenchanted when it fully comprehends this inexorability, places before us the bleak vistas of universal bureaucratization, the death of art and impulse, the suffocation of instinct. In this last third of the twentieth century, most men of years and wisdom agree that there is bitter truth in these insights.

But it is neither the truth of historical doom nor the truth of science that speaks through Weber's pessimism. Despite disquieting similarities between our world and the "iron cage" in which Weber saw himself trapped, our options are far more open than his, our values more fluid, and our youth determined to wrest control over their fate from impersonal bureaucracies. At the heart of Weber's vision lies only the truth of his epoch, his country and his station, the truth of a bourgeois scholar in Imperial Germany. It was developed under agonizing personal pressures, themselves exerted and maintained by the dilemmas of family, social milieu, and historical position. The broadest ramifications of these dilemmas have been sketched by Talcott Parsons in his essay on "Social Structure and Democracy in Pre-Nazi Germany."[1] They are the dilemmas of a man of passion in a highly repressive family situation and society which, in parallel ways and under the threats of madness and social ostracism, blocked the expression of passion.

Weber's world was dominated by a rigid cultural super-ego,* an overstructured cosmos of values and institutions which appeared to him as a permanent threat to his autonomy and freedom. His lifelong alternatives were either to accept unquestioningly his enslavement to this reified† world or, at

---

* The term "cultural superego" will be used in this work to designate a set of values which is transmitted to individuals in any given social system through the institutions of that system and which inter-acts with the parentally inspired "superego" (as defined by Freud) of these individuals. The term is implied by several branches of post-Freudian theory: the Freudian revisionists (Fromm, Horney, and Sullivan); their opponents, such as Marcuse and Brown; and Erik-sonian ego-psychology. Marcuse's notion of a "performance principle" as the dominant code of industrial society is one example. The concept, however it is phrased, is indispensable to the methodical application of depth psychology to historical and social problems. (Freud's own definition and discussion of the superego, as a psychic device by which children internalize the norms of their parents, appears in *The Ego and the Id, Civilization and Its Discontents,* and other of his later works.)

† The concept of reification, one of the most important legacies of the German intellectual tradition to modern social thought, has been recently discussed by Peter Berger and Stanley Pullberg in "Reifica-tion and the Sociological Critique of Consciousness," *"History and Theory,* 1965, pp. 196–211. They define reification as "the moment in the process of alienation in which the characteristic of thing-hood becomes the standard of objective reality" (p. 200). Though Schiller, Hegel, Marx, Simmel, and others have worked with the idea (if not always the term) of reification, Weber himself etched the concept perhaps most vividly in one of his jeremiads against bureaucracy when he wrote: "A lifeless machine is the materialization of mind. This fact alone gives it the power to force men into its service and to determine so coercively their everyday life in the factory . . . Also a materializa-tion of mind is that living machine which bureaucratic organization represents, with its trained, specialized labor, its delimitation of areas of competence, its regulations and its hierarchically stratified relations of obedience. In union with the dead machine, it is laboring to produce the cage of that bondage of the future to which one day powerless men will be forced to submit like the fellaheen of ancient Egypt. This will certainly be true if a purely technically good (i.e., rational) bureau-cratic administration and welfare system is the ultimate and unique value, which is to decide the way their affairs are run."

whatever the risk of *anomie,* to probe, challenge, and defy it. Through most of his life Weber followed this latter, more dangerous course, thereby defying what he paradoxically (and misleadingly) called the "inescapable destiny of mankind." Indeed, one who knew him well summarized his ethos as a *"metaphysic of human heroism,"* and went on to write:

> Max Weber vowed a struggle unto death against every Institution, State, Church, Party, Trust, School, i.e., against every super-individual structure, of whatever kind, that claimed metaphysical reality or general validity. He loved every man, even a Don Quixote, who sought, against the unjustified claim of an institution, to assert himself and the individual as such. . . . Gradually, such men came to him automatically; indeed, the "last human hero" drew them with positively magical power into his circle. . . . In those days this archetype of all archheretics gathered a whole horde of men around him, whose best features, perhaps without their knowing it, lay in the fact that they were all somehow at least outsiders, if not quite a bit more.[2]

It is, at first glance, odd that one should speak of "magical power" in discussing the principal exponent of cosmic "disenchantment" in Western thought, but the oddity disappears if we recall the interpretation, now over forty years old, of Albert Salomon, who analyzed Weber's historical perspective in terms of a dynamic tension between the opposed revolutionary forces of charisma and rationalization.[3] In terms of this approach, "rationalization," with its accompanying disenchantment of the world, may well be inevitable, but the "emotional life forces" epitomized in the "charismatic hero"[4] are nonetheless pitted against this rationalization in a "struggle unto death."

When we attempt to superimpose Salomon's interpretation on all of Weber's work, basic problems arise. Disenchantment as the result of an irresistible process of rationalization, charismatic heroism as doomed to wage a hopeless struggle against it, indeed, the very methodological theory which purports to allow one to treat these phenomena in an objective mode—all these appear significantly in Weber's work only after 1902, when he was approaching the age of forty. In an earlier period of intense productivity, between 1890 and 1897, these ideas appear, if at all, only in grotesque inversions of their later relationships. The idea of political progress appears not in antagonism to "enchantment" but— to the contrary—dependent on what Weber twice refers to as the "enchantment of freedom" (*"Zauber der Freiheit"*). And far from espousing a value-free methodology, he demands that the work of the political economist serve exclusively the interests of the nation-state.

Between the earlier and later periods yawns an abyss of six years of psychic collapse, a collapse which overwhelming evidence compels us to associate with the all-too-successful conclusion of Weber's prolonged crusade against the authoritarian spirit that dominated his own family: his father. In June 1897, Weber was finally able for the first time openly to defy his father, and he ordered the old man out of his house. He never saw his father alive again. Seven weeks later, the father died, of what *may* have been an ulcerated colon. Unmoved at first, his guilt-ridden son gradually, in the latter months of 1897 and the first half of 1898, fell into a melancholic depression that led to his intermittent institutionalization in the years 1898–1902. Though in 1902 he gradually began to emerge from this collapse, another fifteen years were to pass before Weber could again take on teaching responsibilities.

Part I of this book will argue that Weber's view of the world in the years before 1897 was shaped by his struggle to escape from and finally challenge the dominance in the Weber household of his father, a dominance which he identified subconsciously with the political hegemony of the Junkers over the landworkers in particular and the German people in general. Part II will maintain that his view of the world in the years after 1902 was structured by the lessons he

drew, consciously or otherwise, from the agonizing collapse
which resulted from this struggle.

THE PURPOSE of this inquiry is in no way antiquarian or nar-
rowly pathographical. By showing the connection between
Weber's evolving perception of the world and his personal
fate in the half decade before his breakdown, I intend to illuminate two patterns which concern most historians, political scientists, and sociologists of twentieth-century Europe:
First, the psycho-social conditions in which the ideology of
German imperialism developed around the turn of the century; whatever the "objective" or "material" interests which
underlay the demands for a strong fleet and a place in the
sun, the basis for the acclamation of these demands by in-
fluential publicists and intellectuals may be shown, through
an analysis of Weber's popular appeal for a liberal imperialism in the '90's (and of the propaganda tracts which took up
his line of thought), to have rested ultimately in the suppressed hostilities of sons against fathers. Second, the suffocation of Weber's generation of late-liberals in the institutions
created by its parents. The first pattern will emerge directly
from the narrative of the following chapters. The second requires, I believe, some preliminary speculation to clarify the
direction of my work.

My ultimate interest is in that strange prelude to the
age of world war and totalitarianism, when the heirs of bourgeois liberalism saw the world created by the constitutional
victories of their parents' generation as a prison locked by
Reason and History—a prison to be escaped only by rationally
inexplicable, indeed miraculous, acts of will. This turning
point in the world view of the European liberal intellectuals
has been brought to light in H. Stuart Hughes's work *Consciousness and Society* and has been beautifully captured, for
Viennese society, in Carl Schorske's study of *fin de siècle*
Vienna.[5] Schorske's analysis, however, is applicable in detail
only to Vienna, and Hughes's more comprehensive account of

European thought between 1890 and 1920 only rarely (as, for example, in his magnificent treatment of Sorel) makes the connections between an individual's specific historical milieu, his personality, and his work that intensive research can discover. Morever, in distinguishing the generation of the 1890's from the generation of 1905, Hughes exaggerates the extent to which the earlier, social-scientific focus on individual will as an explanatory device may be opposed to the later, metaphysical glorification of will as ultimate value. For it is arguable that in the work of Weber, precisely during the period after 1905, the two are joined in such a way that the value on the striving, Faustian will is the more basic component. And one can trace to his earlier period as well the voluntarist ethos in his work.

This voluntarism is no doubt comprehensible as a response to the estrangement evoked by an overrationalized, reified world. But to explain, in part at least, why the phenomenon gains sudden power at about the turn of the century, I should like to offer a hypothesis concerning the social, political, and above all, deeply personal plight of the European bourgeois intellectual of Weber's generation.

The bourgeois ascendancy in France, Italy, Germany, and Austria culminated in the establishment of constitutional regimes in the 1860's or early 1870's. The generation of bourgeois publicists and idealists that came to maturity in these decades was the first in European history that could feel it had made a decisive breach into the ancient fortresses of aristocratic reaction. Yet, by its success, it condemned its progeny to a status never before imposed on the sons of the third estate: that of epigones.

I would argue that in the generations before the 1860's it was the archrepressiveness of the Victorian superego that inspired both the economic triumphs of the European bourgeoisie and its demands for social status and political power. As long as the bourgeoisie remained politically unsuccessful, there was a certain equilibrium in this situation: an equilibrium created by the continued deflection of the aggressiveness that was not absorbed by the conquest of nature into the concealed *Ressentiment,* conscious hostility or open struggle against the traditional powers. In other words, there was a rationally defensible political outlet for the psychic bile accumulating in the souls of those energetic Victorians, and because the struggle of bourgeois against aristocrat seemed to make sense, the oedipal hostilities and the struggle for release of the shackled, built-in aggressions of the nineteenth-century bourgeois could be rationalized in the name of Progress and Reason. But when the last generation of rebellious bourgeois achieved success in the 1860's and early '70's their descendants, no less repressed and hostile than themselves, were deprived of those glorious visions of terminal conquest by means of which the earlier generations had sublimated their hostilities. Aggressions masquerading as political passions had formerly been unleashed against the aristocracy. But now the older generation of bourgeois politicians ruled either in place of or alongside the conservative aristocracy: revolt against the generation in power no longer permitted the easy transference of patricidal aggressions to enemies condemned by Reason and History.

Although the same generational dilemma of the late-bourgeois intellectual existed in all the European nations where liberal constitutionalism seemed to emerge victorious in the last third of the nineteenth century, Germany comes as close as any to offering what Weber might have called an ideal type. France is a less clear case, for the prolonged precariousness of the Third Republic and especially—as Hughes points out—the Dreyfus case permitted the spirit of bourgeois radicalism to flourish there until the turn of the century. But the liberal politicians who experienced the unification of Germany were co-opted into a stable power structure that retained more of the authoritarianism and paternalism of the old regime than any of the others I have mentioned (with the possible exception of the Austrian). The internal psychic pressures of the Victorian superego remained, and the harsh goad of the old regime also persisted. But when the conserva-

tive aristocrats allied their power to that of the liberal constitutionalists, the young bourgeois of Weber's generation
could only directly express his hostilities toward the power
structure that oppressed him by a rebelliousness which bor-
dered on patricide.

Of course, alternative channels for filial aggressions were
appearing about this time. Harry Pross has argued that
the gradual emancipation of German women during the last
decades of the nineteenth century from *"Kinder, Küche,
Kirche"* created more opportunity than hitherto for a rebellion of sons, and he explains the antibourgeois German youth
movement on this basis.[6] But Weber was about fifteen years
too old to become directly involved in the youth movement,
though his mother certainly smoldered with the kind of rebelliousness against his father that, according to Pross, precipitated the youth movement, and he became one of the few
older people to whom the youth looked (unsuccessfully) for
leadership in the period around World War I. Weber's alternative to a direct assault on the older generation was nationalism.[7] His nationalism was so permeated with hostility
for his father's generation, however, that it seemed to make
open conflict with his father more possible rather than less.
Indeed, von Krockow characterizes the main components of
German social thought in the decades before World War I
as "a struggle of the bourgeoisie against itself. . . . ideological
class suicide."[8]

Such struggle tends to produce neuroses, but not theories
of progress. If the neuroses are to be avoided, some kind of
Nietzschean "transvaluation of values"—Nietzsche is, of
course, the genuine prototype of the new intellectual hero—
is necessary, whereby the psychological locus of paternal
authority, i.e., the superego and all its ethical manifestations
in the traditional moral code, are deprived of the transcendent
value given them by Victorian society and subordinated to
the creative power of the ego—thus, the *élan vital*, the ethic
of Will. But before the theorists of this age became viscerally
aware of the necessity for this transvaluation, they sometimes

had to proceed through some kind of *Höllenfahrt*, a journey through a most personal hell, precipitated by the attempt to cope with the new problem of authority in the old way and with the old ideological apparatus.

Weber's abortive struggle for personal realization and autonomy—a struggle which he repeatedly viewed in generational terms—was, then, far from unique. In particular, it had much in common with the similar struggles of Werner Sombart and Robert Michels, coeditors with Weber of Imperial Germany's most important journal in the social sciences, the *Archiv für Sozialwissenschaft und Sozialpolitik.* The fathers of all three men had been powerful figures in the creation of the new Germany, had all joined their fortunes to those of the Bismarckian state, and it was precisely this merging of the bourgeois spirit with the spirit of the state that made it impossible for these sons of the German bourgeoisie to maintain their generational hostility in the heretofore traditional manner of bourgeois radicalism: as an attack from rational grounds on the irrationality of state and society.

If, as was clearly the case with Michels and sporadically true of Sombart and Weber, they attempted to project their aggression into the struggle for proletarian liberation, they discovered that the socialist movement, like the liberalism of their parents' generation, was becoming absorbed into the machinery of the bureaucratic and capitalist state.[9] The younger generation of middle-class intellectuals thus found themselves and all the vast stores of aggression that Victorian morality and authoritarian fathers had built into them, bereft of the faculties of rational protest that had for generations been available to the bourgeois not yet ensconced in the mansions of power.

Since the publications and meetings which commemorated the one hundredth anniversary of Weber's birth in 1964, sufficient biographical and autobiographical material has become available to permit a close analysis of the relation between his personal development as a bourgeois "epigone" and his *Weltanschauung.* Through this close analysis, I hope to show: (a) that generational conflict, aggravated both by the special tensions of his family and the suffocating character of bourgeois society in Imperial Germany did, indeed, underlie Weber's scholarly and political perceptions; (b) that his formulation of liberal-imperialist ideology reflects a stage both in his personal evolution and in the psycho-social development of the German bourgeois; and (c) that the "heroic pessimism" of the late Weber was in large measure a result of his shattering conflict with his father, an experience which, once he had recovered from it, permanently shrouded his view of the world. But the main point I would like to suggest is that the course of Weber's generational conflict with his father, though perhaps unique in the harshness of its outcome, reveals in its contours the underlying conflict of younger and older generations in *fin de siècle* Germany and that a similar hopelessness as to any conceivable alteration of the merciless course of rationalization and bureaucratization is the source of a great deal of the estrangement and voluntarist irrationalism of the age.

PART I

The Late-Bourgeois Generation

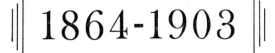

1864-1903

Weber's Family Background and Youth (1864-1886)

W EBER'S PROMETHEAN DEFIANCE of the political and intellectual forces of his day was in many respects an attempt to transcend history: the history of his epoch, of his own experience, but also, in a very real sense, of his ancestors. For the masterful analyst of the relationship between Protestantism and capitalism, and the rebel who was pursued through his mature years by the avenging furies of his own psyche, were welded together by genealogy. On both sides of his family, Weber descended from Protestants who had fled their homelands to escape the wrath of outraged Catholicism; but from refugees in the name of true religion, they had somehow, by the nineteenth century, become capitalist magnates. For their tormented descendant, sorting out the strange relationships between religious rebellion, asceticism, and productivity was to become—after his breakdown—a form of autotherapy, a means of tracking down the elusive demons within him by the techniques of historical scholarship and sociological insight.

On the paternal side, Weber's ancestors had been driven

from Salzburg because of their "evangelical" convictions.*
Karl August Weber, the grandfather, had been a member of
the merchant patriciate in Bielefeld. A linen dealer, he
became for his grandson a model of the early capitalist entrepreneur, still dominated by a traditionalist view of the world.
Marianne Weber said of him, "Making money was neither
an end in itself nor a sign of probity, but stood mainly in
the service of a comfortable, customary way of life. Accord-
ingly, the labor tempo was moderate." This man married
Lucie Wilmans, the daughter of a prominent Bielefeld
physician; she bore four sons: the eldest and youngest of
these were Karl David Weber and Max Weber, respectively,
uncle and father of the author of *Die Protestantische Ethik.*†

Karl David Weber, the eldest brother of Max Weber,
Sr., continued the family linen concern in Bielefeld but
radically transformed the old patriarchal business methods
to meet the competition of modern, machine-made cloth. He
systematically organized the cottage industry of the area by
enticing the peasants from their sandy soil to engage in
permanent rather than casual home weaving, and delivered
yarn to them. He also sought the wholesalers, bringing them
samples rather than waiting for their visits. K. D. Weber's
colleagues had previously avoided such methods, and viewed
his innovations with disgust, until they decided to emulate
him. In his nephew's work on the spirit of capitalism, this
uncle served as a prime example of the modern entrepreneur,[1]
the affirmation of whose creative energies contrasted sharply
with Weber's lifelong condemnation of the eudaemonistic
ethic represented by his own father.

---

* Marianne Weber: *Max Weber, ein Lebensbild* (Heidelberg,
1950), p. 29; this work will be referred to hereafter as *Lebensb.* The
*Handbuch der Geschichte Österreichs und seiner Nachbarländer Böh-
men und Ungarn* (Graz, Wien, Leipzig, 1927), Vol. 1, p. 287, links
the flight of the Salzburg Protestants to an expulsion order of Arch-
bishop Leopold of Firmian in 1731.

† *Deutsches Geschlechterbuch* (10. Hamburger Geschlechterbuch), p. 441. This source also says that Max Sr. was a twin brother
of Ottilie Eleonore Weber.

Max Weber, Sr., was born in 1836, studied law and, about 1860, worked for the city government of Berlin while editing a liberal weekly. Never a democrat, he belonged in the early '6o's to the Constitutionalists, a splinter party that stood for "a strong Hohenzollern monarchy and full recognition of the rights guaranteed the people."[2] He married Helene Fallenstein in 1863 and moved to Erfurt, where he became a magistrate. Max Jr., the first of eight children, was born on April 21, 1864. In 1869, Weber Sr. moved his family to Berlin, where he became first a city councillor and then a member of both the Prussian House of Deputies (1868–97) and the Reichstag (1872–84).[3] In Berlin, Weber Sr. became part of a circle of liberal intellectuals and politicians that included Treitschke and the elder Rickert. He followed Bennigsen's pro-Bismarckian lead in the National Liberal Party and, though he once appeared to be on the left wing of his party,[*] he seems to have developed in his maturity a satisified, comfortable view of life which forbade any political idealism that might require personal sacrifice.[4]

Max Weber, Sr., thus carried into the plane of political life the comfortable, patriarchal bourgeois patterns of his father, except that, unlike his father, he was not his own master. The Prussian state determined what was possible for him, and a certain hedonistic abhorrence of suffering encouraged in him, at least in the eyes of his daughter-in-law, a spineless acquiescence to the status quo.

The sociologist's maternal grandfather, G. F. Fallenstein, was born in 1790 in Thuringia, the son and grandson of schoolteachers. Educated both in natural science and in

---

[*] Max Weber: *Jugendbriefe* (Tübingen, 1936), letter to Herman Baumgarten, July 14, 1885, p. 170. Future references to this work will be designated by the initials *Jb.* followed by the initials of the recipient (Max Weber, Sr.; Helene Weber; Hermann Baumgarten; Emmy Baumgarten; Klara Weber; Alfred Weber; Fritz Baumgarten), the date and the page. Wherever possible, cross-reference will be given to the more easily available selections from the letters in Eduard Baumgarten: *Max Weber, Werk und Person* (Tübingen, 1964), hereafter designated as *Baumg.*

languages, he was in his youth a tutor, secretary, translator, and romantic poet. Inspired by Jahn, he enlisted in the Lützow Freikorps in 1813 to aid in Prussia's liberation from Napoleon. In 1816, when the wars had ended, he took a position as a civil servant in Düsseldorf, where he became the model of a diligent, self-sacrificing bureaucrat. Despite abundant praise from his superiors, he was not advanced, because his democratic beliefs made him an advocate of political equality and a foe of the dominant reaction in Berlin. Only in 1832 did he receive an appropriate position in Koblentz.[5] Shortly before he started work in the new position, his wife died; in 1835 he took as his second wife Emilia Souchay.

Emilia's great-grandfather, Jacques Souchay, though born in Orléans in 1689—i.e., four years after Louis XIV had outlawed French Calvinism by revoking the Edict of Nantes —had emigrated as a young man to Geneva, where his brothers were already settled, and from there had made his way to Hanau, where he settled down as a goldsmith. In the next century his descendants accumulated a great deal of wealth. Emilia, the daughter of a merchant patrician in Frankfurt and a paragon of sorrowing ethical religiosity, became the mother of several daughters, on all of whom she vigorously impressed her religious convictions and one of whom, Helene, in turn did her best to transfer these convictions to her son, Max Weber. Marianne Weber summarizes the moral heritage that Emilia Fallenstein gave to her daughters as follows:

> To all was given a profound emotional existence which made their life both rich and difficult, and a bravery with which they approached their fate fearlessly and calmly. All controlled their lives as much through religious as through vital power. All shaped their daily lives through moral passion and selfless goodness.[6]

By marrying into the Souchay family, Fallenstein ended his financial problems, which had earlier been considerable.

He retired in 1847 to Heidelberg, where he built a large house on the Neckar opposite the castle and became acquainted with a good part of the local professoriat: indeed, he found the historian Gervinus companionable enough to invite him to live in his house and tutor his daughters.[7] Nonetheless, Fallenstein's worldly success brought him little personal happiness. Curiously anticipating the fate of his son-in-law, Max Weber, Sr., he found himself increasingly estranged from his Calvinist wife, in whose eyes his success, based largely on her dowry, must have been less than impressive and whose continuous self-torment over her spiritual imperfection was incomprehensible to him.[8] A man of the world to the end, Fallenstein concerned himself in his last years with the preservation of Napoleonic law, which, despite his lingering hatred for Napoleon, he thought more suitable for the Rhineland than Prussian law and whose arbitrary revocation by the Hohenzollern regime would, he feared, estrange the population from Prussia.

Gervinus, his friend, who was married but childless, continued to live in Fallenstein's house after his death, tutoring his daughters and apparently developing a more than fatherly interest in one of them. When Helene was sixteen years old, she was forced to repel his advances, an experience which left her with a permanent distaste for sensual passion.* Despite his rejection, Gervinus continued to try to dominate Helene's life; soon after his misguided adventure, he tried to marry her off to a student of his. To escape this situation, she fled to her sister Ida in Berlin, recently married to the liberal historian Hermann Baumgarten. It was there that she met and became engaged to Max Weber, Sr., a friend and political colleague of Baumgarten. Two years later, in 1863, they married.[9] Erfurt, where Weber had

---

* Marianne Weber said of her mother-in-law: "the physical side of marriage was no source of joy to her, but a heavy sacrifice and also a *sin,* justified only by the production of children. Thus in the midst of youthful happiness she often yearned for old age as the time of liberation from this 'service.'" *Lebensb.,* p. 36; also, p. 24.

by then been appointed magistrate, was a lifeless city according to Marianne Weber, and at the urging of Ida Baumgarten, Helene spent her time studying the nonconformist theology of Channing and Parker.

As his parents' eldest child Max Weber, Jr., felt throughout his youth and early manhood a strong sense of responsibility for his siblings, who were to include three brothers (among them the sociologist of culture Alfred Weber) and four sisters (two of whom died in childhood).

Unquestionably stimulated by his father's political and intellectual discussions with such men as Bennigsen, Dilthey, Treitschke, Sybel, and Rickert,[10] Max was in addition clearly the possessor of remarkable gifts. Indifferent to his school assignments, he read avidly on his own: Machiavelli at age twelve; soon after, the Greek and Roman classics; then, in the years before university study, Spinoza, Schopenhauer, and Kant. To escape the tedium of the classroom, he gradually read through secretly, at his desk, a forty-volume edition of Goethe. Letters from the fourteen-year-old Max to his older cousin, Fritz Baumgarten, who had attended the university in Berlin, show an extensive and critical knowledge of Homer, Herodotus, Virgil, Cicero, and Livy; the earliest of these letters brought on the (unmerited) rebuke from Fritz that Max had stolen his insights from Mommsen's *History of Rome.**

Tension between Helene Weber and her husband arose early in their marriage and could not have escaped the notice of their eldest son. Even cousin Fritz wrote home to his mother during his 1877 study semester at Berlin: "I understand now why you quarrel so easily with Uncle . . . He has it indeed impermissibly good with his Helene and is a genuine despot."[11] But the trouble, so strangely paralleling the difficul-

---

* *Jb.*, F. B., Sept. 9, 1878 and Oct. 25, 1878, pp. 9–15; *Baumg.*, pp. 6–10. Actually, one of his ideas, in a later letter to Fritz of Dec. 19, 1879 (p. 32), that Homer was naïve while Ossian was sentimental, was almost certainly taken from Schiller's "Essay on Naïve and Sentimental Poetry."

ties of Helene's parents, had begun long before 1877 and arose from the basic incompatibility of the pleasure-loving Berlin politician with his pious wife. From the time of his move to Berlin, in 1869, Marianne writes, Helene found it "increasingly difficult to approach her husband with her own spiritual and religious interests—for they are basically not vital needs for him, and wordly life, office, politics, socialization demand his time." The death of a four-year-old daughter in 1876 crystallized their estrangement. Though Max Sr. at first shared his wife's sorrow, he soon returned to his normal frame of mind and looked on uncomprehendingly at her prolonged and desolate bereavement; "It was . . . his nature to withdraw from prolonged personal suffering, not to permit any long interruption of his enjoyment of life." Helene, as was her custom, refused to make an issue of his coldness, but shared her now doubled grief with her sisters.

> What may long have been evolving now broke through to consciousness: clarity over the fact that the love of her youth is made of quite other spiritual stuff than herself . . . And despite her inclination to modesty and self-deprecation, she applies instinctively unshakeable standards to the emotional life of others, and her husband does not measure up to them—Helene hid behind a veil of renunciation and inner loneliness and thus began a continuing estrangement from her husband.[12]

Compounding this emotional disharmony was Max Weber, Sr.'s, tendency to compensate for the flexibility and compromise imposed on him by the broader political arena by maintaining that patriarchal despotism at home of which cousin Fritz complained to his parents. An enthusiastic supporter of Bismarck in the '70's during the Chancellor's alliance with the National Liberals, he became somewhat critical in the '80's, when the Catholic Center Party replaced the liberals in Bismarck's favor, but would never accept the risks of sharp opposition. "Fundamentally," writes Marianne Weber, "he fends off the recognition of any difficult problematic in life. In his later years, he cultivated an inner indolence, and withdrew from suffering and compassion. His liberal political ideals could not work out, and new ideologies, which might have required some degree of sacrifice, did not inspire him."[13] Domestic authoritarianism was the inversion of this political softness. Marianne writes that he was "too strongly convinced of his own superiority and of his permanent right to prestige and authority" to be much of a companion to his sons, and that "some characteristics, e.g., his way of letting himself be served by his wife, evoke secret criticism in the children, although they follow his example."[14]

These tensions imposed on Weber, as an adolescent, the necessity to choose between his parents, a necessity which was later to be objectified repeatedly in the voluntarism of his doctrine of values, his insistence on strictly personal responsibility for ultimate standards of judgment.[15]

Under the pressure of these competing domestic allegiances Weber's earliest choice did not, however, go to his mother, but to his father. For the father's defects were balanced by a goodnaturedness when not crossed, worldly eminence, and most important, a stimulating intelligence, manifested in lively parlor discourse with political and intellectual friends— which supplied a vital need for the observant boy and which the mother could not offer. Moreover, Helene Weber too had her authoritarian inclinations, especially in her younger years,[16] and her real qualities of understanding, compassion, patience, and deep religiosity had little significance for the youth who, inspired by Machiavelli, found Cicero pusillanimous in dealing with Cataline.[17] Thus, his early choice between his mother's "ethic of conscience" ("*Gesinnungsethik*") and his father's "ethic of success" ("*Erfolgsethik*") was clearly for the latter.[18]

. . .

WEBER LEFT HOME at eighteen to attend the university in Heidelberg, where his mother had grown up and where one of her married sisters was then living. The youth who left Berlin was thin, studious, and, because of his precocity, shy and virtually without companions of his own age. During his three semesters at Heidelberg, he underwent a transformation in both physique and personality. After some initial reluctance, he joined the Alemanni, his father's dueling fraternity, where he learned, beside the art of fencing, that of drinking enormous quantities of beer—which put a permanent end to his willowy boyishness. Indeed, getting away from home seemed to induce a sudden flowering of masculinity in Weber, and if, as Marianne Weber says, the youth identified more with his father than his mother his first semester at the university could only have strengthened this identification. Apart from joining his father's fraternity, he chose as his major field of study his father's profession of law. Weber later said of these years, "The customary posture of decisiveness in fraternity life and as non-commisioned officer undoubtedly had a strong effect on me at that time and did away with the characteristic inner shyness and insecurity of the boyhood years."[19]

This is by no means to suggest that Weber's intellectual growth ceased at Heidelberg. In his first semester, apart from his law courses, he studied political economy with Knies, whose place on the Heidelberg faculty he was to take in 1896, medieval history with Erdmannsdörffer (reading two of Ranke's major works), and the history of philosophy with Kuno Fischer. In Heidelberg, too, he was close to his relatives. Apart from a somewhat misanthropic uncle, the church historian Adolf Hausrath, he became friendly with another of his Baumgarten cousins, Otto, who was then finishing his studies at the university. Together with Otto, he read a wide range of theological and philosophical works from Plato through Schleiermacher, D. F. Strauss, and Lange's *Geschichte des Materialismus.* But the intellectual development had begun long before Weber entered Heidelberg; the physical maturity had not. Certainly his mother recognized the change, when, on his return from Heidelberg, she greeted his bloated, saber-scarred face with a resounding smack.

IN THE FALL OF 1883, after three semesters at Heidelberg, Weber moved to Strassburg to fulfill his year of military service. Probably an important motive for his choice of the Alsatian city was a desire to be close to the Baumgartens, with whom he had become well acquainted through cousins Fritz and Otto. At any rate, by the end of a year of suffering quietly the inanities of Prussian military discipline, which he sporadically escaped by attending Hermann Baumgarten's history seminar, this man and his wife Ida, Helene Weber's sister, had assumed decisive importance in shaping the political and ethical ideas of the young Weber.

Baumgarten had earlier been a liberal friend and comrade of Max Weber, Sr. Unlike the elder Weber, however, he did not acquiesce internally in the evolution of the new Reich. While his nephew Max was still in Heidelberg, Baumgarten had published a withering critique of the work of another old liberal comrade, Heinrich von Treitschke, of whose glorification of the Hohenzollerns he wrote: "One sees the old *sine ira et studio* does not exist for this historian. Impartial love of truth, careful calm research, fairness of judgment, these first and most essential qualities of every historian, which cannot be replaced by a dazzling vocabulary or by dynamic eloquence, are lacking here to an exceptional degree."[20] The young nephew in Heidelberg, who had already registered disapproval of his professors' tendencies to substitute eloquence for objectivity,[21] could not but agree with Baumgarten, but when Weber attempted to defend him before the Heidelberg uncle (Adolf Hausrath), he was sharply attacked.[22] Another sign of family tension over Treitschke is yet more significant: Max Weber, Sr., had praised to his son the same work which Baumgarten was attacking.[23] Indeed, those liberals who by 1883 still retained enough of the spirit of '48 to oppose Treitschke's transfigured image of Prussia were a small minority in Germany, and in his defense of Baumgarten, the young Weber was setting himself against that dominant trend of National Liberal politics with which his father was so comfortably aligned.

Baumgarten had not always been hostile to Prussia, and even now his criticism was directed less toward Prussia's historical role than toward Treitschke's exaggerations and his denigration of South German liberalism. In his youth, Baumgarten, with Treitschke, Sybel, Dahlmann, and others, had striven for the unification of Germany under Prussia, as the liberal alternative to unification under reactionary and authoritarian Austria. The struggle for national unification had given meaning to Baumgarten's generation, and when it was attained, Baumgarten's friend Sybel wrote to him: "How do we deserve God's grace that lets us witness such great and mighty events? And how shall we live after this? . . . Where can I, at my age, find a new goal for my future life?"[24] As Marianne Weber remarks, this lack of any new meaning was to be the tragedy of Baumgarten's generation of liberal bourgeois patriots; for participation in the political leadership of the Reich they had helped to create was forbidden them— only Bismarck, as Chancellor, wielded power, and it was never his intent to share it.[25] Baumgarten, who, unlike his brother-in-law, renounced any further political activity under these conditions, saw with uncommon clarity the consequences of Bismarck's ruthless rejection of parliamentary control: glorification of the Prussian power state, militarism, and the consequent endangering not only of traditional German humanism, but of the political stability of the newly unified nation as well.* Thus, writes Marianne Weber, "The imperiling of his constitutional ideals by the Bismarckian colossus

---

* He was particularly incensed by the Reich's heavy-handedness in dealing with German-speaking Alsace, taken from the French in 1870.

filled him with growing discomfort, and he saw in the unconditionally deifying devotion of the young generation to this genius a dangerous exaggeration, which would take its revenge through the loss of any sense of proportion for other values. 'The legacy of the great man will be a great misery.' "[26] It was out of this accumulating tension that Baumgarten, the representative of a dying German liberalism, released his attack on his former liberal comrade, the historian Treitschke.

It is unlikely that his uncle's attack on Treitschke contained anything startling for Weber. The condemnation of Bismarck was not drastically different from that of his father, who, Weber wrote in 1884, generally agreed with the anti-Bismarckian critique of a French author that "Bismarck tried to destroy all capable and independent forces around him and . . . once gone, will leave behind a chaos, an inextricable human machine for which the driving force is missing."[27] But two things seem to have distinguished the father's attitude from the uncle's. First, the thought of risking his secure position in the center of Berlin political and social life was probably so repugnant to Weber Sr. that he could never, publicly or privately, have assumed the uncomfortable and exposed position taken by his maverick brother-in-law. Bismarck might have his defects, but that did not give one license to attack Germany's most popular historian for failing to notice them. In contrast to Weber Sr.'s pharisaical morality was the posture of the uncle, similar in many ways to the intransigent ethical rage of those Old Testament prophets with whom his nephew was later to identify in his religious sociology; and he thus offered an example of moral heroism completely lacking in the father. But in addition to this, the student perceived clearly the different attitudes of father and uncle to himself. Marianne Weber, whose principal source of information on these matters could only have been her husband, wrote of the father that he "claimed intellectual authority and could not well tolerate deviating opinions from the youth. In conflicts, he always felt himself in the right."[28] Contrariwise, of the uncle: "The communicative but isolated scholar had the need to express himself to the nephew on all political matters *as to a peer,* and shook off onto him his frequent irritation over the political course of the eighties."[29]

The twenty-year-old student, to be sure, did not share the older man's bleak pessimism as to the impossibility of any future positive evolution in German politics. But he certainly agreed with the sharp condemnation of Bismarck's policies, a condemnation which he had already heard (in private) from his father.[30] And he could not fail to be attracted both by Baumgarten's moral stature and by the Strassburg scholar's confidence in him as an equal partner in discussion. As the *Jugendbriefe* eloquently testify, Weber repaid this confidence by making his uncle the primary confidant of his own political views from the time of his departure from Strassburg in 1884 to Baumgarten's death on June 19, 1893.[31]

At least as important an influence on Weber's development at this time was Baumgarten's wife Ida, Helene Weber's sister. For it was through this woman, his aunt, that Max Weber came to understand his mother's values and to sympathize more keenly with her subjection to his father.

The fundamental difference between the two sisters seems to have been one of forcefulness. Ida was generally successful in imprinting her personality on her household; Helene was not.* Of course, Ida too became aware of the gulf separating her own religious ethics from the political standards of her husband. But Ida's toughness, her refusal to permit herself to be overawed and silenced by her husband, gave her a significantly greater moral authority in her family, particularly over her son Otto. Thus, there was a note of spiritual exaltation in the atmosphere of the Baumgarten home that distinguished it sharply from the Weber house-

---

* "The soul of the Baumgarten house was Ida . . ."; *Lebensb.,* p. 95. Contrariwise, "Helene was much softer than her sister, and her husband's nature was imposed more strongly than that of Baumgarten"; *Lebensb.,* p. 96.

hold in Charlottenburg. Using the Sermon on the Mount continually as an uncompromising standard, Baumgarten's wife found the academic world "socially loveless, arrogant and selfish, moreover in a human sense often miserably small; burdened with vanity and envy."[32] Her persistent efforts to live according to the Gospel in a world so heavy with sin, her sorrowful sense of Christian social responsibility, led her to frequent gifts to the needy. Ida's expensive conscience pained her husband—indeed, one act of charity led to the loss of a daughter, when she took into her house a girl whose sibling had scarlet fever[33]—but, out of love and respect for her values, he rarely interfered.

In this atmosphere of Christian sacrifice and social responsibility, which his mother considered unquestionably superior to that of her own home, Weber at first felt completely estranged. Marianne writes: "He shared his father's view that it was 'eccentric' to want to put every act under an ethical law and to judge by absolutes, and rejected a burden which had no room for smiling tolerance of one's own weakness, which with its 'all or nothing' seemed to do violence to human nature. This 'overtension' was for him inimical to every naïve happiness, which he still at that time demanded of life."[34] Despite this opposition, which he never concealed and which never completely disappeared, Weber found in Strassburg an amiable tolerance for his differences which must have been refreshing when compared with the authoritarian responses of his father. Less than a year after his arrival, the Baumgartens were taking him into their closest confidence over the questionable marriage of Otto to a sickly cousin several years his senior. At this time, Weber wrote to his mother, "My visits in the Baumgartens' house become really ever more pleasant and valuable for me. Particularly since great confidence is shown me from all sides, above all by the uncle, who spoke to me recently, almost to my surprise, exhaustively about Emily and the marriage of his son and their whole history. . . . It was a great sign of confidence on Uncle's side, a real honor to me, that he spoke to me at all

about the matter.* Of yet greater significance at this time
was his sudden fondness for William Ellery Channing—the
favorite theologian of his mother and his Aunt Ida. The aunt
had lent him a volume of Channing during a bout of illness
in his period of army service, and in the same letter which
expressed his joy in his uncle's confidence, he also tells of
his serious interest in the Anglo-American theologian: "For
as many years as I can remember, it is the first time that
something religious has won a more than objective interest
for me." Though he finds Channing's theoretical basis naïve,
"the practical results which he draws from it are in part so
directly illuminating, and the clear and quiet idealism which
he draws from his observation 'of the infinite worth of the
individual human soul' is so understandable to all, even
those distant from his views, that there can be no doubt
of the universality of the conception and of its foundation in
real needs of man's spiritual life."[35]

The lifelong influence on Weber of parts of Channing's
moral philosophy becomes clear in the light of Marianne
Weber's description of that doctrine:

> We grasp God not in ecstatic emotionalism, but in the
> fulfillment of clear and simple duties: "The sacrifice
> of a desire to the will of God is more important than
> all raptures." Highest good is the moral energy of a
> holy resolve, spiritual† freedom. Its essence is: to be
> master over the senses, to be master over the material,
> to be master over fate, over all fear, over custom, in-
> dependent of every authority: "I call that soul free
> which vigilantly protects its own freedom and inde-
> pendence, which defends itself against submersion in
> others, which is dissatisfied with an inherited or passive
> belief, which accepts every new truth as an angel from
> heaven, which holds power over itself to be more

---

* *Jb.*, H.W., July 8, 1884, pp. 121–2; also *Baumg.*, pp. 30–1. The
uncle was, of course, bitterly opposed to the marriage; his wife and
most of the children were for it. The girl died a year after the wedding.

† In German, *geistige*, which means "intellectual" as well.

important than power over the whole world, which, transcending the limits of time and death, hopes for everlasting progress, and which finds in the prospect of immortality an inexhaustible force for its action and suffering."[36]

In his work on the Protestant ethic and the spirit of capitalism, Weber himself showed us how to derive from a religious statement like this its significance for wordly activities. If we wish to use the same technique on Channing, asking only in this case what sort of political, rather than economic, spirit would develop from such a philosophy, all we need do is substitute *Staatsraison* where Marianne Weber or Channing wrote "God" or described some divine attribute or consequence. The result is a political philosophy which argues that true moral and intellectual freedom arises not from the unleashing of instincts and certainly not from blind acceptance of custom, but exclusively from rational control over one's instincts, the sacrifice of hedonistic or selfish desires to the interests of the commonweal. Indeed, only through such rational self-control and such renunciation can the individual ever come to grasp the genuine needs and interests of the polity.

This value model, as will be evident below, runs like a red thread through all of Weber's political sociology. Accompanying it is another view found in Channing, that, rather than the individual existing merely for the good of the state, "the goal of state and social institutions is the unfolding and protection of God-like humanity."[37]

Now none of this can have been new for Weber, who had read enough philosophy to know that, taken out of its naïve theological framework and placed in the context of German idealism, what he was dealing with in Channing was a version of the Kantian ethic. Furthermore, rejecting as he did the Sermon on the Mount as a unique guide to personal behavior, he vehemently denounced Channing's pacifism when he read some more of the minister's work the following year and perceived clearly the conflict between basic Christian values and the demands of the modern state.[38] But despite his familiarity with Kant and despite his rejection of those aspects of Channing's moral philosophy which directly conflicted with political realities, the young Weber must have been impressed by the fact that his aunt was not content merely to preach Channing's ethic of rational responsibility, but actually lived it. Indeed, Marianne Weber points out that it was his aunt's influence that made him conscious of the necessity to choose between his parental models—and to make this choice not on emotional grounds but only through a moral decision.[39] And after Ida Baumgarten's death, he clearly acknowledged her influence and her importance in changing his attitude towards his parents in a letter to her daughter:

> If I say that your mother was a second mother to me, then you know, dearest friend, more than anyone else, how profoundly true that is. I am altogether incapable of subtracting from my life the inextinguishably deep impressions and moral influences on the formation of my personality, which I received in your house with all their after effects, without seeing all that is dear and elevated in my life begin to shake. That there are other things and tasks than just the fulfillment of duty in a man's external profession I first learned to dimly perceive under the impact of your mother's personality, and only later fully grasped it when my eyes opened up in my own family circle.[40]

If Weber was later convinced, according to his wife, that he bore within him the opposing dispositions of, on the one hand, "becoming a robustly egotistical, essentially amoral hedonist who by intellectual superiority could have . . . ruthlessly subjected others to his ends" and, on the other hand, "someone who early set his mind to rest and found satisfaction in a securely comfortable position—e.g., judge in a small city"[41]—he could only have been extrapolating the opposed potentialities offered him by the example of his father and his father's political friends. That he was able to transcend these extremes, to view them both as unworthy, and to juxtapose to them an energetic moral heroism is due as much to his belated understanding of his mother—mediated through Ida Baumgarten—as to the model of Jeremian prophecy offered by his uncle.

But the abandonment of these unworthy alternatives by no means freed Weber from the tension of inner ethical conflict, for that elusive synthesis of Christianity with a practical worldly ethic that he had early criticized Channing for not finding[42] proved nonexistent after all. Throughout his life Weber was to be haunted by another Either/Or, which was superimposed on the first. With ruthless logic he drew as the ultimate radical consequence of Channing's ethic—and his aunt's and mother's—the Tolstoian refusal, based on the Gospel of Brotherhood, of all cooperation with evil. He never lost his respect for this position and accepted it as an ultimate value for personal life; but the man who read as a boy and never forgot Machiavelli's praise for those Florentines who risked their immortal souls for the salvation of their city also never ceased to maintain against the Tolstoian ethic "the worldly values . . . the active hero-ethic; the service for impersonal cultural possessions which elevate life in this world."[43] It bears repeating, though, that in juxtaposing these value systems, Weber was no longer simply trying to choose between his mother and father as models. His father's qualities were summarized in the unworthy alternatives he fought against: aggressive versus passive hedonism. Instead, just as Ida Baumgarten became a "second mother," her husband, with his lonely, embittered denunciations of the Establishment, must have become a second father, a most important one as far as Weber's values are concerned. Through the Baumgartens then, Weber came to a profound, if belated, appreciation of his mother, and a tendency to dismiss his father from serious consideration as a moral example. Concomitantly, he came to resent with increasing bitterness his father's rigidly authoritarian treatment of his mother. Only after a decade of rising tension did he unleash his hatred for his father's domestic tyranny, and when he finally did the results were catastrophic.

During this decade, from the mid-'80's to the mid-'90's, Weber's life came to be increasingly dominated by this tense synthesis—always in danger of polarization—of the moral example of his uncle on the one hand, and of his mother and her sister on the other. The strain created by this moral legacy must have been enormous. Marianne Weber tells us, for example, in her oblique Victorian way, that his mother's influence kept Max Weber chaste in his Strassburg student days:

> Yes, the young student had surrendered to the rude exuberance of student life, drunk much, spent far more money than was necessary or expected by the parents, and he had had companions in Strassburg who satisfied their sensuality in crude, irresponsible and heartless forms. But the mother could be thankful. Without a word—for in those days, one left deeply hidden the dark underground of existence and its threatening problematic—only by the holy purity of her conduct, she had implanted indestructible barriers in him against any surrender to the instinctual. He resisted the others' example: better that his spirit should be increasingly tormented by the demonic temptations of a robust physicality than pay toll to natural necessity.*

This absolute rejection of any surrender of rational control to instinct (found, as shown above, in Channing and Ida Baumgarten as well as his mother) was later to be objectified in Weber's scorn for any social theory which justified instinctual or irrational social behavior of any sort. But during his years as a student this sexual repression was compounded by his intense and exclusive family relationships.

---

* *Lebensb.*, p. 107. Weber made explicit his belated appreciation of his mother's moral example in a letter to her of May 3–7, 1884. *Jb.*, pp. 114–15; *Baumg.*, pp. 27–8; *Lebensb.*, pp. 106–7.

For Weber was in his Strassburg days so closely tied to the Baumgartens that there was never any inclination or need to satisfy his desires for intimate companionship outside of the family, and this closeness excluded any non-familial female companionship as well. Thus his first love was the Baumgarten's daughter Emmy, a first cousin. This relationship, burdened simultaneously by Weber's repressions, by the frail state of Emmy's mental and physical health, and perhaps by lingering taboos on endogamy, lasted from 1886 to 1892. During this time their communication was largely by post, as the warm, bright, lengthy, but pre-eminently cousinly letters in the *Jugendbriefe* show. On one of the few occasions when they met (in somewhat melodramatic circumstances: Ida had sent her daughter to live with a brother to keep her away from Max): "They feel one another's love, but no word is spoken, no gesture breaks through the chaste distance, only on leaving do the young man's eyes dampen for a moment. Otherwise, everything remains concealed; even the suspecting mothers are silent."[44] After six years, filled with painful doubts and guilt feelings, Weber ended the relationship to permit his engagement to Marianne Schnitger, the daughter of yet another cousin, on his father's side, the granddaughter of his father's capitalist elder brother, Karl August Weber.

In the fall of 1884, after a year in Strassburg, Weber returned to his parents' home in Charlottenburg to spend his fourth and fifth semesters at the University of Berlin.* The return was made at his parents' request, and both their desire to control his apparently unexpected high spending and his father's wish to remove him from the influence of his brother-in-law's family seem to have motivated their decision.

But removal from Strassburg could not erase Max's experience there. The young man who came back to Charlottenburg needed no motherly slaps to warn him against

---

* *Lebensb.*, p. 110. Charlottenburg is a suburb of Berlin.

his evil ways; he had benefited enormously from the mother's standpoint, both through being opened up to her social-religious views by her sister and in the more general sense of having grown in personal understanding through his sympathetic immersion in the problems of the Baumgarten family. From this point on, Weber maintained a respect and sympathy for his mother's convictions which led him into one of his first political experiences in the *Evangelisch-Soziale Verein* (Protestant Social Union) and to close friendships with the Protestant social reformers Paul Göhre and Friedrich Naumann.

It was during this year in Berlin that Weber personally encountered, and found repellent, Treitschke's academic demagoguery. Treitschke, the friend of his father and ex-friend of his uncle, henceforth became an important foil through which Weber translated intimate passions and ambivalences into scientific objectivity and balanced historical judgment. It is, of course, widely known that throughout Weber's later life Treitschke, his own teacher and a friend of his father's, was to remain the prime example of a breed he detested: the professorial agitator—the only alternative to which was the value-free social scientist. What is less common knowledge is that Weber showed a marked ambivalence about the source of this demagoguery, that the same ambivalence appears in his youthful analysis of Bismarck, and that he was probably projecting onto both of these eminences his confused feelings about his own father.

Thus, in a letter to Hermann Baumgarten of 1887, he wrote of an attractive idealism buried in Treitschke's poetry, the eclipse of which by the historian's glorification of *Realpolitik* was as much due to the crudely chauvinistic immaturity of his student admirers, which he had inflamed but not created, as to the nature of the man.[45] And Weber saw the excesses of Bismarck in the same light as those of Treitschke:

> If the nation knew how to treat and value [Bismarck] properly, supporting him at the right time and giving

him its trust where he deserved it—or rather, if they
had earlier understood this, for now it is too late—
then the variously devastating effects of his personal
politics could not have assumed these dimensions. And
if among people of my age, worship of military and
other forms of ruthlessness, the culture of so-called
"realism," and the philistine mistrust of any efforts
which hope to achieve their goal without appealing
to the bad side of men . . . if all these were not already
the mode, then the innumerable and often crude
biases, the passion of the struggle against other opinions and the preference, evoked by the powerful
impact of success, for what one today calls *Realpolitik*,
would not be the only things they would take from
Treitschke's lectures. They would reserve their opinion
on them or see them as unhappy deformities, and
instead perceive under and in part precisely *in* these
extravagances of political passion and one-sidedness
the great and passionate striving of the man for ideal
foundations and take some of that home with them.
But now of course the result is only that serious, conscientious work concerned only with the truth is held
in low esteem, and a loutish sense of satisfaction which
often becomes unbearable here in conversations, and
an uncommon crudeness of judgment against all non-
opportunistic views, is becoming widespread.[46]

The ambivalence in these letters has a curious ring to
anyone familiar with Weber's letters on family matters, for it
echoes, if only in part, his attitude toward the strong man in
his own family: his father.[47]

In June 1885, Weber replied to a letter from his mother
which apparently discussed the sad fate of a family well
known to both mother and son, where the husband had become accustomed to unrestrained tyranny over his wife.
According to Marianne Weber, her husband's letter on the
subject may have been an attempt "to say something to
Helene between the lines that filial piety did not otherwise
permit him to express." In Max Weber's judgment on this

unhappy couple, their relationship so terribly similar to that of his parents, he approximated closely his diagnosis of the relationship between Treitschke and Bismarck and their servile publics: powerful men need open and conscientious resistance to curb their tyrannical inclinations. In the case of Mr. and Mrs. X, Weber saw the wife's practice of secret opposition to her husband's wishes as only embittering him, since he knew perfectly well what was happening. But,

> perhaps an openly independent behavior would make him somehow aware that he is attempting to suppress a conscious right, that of free thought and speech, indeed of freedom of the personality. Perhaps he would, despite it all, get the idea that there are not all kinds of cliquish and concealed machinations and conspiracies being directed against him, as he imagines in his misanthropy, but the simple consciousness of personal rights. Perhaps, through this dim recognition, his self-certainty and his deeply held conviction of the meanness of the whole world would be somewhat shaken.[48]

The man who did stand up to Treitschke—and, by subconscious transference, to Weber's own father—was, of course, his uncle Hermann. And, as I have suggested above, this example of political heroism took its place in Weber's fragile pantheon of virtues next to the social ethic of his mother and aunt. But it is clear from the ambivalence of the letters cited above that Weber did not fully share his uncle's embittered negativity and that he believed that, with the proper kind of responsible opposition, the imperial ideal embodied in the credos of Bismarck and Treitschke was also a value to be striven for.

Thus, until his violent personal upheaval of 1897, Weber's activity centered around the many-faceted struggle in his private and public life for the preservation of some harmony between these three ultimately incompatible ethics: political responsibility, Christian social conscience, and power. He became active in the *Evangelisch-Soziale Verein,* a Protestant effort to implement the Christian social ethic among the victims and overseers of German capitalism; but he was brought to its meetings by his mother, and it was her ethic that inspired him and kept him there. He worked furiously for the *Verein für Sozialpolitik* (Union for Social Policy), churning out thick studies of the agrarian problem in East Prussia for an organization dominated by men of his father's generation. And while he wrote them he was living in his father's house without an income of his own, choking back his anger at Max Sr.'s treatment of Helene. In 1894, the son left his father's city and his father's profession of law to teach political economy in Freiburg. His inaugural lecture the following year was a magnificent synthesis of all three ethics: responsibility, Christian conscience, and power. But it was explicitly based on the need to overcome his pathetic sense of generational inferiority (*"Epigonentum"*) to his father's age. And when, two years later, Weber, by then living again in his mother's childhood city of Heidelberg, finally released his volcanic hatred for his father's tyranny over Helene Weber, the consequences of this lapse into a pure act of conscience were to leave him incapable of any work for five years and to force him to abandon the classroom for two decades. But all this can only be made clear through an examination of certain aspects of Weber's life, both private and public, in the years before his breakdown.

In the Father's House (1886-1892)

Every free spirit would be set thinking,
provided he had ever stopped thinking,
just as it once happened to Buddha:
"Close and oppressive is life in a house,
a place of impurity; to leave the house is freedom"
and, thus meditating, he left the house.

NIETZSCHE, Genealogy of Morals,
Third Essay, VII

IN HER BIOGRAPHY of her husband, Marianne Weber tells us that the death of a younger sister when Max Weber was a boy resulted in an estrangement between his parents, based on his father's inability to share his wife's prolonged grief, that was to continue and grow until the father's death. We cannot know if the son was aware of this estrangement at the time or, if so, how it affected his attitudes toward his parents or whether it influenced his later hostility to his father. But there was apparently another, similar incident of parental estrangement in Weber's childhood of which he could hardly have been completely unaware, since he was himself the cause of it. At the age of two years, he was afflicted with meningitis, a disease which can lead to imbecility or death. As a result, according to autobiographical notes written by his mother, Max remained sickly for the next five to seven years, and his mother's worrying over him in this period angered his father because it threatened his "fundamental optimism and boasting of his joy in life."*

Now there is an excellent chance that even if Weber forgot the emotional strains of this period, his mother reminded him of them during the period of her and Max Sr.'s intensified antagonism, for in 1918 Max Weber wrote, in an explanatory letter to his siblings which accompanied the notes, that "At the time of these difficult conflicts, 1885–1897, Mama herself was unable to speak of them, *except to the children who were already completely grown, who had experienced it.*"[1] As the eldest son, then, and as one who was already inclined toward the mother's side, it is quite likely that Max heard more than once the story of his father's infamous indifference toward his childhood "sickliness," of his father's resentment at his mother's ministrations.†

---

* Eduard Baumgarten's paraphrase; *Baumg.*, p. 629. Baumgarten offers only two very brief direct quotes from the notes, but reproduces all or most of a letter Weber sent to his younger brothers and sisters accompanying the notes, in 1918, which explains some references in them that apparently needed elaboration. Apparently the notes were written somewhat earlier (but well after the death of Weber's father in 1897) to explain the mother's antagonism to her husband in detail to her oldest son and daughter (Max and Klara); and, by 1918, Max decided they should be seen by his other siblings as well. Marianne Weber describes her husband's childhood illness on pp. 38–9 of the *Lebensbild*.

† Meningitis is a disease which lasts a few weeks and ends in either imbecility or death, or recovery, but not in five to seven years of sickliness. It is not unusual, however, for young mothers of a first male child, excluded from any practical concerns (as was Helene Weber in Erfurt), to invent just such a plausible pretext as the prolonged convalescence of a delicate child as an excuse for overprotectiveness; furthermore, it would be eminently reasonable for a woman with as vast a loathing for carnal intercourse as Helene Weber is said to have had to wear her sorrow as a protective talisman against her husband's physical needs. One wonders if this, rather than, as in Helene's version, her husband's refusal to take life seriously and join in her concern for

In any case, Weber's wife depicts him as having been frequently bitter and upset, during the years following his successful passing of his law examination at Göttingen in 1886, because of his prolonged dependence on his father's pocketbook and hospitality.

It may be useful to summarize briefly the more external facts of Weber's life in these years as a scaffolding on which to situate his emotional difficulties. During his four years as a junior barrister (1887–91)[2] and his two years of work on his doctoral thesis (1887–9), Weber had virtually no income of his own, and his only major departures from his parents' house in Berlin-Charlottenburg were his second and third tours of duty as a reserve officer, once in early 1887 in Strassburg, then in 1888 in Posen.* In 1890 he applied to the city of Bremen for the position of legal adviser that Werner Sombart had previously held, only to be turned down in favor of a local man.[3] In 1892, he took over the lectures of Goldschmidt, his ailing thesis adviser at the University of Berlin, and represented an attorney at a Berlin court. A year later his future began to take shape: he almost received a position at Freiburg and, after some unpleasant dickering with Althoff, the Prussian Minister of Education, he did obtain a temporary post in Berlin. In the

---

her son, may not have been the real cause of their estrangement. One also wonders about Helene's prolonged grief in these early years over the death of two small daughters, the other cause of initial estrangement between her husband and herself. Could this too have been interpreted by Max Weber, Sr., as an excuse to avoid intercourse? Or, if Helene's grief was real, could it have been so prolonged because she was accusing herself of neglecting the daughters to care for the more delicate son. And could her husband also have been silently accusing her of such neglect in his coldness toward her mourning?

* Marianne Weber writes that after passing his law exam in May 1886, "Weber returned to his parents' house and lived there, since he was not yet earning any money, seven years, until his marriage." But he probably received some compensation for his teaching at the University of Berlin in 1892–3 and for his work as *Assessor* (magistrate's assistant) in these years.

same year he married a first cousin once removed—the granddaughter of his father's brother—and in the spring of 1894, after renewed negotiations, the Freiburg faculty finally offered him a most desirable *Ordinariat* (full professorship) in *Nationaloekonomie*. He accepted, and moved there in the fall of the same year.

Weber's appointment at Freiburg was the result of his extraordinary productivity. He "promovierte" *magna cum laude* in 1889 with a doctoral thesis on the history of medieval trading associations[4] and "habilitierte" (the postdoctoral step necessary for a university teaching position) in 1891 with a study of agriculture in Roman antiquity. In 1888 he joined the *Verein für Sozialpolitik* and in 1890 took part in the founding meeting of the *Evangelisch-soziale Verein;* in the latter year, he took charge of a study of the situation of East Elbian land workers for the *Verein für Sozialpolitik* and shortly thereafter (1892) supervised a similar study, based on questionnaires sent to ministers in farming areas, for the *Evangelisch-soziale Verein*. A flood of scholarly studies was the issue of these inquiries. The study of East Elbian agriculture alone was 891 pages long; it was written in about a year, during which Weber was also teaching and holding down a full-time job as a junior barrister.[5] Of his thirteen collaborators in the *Verein*'s study of German rural workers none wrote even half as much as he did! His closest competitor for the title of "Hercules of Scholarship" was a man who filled 399 pages: Dr. Kuno Frankenstein.

In these years, however, the real significance, both of Weber's massive body of work and his intense political activity, will appear only in the context of the psychological tensions that began to plague him during his six years' residence in his father's house in Charlottenburg, and that led to the abrupt ending of his productivity during the half-decade after 1897.

Weber's wife describes his position in his father's home after 1886 unambiguously:

Inclusion in the framework of family life, whose daily rhythm is determined by the master of the house, and then the forced, long-lasting pecuniary dependence on a father who becomes more alien to him with each year are like pressures and dark clouds that weigh increasingly on his life.[6]

His sense of humor, Marianne tells us, helped him in this situation, but not enough to dispel the clouds,[7] particularly since he was never able to express clearly to anyone his antagonism toward his father. Nonetheless, bitterness over his forced preprofessional incubation overflowed in at least two of his letters to his relatives. The later of these, written to Emmy Baumgarten in 1893, shows most sharply his sense of estrangement during the half-decade after 1887:

In these last years, on whose joyless barrenness I think back with horror, I have been immersed in such a total and bitter resignation that, apart from the melancholy gleam cast into my bookish existence by some rich and beautiful memories of earlier years, I have become exclusively absorbed in the, so to speak, automatic continuation of my obligatory professional work . . .[8]

Whatever the subsurface hostility between father and son that may have been triggered by trivialities, there were two major events during the earlier part of Weber's seven years in Charlottenburg that bred conscious antagonism. They concerned his mother.

In 1886, Weber's mother was forty-two years old. With her childbearing period over* and her oldest son at home and able to take over some of her responsibilities to the younger children,[9] Helene, inspired both by her sister Ida and by the writing of Channing, had earlier developed strong religious and social concerns, which she now wanted to put into

---

* Her youngest daughter, Lilli, was born in 1880 and was probably starting school.

practice. But "To papa . . . religion was basically hypocrisy and theologians, hypocrites."[10] Moreover, as a confirmed nineteenth century liberal, Max Weber, Sr., saw compassion and charity for the downtrodden as senseless.[11] Helene, unable to stand up to her husband's ridicule, suffered his antagonism quietly, but, as mentioned above, unburdened herself to her eldest son.[12] She also took a part of the money given her by her husband for the employment of domestic help and gave it to charity; she did the work herself, "continually pained by the feeling that too much happened for her own comfort, but not enough for others!"

In the general context of this situation, two major quarrels occurred, one over Helene's inheritance, the other over a theological student she had employed to tutor a younger son.

Helene's mother died in 1881 and left her a large fortune, the income from which exceeded her husband's salary. Not unnaturally, she sought to use this inheritance to escape her husband's tightfisted control over her expenditures. In 1918, Weber explained the position of both sides in the letter to his siblings:

> Mama wanted free use of a small part of the *interest* of her estate, to cover the costs of her own needs and also *social* goals, since the lavish style of our life then went against her nature, if she could not, along with it, yield to that need of her heart. This point of view was most deeply contradictory to Papa's energetic nature. He had grown up in an old-liberal age which still knew nothing of these social problems, and, although he was a kindhearted man by nature, the demand that he should give his wife independent means contradicted all firm traditions.*

Marianne Weber, attributing the elder Weber's parsimony to "the patriarchal power need of that generation" (and neglecting the odd coincidence that he was by profes-

---

* See note, p. 40.

sion a member of the budget committee of the Prussian House of Deputies), narrates the result:

> Thus, in the fifth decade of her life, Helene, in accordance with the tradition of these circles, has at her disposal neither a fixed household allowance nor a special sum for her personal needs. Rather, with her expense books, which never want to balance, in her hand, she must request what she needs for the house and for herself from case to case. She is thus subject to continual control and—equally typically under this regimen—to the frequent criticism and amazement of her husband at the great expenditure, whose inevitability he cannot really judge. Since over half of the family income flows from her own estate, she experiences this situation as increasingly contradictory and burdensome.*

Helene, unable to fight her husband, poured out her grief to her eldest son, who, equally unable to stand up to his father, thereby found—if he did not yet have one—an excellent reason for hating him.†

The second incident was the dismissal, by the head of the house, of Karl Weber's tutor; it, too, was related to Helene Weber's religious convictions. Karl, her third son, was six years younger than her first. About the time that this first son returned from Göttingen, his brother began running around with the kind of boys which we would probably describe today as juvenile delinquents. Karl abandoned his

---

* *Lebensb.*, p. 163. Max Weber had himself experienced the annoyance of his father's tight purse strings only a year or two earlier. His letter to his parents of September 2, 1884, is one long defense of the expenditures his father had been complaining about. Later letters to his mother, such as the one from Gnesen, September 14, 1888 (*Jb.*, pp. 309–10), and from Schrimm, June 17, 1891 (*Jb.*, p. 332), show a similar need to defend his expenses as a reserve officer.

† "For now the pressure on her often became so severe that she had to unburden herself to the grown son. Thereby, however, she unintentionally brought him over to her side against the father." *Lebensb.*, p. 164.

studies and, though he might earnestly promise his mother time and again to obey the moral law, as soon as he walked out the front door he rejoined his delinquent comrades.[13]

To counteract these baleful influences, Helene Weber resorted to the employment of a young theologian as a special tutor and companion for Karl, a Herr Voigt who lived in the Weber household between the spring of 1886 and the spring of 1887.[14] Marianne Weber's description of this young man makes it clear that his function in the house was not only to supply Karl's needs for continual moral support, but also to satisfy Helene's desire for a son as close to her own values and interests as her nephew Otto—also a theologian—was to her sister Ida's. "What she could not obtain from her own sons," writes Marianne Weber, "she received through him [Voigt]: complete insight into a struggling young soul of great purity. Here she could influence the development of someone who, through his religious endowment, was more closely related to her than her own children."[15] But the situation must have been as transparent to Helene's husband as it later was to Marianne, for "the joy of this domestic communion with a young man whose soul was tuned to the same pitch as her own, did not last long. By his nature, her husband could not want his wife, whom he loved passionately and wanted to continue to master, to slip away increasingly into interests unsympathetic to him and so come close to all kinds of people who meant nothing to him. He dismissed the young man before his task was fulfilled, which Helene felt as unjust to him as well as to her son; it was a long time before she got over it." It may have taken her eldest son even longer. Thirty-one years later he wrote of Herr Voigt's dismissal: "The nasty correspondence which resulted from it at the time completely estranged me too from papa."[16]

Indeed, there are indications that Weber never fully overcame his antagonism toward his father. In 1892, Helene Weber wrote to her sister: "Max very changed. Max Sr. continually at home." Shortly before World War I, Weber curiously bowdlerized a New Testament reference in his *Religionssoziologie*, to read: *"Wer nicht seinen Vater hassen Kann, Kann nicht Jesu Jünger sein."** Perhaps most significant is a note he wrote in 1919 just after his mother's death: "On Saturday, then, she will be buried in the enormous stone field of this southern cemetery at Kreuzberg, where my father lies. It goes against my every feeling, but is unavoidable in view of the siblings here. . . . I will *never* go there. For me she is in the Heidelberg garden [i.e., the garden of the house in which his mother was raised and in which he had been living for most of the previous decade]."[17]

All available evidence then, suggests that Max Weber, a man whom his contemporaries frequently described as the possessor of a "volcanic" temper, spent the eleven years between his arrival at his father's home in 1886 and his father's death in 1897 accumulating a vast but inexpressible loathing for this man and a deep sympathy for his maltreated mother. If we make the elementary hypothesis that a man so consumed by emotions he cannot express vocally must express them in some other way, we are led to investigate the relationship between these inexpressible, but clearly quite conscious, passions of Max Weber and the apparently non-familial dimensions of his life in those years: his scholarship and his politics. For both in his manner of work and in the values inspiring the results of that work, Weber betrayed the hatred that conventional inhibition forebade him to unleash.

ONE CANNOT POSSIBLY produce as much and as well as Weber did in the years before 1897 without enormous self-discipline, and it is therefore not surprising to find that as early as his year of study in Berlin (1884–5) Weber subjected himself

---

* *W.u.G.*, p. 449: "Whoever cannot hate his father, cannot be [my] disciple." See also *Baumg.*, p. 628. That Weber may have been right in spirit if not in letter is suggested by N. O. Brown in *Love's Body* (New York, 1966), pp. 3–31 *passim*.

to a ruthless work schedule.[18] In the following semester in Göttingen, "he continues the rigid work discipline, regulates his life by the clock, divides the daily routine into exact sections for the various subjects, saves in his way, by feeding himself evenings in his room with a pound of raw chopped beef and four fried eggs."[19] One can only infer that, in the course of transferring his loyalty and sympathy from his father to his mother while at Strassburg, Weber had taken over his mother's Huguenot asceticism. Certainly, the adoption of such a severely repressive asceticism functioned as a means of retaining his mother's good will.

Marianne Weber comes back again and again to the theme of the "uninterruptedly laboring mind"[20] of her husband in these years. The initial, conscious motivation may well have been merely the desire for advancement: from 1886 to 1890, Weber was preparing himself for two legal careers at once—he was an apprentice lawyer at the same time that he prepared himself for the more difficult goal of joining the Faculty of Jurisprudence at the University of Berlin. But in the same passage that his wife informs us of this she also points accurately to another strong motive for her husband's early choice of "work asceticism"[21] when she says that he "rescued himself through intense pursuit of his studies from the mental tedium of this period [as an apprentice lawyer] and from the danger of becoming comfortable."* We need only recall that the "danger of becom-

---

* *Lebensb.*, p. 170. Weber expresses his fear of "being drawn down like a lead weight onto the couch of intellectual needlessness and comfort" in a letter of February 18, 1892; *Baumg.*, p. 79. In another letter, written to his mother while on maneuvers in 1891, Weber plays lightly with the connection between the dangers of too much comfort and his need to work. He reports that his situation is "extremely comfortable" because he has an orderly to "spoil" him, i.e., help him dress and prepare his meals, and put his papers in order. Then he says, "Free from all care over the necessities of life, I could thus devote myself, in the time left over from my service, to my scholarly activity." Thus, with his orderly there to spoil him by taking care of his manuscripts, proofs, and papers, Weber is able to sandwich in about five hours of work between the nine and a half hours required each day

ing comfortable" was for Weber a lifelong peril, emanating from his father's nature, to understand the intimate relationship between Puritanical work morality and antagonism to his father's authority in his life. Of course, the abjuration of Max Weber, Sr.'s, good-natured, easygoing temperament may not have been originally intended—consciously or otherwise—as an act of hostility, but the likelihood remains that it became interpreted as one during the long years of the son's virtual imprisonment in his father's house. In any case, Weber's work routine became no less arduous in the years after he had attained his goals: in 1893 he took an academic position at Berlin, in 1894 an even better one at Freiburg; but his pace did not slow until his father died in 1897.

Weber himself was perfectly aware of his compulsive need to work, and related it at least twice, once before and once after his breakdown, to a pathological condition. There is, however, a marked difference in these two diagnoses. A few months after his marriage, in the winter of 1893-4 (i.e., at a time when his academic future was secure), his wife wrote him of her fear that he was ruining his health by overwork. He replied:

> When I had finally come to an inner harmony [through marriage] after years of a nasty sort of agony, I feared a deep depression. It has not occurred, to my mind, because, through continual work I did not let my nervous system and brain come to rest. Quite apart from the natural need for work, therefore, I am most unwilling to allow a really marked pause in my work; I think that as long as I am not positive that I have gone past the stage of convalescence, I can't risk allow-

---

by the King of Prussia: he is revising his study of Roman agrarian history. Later letters in the summer of 1891 also discuss the scholarly work he is doing while on maneuvers. See *Jb.*, pp. 330-7. See also the letter to E. B. of May 8, 1887 (*Jb.*, p. 236): "I must, as a result of attending lectures, get up at seven and other hours just after midnight, which is nasty for a worthy royal Prussian official like myself."

ing the present composure—which I enjoy with the feeling of a really new happiness—to be transformed into relaxation.[22]

Even the prose sweats in these lines. For Weber, as for his Calvinist ancestors, any lapse from steady labor bore the risk of *Erschlaffen* (relaxation), that loathesome condition of the damned in general and his father in particular.

Sometime during the total nervous collapse of the late '90's, Weber saw his compulsiveness in a very different light, as a symptom of his approaching breakdown:

> Such an illness still has its very good side . . . I could say with John Gabriel Borkman: "An icy hand has let me go." For my sickly disposition expressed itself in past years in a desperate clinging to scholarly work as to a talisman, without my being able to say why.[*] That is quite clear to me, and I know that sick or healthy . . . the *need* to feel submerged under a work load is extinguished.[23]

The implications of this statement for Weber's breakdown and subsequent recovery are considerable; it is hardly accidental that his study of Puritanism and the capitalist spirit followed shortly after the worst phase of that misfortune. But well before the breakdown, Weber's ideas about politics and scholarship mirrored his rigid antagonism to his father's "comfortable" nature.

WEBER NEVER DID succeed in totally eradicating his father's nature from his own spirit. The twin dangers of succumbing to a ruthless egotism on the one hand, or to the servile comfort of an easy bureaucratic routine on the other, haunted him all his life; his inability to shake loose from these ghosts was a most important factor in his breakdown. The political

---

[*] There may be significance in the precise meaning of the word I have translated here as "why." The usual word for "why" is *warum*. Weber uses *wogegen*, which means literally "against what."

corollary of this partial internalization of his father's values
was Weber's lifelong retention of his father's National Liberal reverence for the German power state. This ideal, however, if left unmodified, tended to incorporate both of the
demons Weber fought against: the cynical ruthlessness
represented by Treitschke (and by Weber Sr. in his despotism over his family) and the comfortable servility of the
Untertan (the face his father showed to his superiors).
To ward off the demons, Weber put two conditions on his
sanction of the *Machtstaat* (power state) which alone gave
legitimacy to it. Its components of ruthlessness and bureaucratic servility were jointly subordinated to the ideals represented by his mother and uncle: his mother's insistence on
a sense of social responsibility that was both moral and rational and his uncle's value on incorruptible intellectual and
political independence.

In the period between 1886 and 1897, these values—
that of the *Machtstaat* and of its two moral counterbalances
—are gradually worked into a coherent political *Weltanschauung*. But it is naïve: the values work largely unconsciously, without any serious reflection on them. In 1903,
after five years of hell, Weber will begin a completely new
phase of his work, in which he maintains his sanity only
by subjecting some of his values to a searching examination, by transforming others, and by establishing a methodology which permits him to keep all the various gods who
rule him from confronting one another and fighting it out.

IT WAS PROBABLY Weber's chaste love for Emmy Baumgarten
which first woke in him the powerful desire to live up to
the two countermodels he set against his paternal superego,
to prove himself worthy, that is, of being his mother's son
and his uncle's disciple.

Although Weber had spent his year of military service
in Emmy's city of Strassburg, the relationship apparently
only became serious when he returned to the Alsatian

city for his reserve-training duty in the early months of 1887.* Then it became, if not wildly passionate, serious indeed. The spring of that year was the time of Max and Emmy's clandestine rendezvous at her brother Otto's home in Waldkirch,† and the *Jugendbriefe* contain six letters from Max to Emmy, covering forty-three pages, in the six months from April to October 1887. In the following year there were only two letters; the year after, one; then a two year gap, followed by one in 1892 and two in 1893. But in the latter year, Weber married Marianne Schnitger, and his letters to Emmy were then explicitly brotherly. So we are left with the year 1887 as the crucial one,** and must pose two questions about it: Why did the relationship begin then? and What occurred to reduce its intensity so abruptly?

The answers lie to a great extent in the letters themselves. First of all, the whole context of Weber's brief stay in Strassburg must surely have encouraged him to see himself in a more mature and masculine light. Not only was he there for military training—that had also been the case three years earlier—but French *Boulangisme*, with its demands for revenge, had created a serious threat of war. This at any rate was the view of the military men around Weber,[24] and Strassburg, seized in 1870, was the crucial prize to be defended against the French.

At the same time, Weber's position between his father and mother was approaching a crisis. In his first letter to Emmy after returning from Strassburg, he discusses the issue of Karl's tutor, whom his father had just dismissed. And we know both from the *Lebensbild* and from Weber's letter of 1918 to his siblings that his father's refusal to allow

---

* In his letter of proposal to Marianne Schnitger of January or February 1893, he refers to his love for Emmy as having begun six years earlier; *Lebensb.*, p. 206.

† See above, p. 34.

** Emmy later confirmed that the relationship became serious at the time of his military training period in Strassburg in early 1887, but that she was only sure that Max's feelings toward her were more than brotherly for a short time thereafter; *Lebensb.*, pp. 213–14.

his mother to touch her inheritance had upset him a year or so earlier. Both of these situations were combining to turn him against his father and, by the mechanics of the situation, toward his mother, with whom, as we have seen, he must have had an extremely close childhood relationship during his "five to seven years long sickliness."

The filial duty incumbent on Max Weber in these circumstances was to return the devoted love and protection he had received during those years by openly standing up to his father and demanding more humane treatment for his mother. Such defiance, however, bore with it two possible dangers, neither of which Weber could face at that time: the more certain of these was a direct and possibly violent altercation with the family despot, something the twenty-three year old apprentice lawyer, living in his father's house without independent means, found impossible to risk. The less certain danger—but plausible if one accepts Freudian assumptions—was that of bringing perilously close to consciousness repressed childhood desires for his mother. But apart from these, a third and considerably more conscious motive was probably restraining any ardent espousal of his mother's cause: Weber had absorbed enough of his father's (and uncle's) liberal skepticism toward religion to be decidedly ambivalent about the substantive issue—his mother's wish to implement the Sermon on the Mount in Imperial Germany. The ideal emotional solution would have been to project his hopeless desire to protect his mother onto someone else, whose love entailed neither of the risks he could not face but who was sufficiently like his mother so that at that deeper level of the mind where new feelings find and merge with their archetypes, he could retain his love for his mother and need not feel he was betraying her.

Now we know that the personality of Emmy Baumgarten, the daughter of his mother's spiritual mentor and sister, reminded Max Weber of his mother: we know it because, in the waning stages of their relationship, he told her so.[25] Thus, the scene was fully prepared for the classical dénouement described by Ernest Jones in his study *Hamlet and Oedipus:*[26]

> When the attraction exercised by the mother is excessive it may exert a controlling influence over the boy's later destiny . . . If the awakened passion undergoes an insufficient repression, then the boy may remain throughout life abnormally attached to his mother and unable to love any other woman, a not uncommon cause of bachelorhood. He may be gradually weaned from the attachment if it is less strong, though it often happens that he is able to fall in love only with women who in some way resemble the mother; the latter occurrence is a frequent cause of marriage between relatives . . .*

---

* The fact that, through the death of two sisters in their early years, Weber's closest sister was eleven years younger than him, may also be important. In the Freud-Bullitt study of Wilson, one finds: "Little boys who have sisters possess an enormous advantage over little boys who have no sisters . . . The little boy who has a sister normally transfers to the sister a portion of the libido which has been attached to his mother, and from the sister transfers it to friends of the sister. Thus by easy transfers, his libido reaches women outside the family. The ego of a little boy who has no sister is compelled to transfer his libido directly from the mother to some woman outside the family, which is a much more difficult task, and to many men presents an insuperable difficulty. The libido of such men may remain fixed on the mother through life." "Woodrow Wilson," *Encounter*, Jan. 1967, p. 8. Despite the meager reputation of the Bullitt-Freud manuscript, Weber himself gives substance to the point that sister-relationships mediate the jump from mother to wife by suggesting that both Emmy and his sister Klara became objects of particularly strong brotherly affection just at the time of his engagement and marriage. Shortly after his engagement in March 1893, he wrote to Emmy: "Your friendly lines for my birthday . . . showed me—as I hoped—that we have remained as close as ever and that I will retain in you the sister of my own age, which I have always painfully missed." *Jb.*, E. B., April 22, 1893, p. 366. And in the period from September 21, 1892, to January 31, 1893, Weber wrote nine letters to his sister Klara—by this time, seventeen years old—of which five were concentrated in the month of January. (There are fifteen letters to Klara Weber in *Jb.*, 1889–93.) January was the month in which Max Weber had to make up his mind about Marianne, for a friend of his had decided to ask her to marry him at that time, and Helene Weber, who apparently thought Emmy alone a suitable match for her son, encouraged his friend's efforts. *Lebensb.*, p. 204; *Jb.*, K.W., Jan. 9, 1893, p. 359.

At the time, therefore, when Max Weber, Sr.'s, despotism was arousing all his son's desire to return the love and protection his mother had offered him as a child, the son was able to deflect this dangerous emotion—which bore within it the explosive potentialities of a direct, and perhaps violent, confrontation with his father—onto his cousin Emmy.

Of the topics Max discussed in his letters to Emmy, two in particular show the extent to which he superimposed his relationship with her over that with his mother: his comparison of Goethe and Schiller and his comments on his brother Karl.

The discussion of the two great figures of German classicism was triggered by his pleasure in finding that Emmy enjoyed Schiller. For Max, the exclusive adulation of Goethe by literary people had generally put Schiller into disfavor, which he found appalling in view of the greater moral value of Schiller. Goethe's morality suffers from a one-sided eudaemonism:

> For, in general, men do not tend to view their life as though it were only a question of feeling well in their skin and of gaining from life a means for enjoying it. And they are also in no way *only* faced with the question of what path will or will not lead them to happiness and inner satisfaction. But, if we take the matter soberly and exactly, this question is the deepest one that we find—e.g., certainly in Faust—in Goethe's work, and everything, even the most difficult ethical problems, is illuminated from this standpoint. See, it is characteristic that Goethe only felt the unworthy as such, if it was at the same time the ugly and small, but he had no clear perception of it when it appeared under the form of certain beautiful feelings—*cf.* the "Elective Affinities"—or in monumental greatness—*cf.* his encounter with Napoleon . . . I could well imagine that your mother would be in agreement here.[27]

It is, of course, undeniable that the moral opposition presented in this passage is a reflection of the prevailing nineteenth-century conflict between a utilitarian ethic based on the pleasure-pain calculus and an idealist ethic based on moral imperatives. But it is surely no coincidence that the first sentence I have quoted contains just that criticism of his father's ethos which Weber's mother and aunt had for years been offering to him; and it is completely in character with this situation that he sees his aunt as agreeing with him.

In Weber's letter to Emmy of July 5, 1887, his attitude toward his brother Karl is, again, a near-perfect image of his mother's values. Karl's chums have accustomed him to considering himself heroic and emancipated at school, "and thus he exploits the momentary situation both there and at home with the aim of a momentary feeling of well-being and protects himself anxiously from any second thoughts which could ruin the enjoyment of the moment for him."[28] For Max, it was a characteristic of adolescence, a "form of humbug" which, he said, he unfortunately knew from his own experience. Indeed, when Max was about Karl's age, during his first year in Heidelberg (i.e., during the time when he, too, had chosen his father as the model to follow), his cousin Otto wrote home to his father in Strassburg:

> Max runs ever greater danger from the Alemanni [the dueling fraternity Weber joined]; I am glad that his mother can now soon support me; meanwhile the task looks hopeless. "Marriage an animal institution" and similar fruits of Naturalism spice the conversation. Yet our acquaintance is and remains valuable.[29]

In 1887, Max feared that his mother's attempts to bring Karl around by showering him with love were misguided, at least for the moment. Though he clearly acknowledged the beneficent power of this love for his own development ("even to the point of being able to say . . . in what special connection"), he did not think it was meaningful yet for Karl:

> For he will still be for years too immature for a real assessment of the care and love of his mother. To be

sure, he makes use of the advantages of this love, but otherwise he brushes it aside as something uncomfortable. Thus, he reaches an indubitable crudity, a kind of hardness in his conception of these things, which makes him incapable of attaining later the understanding for them that he now lacks.

For the moment, Karl's problem was being handled by the return of his tutor Herr Voigt.[30] We do not know how Weber Sr. had been brought to agree to this, but the fact that Weber's parents were spending at least part of the summer in Heidelberg and therefore could probably agree that Karl needed some kind of moral presence in their absence may have had something to do with it.[31]

Judging by Max's letter to Emmy of October 21, 1887, his relationship with her seems to have come to an awkward standstill as a result of her pressure for him to do the very thing which he had sought to avoid by turning to her: stand up to his father for the sake of his mother. This emerges only obliquely from the text of the letter, but a close examination of it makes such a conclusion inescapable.

We discover from the first paragraph that in Emmy's prior letter she had written that if what she said angered him, he should throw the letter away. (He jestingly replied that she should have put that at the beginning of her letter, "for what good does it do me to throw it away *after* the anger.") After a brief description of his unceasing labors for Professor Goldschmidt's seminar—which delayed his reply for six weeks—he entered the treacherous ground onto which Emmy's letter had forced him.[32]

In July, Max had written to his cousin that his mother would be stopping in Heidelberg during the summer[33] and suggested that Emmy visit with her there a couple of days. It appears that Emmy and his mother did get together over the summer,[34] and the result was that Emmy's letter of early September seems to have raised, directly or indirectly, two very embarrassing questions: (1) (probably directly) Why don't you spend more time with your mother? and (2) (probably indirectly) Why don't you keep the bully from pushing her around all the time? These, at any rate, are the questions which Weber answered in his letter of October 21, 1887.[35]

The answer to the first question was that though he found unpleasant the thought "that I am not offering my mother what ought really to be expected of me," he felt himself terribly pressed for time. He referred to his interrupted and irregular university studies, and to pressure, both from his family and from hers, to finish his doctorate quickly. The only time when he and his mother were both free was in the evening, and by then she was so exhausted that she could only listen to his reading with effort. And some days he had no time in the evening either, "for it is a kind of dogma for me that certain things which one has firmly resolved to finish may not be left undone, and I cannot conceive that my mother could find that improper." He certainly could not limit his socializing any more than he had: for long periods of time he was out no more than one night a month. So what else could he do?

Then, gradually, Weber turned to the vexatious problem which seemed to be the real issue raised by Emmy's letter: his failure openly to take his mother's side against his father. If only his mother had not been so worn out, everything would have been easier. But she always seemed so oppressed and unable to find a focus for her life, a problem which Max felt neither called to—nor in a position to—remedy:

> Enough of this—it is difficult to express here properly what I wanted to say, but I am closely concerned, and you must not think that the thought of it does not grieve me.—Of course, you are not the only one who has the impression.—As I can always say, all that would not be of such great importance if my mother did not, apparently, take some things much harder than earlier; for example, to mention one thing: my father was always sanguine, and his mood was often subject to

sudden change from little external cause; in contrast to earlier years, such a change now often makes a really profoundly painful impression on my mother, which she does not quickly get over, even if the annoyance which produced it was only momentary. I am a son in the house, and you will perhaps grant me—opinions may differ—that it would not correspond to this position and would not help the life of the family if I intervened other than indirectly. And the same in other things. This, moreover, only for you, dear Emmy.—[36]

Then follows a page which contains an extremely insightful and impartial analysis of the difference between his father's and mother's personalities, the avowed purpose of which is to avoid any suggestion that he feels justified in making reproaches against either side.*

The life of a man in an office, according to Weber, shapes his understanding in a particular way. Human relations, when mediated through papers and documents take on "a peculiar kind of ghostly life—a picture as if one saw the outlined shadows of real living men performing a dance on a curtain." We know that real struggles are occurring on the other side of the curtain, "but only the colorless outlines fall on the curtain, often amazingly distorted." The masculine preoccupation with such shadows and, in general, with the "interests of *external* life," makes it difficult for men to understand the reactions of those (such as his mother) "whose calling lies more on the *inner* side." For what comes from men as the mere expression of "an external, momentary mood" is often felt by women "more internally," with lasting pain.

Both the imagery of the shadows and the dichotomy of external (paternal) vs. internal (maternal) are important keys to Weber's later work and values. In fact, this passage and others in the correspondence to Emmy cast interesting

---

* "*Ich sage dies nur, weil ich ungern den Anschein erwecke, als fühlte ich mich zu Vorwürfen nach irgendeiner Seite berechtigt*"; *Jb.*, E. B., Oct. 21, 1887, p. 277.

light on the sociologist's option, after 1903, for a strict separation of science and values.

Weber's justification for not taking sides in his parent's
quarrels—i.e., for not making a value judgment on them—
was, basically, that their actions were set in such different
worlds that it was impossible, knowing both, to judge either.
This was not, however, Weber's first discussion with Emmy
on different ways of viewing human action. In the long letter
of July 5, 1887, he wrote six pages on the subject. Starting
from Emmy's condemnation of one of his fraternity brothers,
he elaborated on three faculties of judgment which existed,
he argued, independent of one another in every man: a
sensual faculty, which tells us what is pleasurable and what
unpleasurable; a rational faculty, which explains how things
come to be the way they are; and a moral faculty, which tells
us what we ought to do, what is right and what is wrong.
None of these faculties, however, can contribute anything
meaningful about the judgments of the others. For example,
our rational faculty may explain the circumstances that
produce a criminal act, but such an explanation has nothing
to do with the moral judgment we bring to bear on the act
itself.

We have become accustomed in the mid-twentieth century
to view Weber's epistemological distinctions in terms of
psychological ones: his faculty of moral judgment in terms
of a superego; his faculty of rational understanding in terms
of an analytic ego, which uses its capacity for conceptual
discrimination to master reality; and his faculty of sensual
appreciation in terms of a bundle of instincts or drives, whose
satisfaction is felt as pleasure. Be that as it may, given his
assumption of separate faculties of judgment, Weber's analysis of his father and mother's differing natures receives an
added dimension. Weber certainly viewed his mother consistently in terms of her capacity for moral judgment and his
father in terms of both the egoistic insensitive man of affairs
and (in general, if not in this passage) the crassly sensual
hedonist. Thus, his refusal to choose between his father and

mother has as its implicit theoretical justification the linking of their personality types with those two utterly distinct categories of judgment: the moral and the rational. As early as its embryonic appearance in 1887, Weber's methodological presupposition of a rigid separation between the spheres of logical analysis and value judgment serves the crucial function of maintaining an equally rigid separation between his attitudes toward his mother on the one hand and his father on the other.

But Weber's first anticipatory effort along these lines was forced upon him by his cousin's pressure to defend his mother. His elaborate defense against this pressure shows how serious it must have been. Indeed, if Max felt challenged by Emmy to stand up to his father, in effect what he was being asked to do was to be as much of a man as Emmy's father, his uncle, whom everyone knew had shown the courage to stand up to that patriarchal despot of the German family of historians, Heinrich von Treitschke; as we know from other letters, Max had a tendency to view Treitschke and his father in a similar light. (See above, pp. 36 *ff.*) Thus, alongside his slapdash theoretical defense of his neutrality appear the dim beginnings of a decade-long struggle to free himself from his father. Indeed, six years later, when this struggle was entering its last phase, Weber acknowledged in his letter of proposal to Marianne Schnitger that at the time of his immaculate passion for Emmy he was "still half a boy" as far as girls were concerned, and that his *Schwachheit* (weakness) as well as his lack of material prospects had stymied the relationship.[37] In the last months of 1887, he betrayed the consequences of this weakness when he reduced —if he did not sever—his ties toward Emmy, became for the time being somewhat closer to his father, whom he could not openly oppose, and immersed himself in an endless work routine, which he saw as the means of his ultimate liberation. But soon afterward he began an intense political career which, though it first gave the appearance of a loyal liberal effort to undermine the stranglehold of East Elbian con-

servatism over German politics, ended with an appeal for a
liberal imperialism that was as hostile to his father's generation of liberals as it was to the Junkers. By the time he
gave his inaugural address at Freiburg in 1895, Weber was
finally able to stand up against, if not his father, the spirit
of his father's generation, and thereby prove himself a worthy
nephew to his uncle.

EVIDENCE OF Weber's retreat, under Emmy's pressure to
help his mother, from the maternal values represented jointly
by his cousin, aunt, and mother, appeared first in the comments he made about Emmy's brothers in his letter of October
1887 and then in the way he viewed Emmy herself in his
letter of February 1888. In these passages, both of which
were written after his labored defense of his policy of non-
intervention, his values are clearly closer to his father's
than his mother's.

Emmy's brothers were Otto, a theologian who was very
close to Max's mother, and Fritz, a more worldly type. Emmy
had apparently described the difference between them in the
following terms: "that while Otto's nature makes it necessary
for him to speak and do what he does, Fritz seeks violently
to be something that he is not."[38] But for Max this analysis
should be reversed:

> On the contrary: the more complicated and artificial
> of the two is undoubtedly Otto. I believe that almost
> everyone will find that *he* is the one for whom it is
> difficult to see things simply as they are and who has
> the need to internalize even external questions and,
> thereby, to put them often rather powerfully in a light
> opposed to any natural conception, both for himself
> and for others.

Only on this basis could Max comprehend Otto's insistence on pursuing a practical career—the ministry—an
insistence which, though it surely sprang from some "great

inner drive," did not correspond to Otto's natural constitution. Though Max did not doubt that Otto was serious and conscientious, he agreed with Fritz that Otto tended to complicate simple things. To be sure, Fritz himself had the very different habit of worrying precisely about being artificial, the result of which was that certain of his potentialities remained undeveloped. Nonetheless, Max continued,

> I think it is not right to say that he does not understand Otto's nature; it seems to me that he understands it well, but holds it to be perverse and one-sided, and *that* he does this is not at all incomprehensible to me.* That you have closer relations to Otto is perfectly natural, dear Emmy; he has gone through more difficulties than many others and stood alone and isolated, and you belong to your sex. But that you find in Fritz so much artificiality and a kind of spirit of contradiction really surprises me, for his feelings are really more direct.

This passage, with its sharp criticism of Otto's tendency to internalize external matters, is followed four months later in Weber's next letter to his cousin by a similar criticism of Emmy herself; and it is here that he mentions her similarity to his mother:

> Every day has its own plague, they say, and I certainly think that applies to you too. And nonetheless, don't you have in addition all kinds of internally plaguing thoughts? I, at least, find . . . that often a kind of resignation appears in your letters, as though you are not doing for your family what you would want to do

---

* In the fall of 1883, Weber, then still closer to his father than to his mother, fended off what he considered his mother's exaggerated praise for the Baumgarten family in very similar terms: "In my view, the Baumgartens' outlook easily leads to an unusual onesidedness in the judgment of other perspectives and men, and to conflicts which otherwise could have been avoided"; *Jb.*, H.W., Oct. 22, 1883, p. 82; *Baumg.*, p. 20.

or be able to do, or did not know how to carry out your
duties properly, or I don't know what? It almost reminds
me of some thoughts which now and then occur to my
mother.[39]

Then Weber enters another brief discussion of the
psychic problems of the fairer sex. The duties of women rarely
consist in the conscious solution of *"externally* important questions," but rather in the fulfillment of daily obligations, the
fruits of which mature only gradually. Thus they rarely see
concretely "the successful result of the fulfillment of their
duties," and this imposes a heavy burden on them.

What he is now doing is discussing Emmy as if she
were his mother and he were a more enlightened version of
his father: it is basically the same standard that he had used to
judge Emmy's brother in October.

Nonetheless, the values of his mother and his uncle had
not been destroyed in him, but only temporarily eclipsed.
Toward the end of the long letter of October 1887, he makes
this quite clear. Against warnings from Emmy that he will
work himself *kaput,* he refers again to parental pressure on
him to complete his doctorate and then writes of his discomfort over his prolonged dependence on his father's bounty, a
discomfort which he sees as having a world-historical significance:

> You know, it is a strange feeling to gradually outgrow
> your student shoes but still have to wait a long time
> before being your own master, at least for me, and
> I must nonetheless swallow the idea almost daily. I am
> also incapable of convincing myself that the feeling is
> unjustified, because *one's own bread, for the man,* is
> the foundation of happiness, the lifelong goal of the
> great majority of men. It was for centuries the point
> around which the history of the world turned.[40]

Thus, the desire for personal independence that he finds
both in his uncle and mother fits in perfectly with his own
inclinations, and indeed the interpretation of major historical

events in terms of the desire for freedom becomes the central idea in Weber's published work from 1889 to 1895.

There is one last value in this letter of October 1887 that deserves mention. It is the bias transmitted to Weber by the two daughters of Emilia Souchay—Helene Weber and Ida Baumgarten—against the Lutheran notion of a "calling" to some specified occupation (*Beruf*) and in favor of the Calvinist notion of "accomplishment" in whichever field offers the greatest promise for it. In the context of his ardent desire to become his own master, Weber discusses the alternatives open to him, of continuing in the legal profession or trying to get an academic position. He is more sure of being able to accomplish something as a practicing lawyer than as an academician, but because he believes he will have a longer wait before reaching his goal as a lawyer than as a university professor, he has chosen the latter. Such concern with practical accomplishment and the attendant indifference for an unequivocal "vocational" choice anticipates a lifetime of wavering between scholarship and politics. This theme, together with several others mentioned above, emerges clearly from a letter Weber wrote to Marianne Schnitger, his fiancée, shortly before their marriage:

> I have for years felt with infinite bitterness the fact that I was unable to reach a position where I could feed myself independently. I never had any kind of respect for the concept of a "calling," since I thought I knew that I fitted into a large number of positions, to a certain extent. The only thing that stimulated me was my own bread, and the fact that it was denied me made my parents' house a torment.[41]

Another letter of this period brilliantly illuminates Weber's scorn for the scholarly life, certainly a legacy of his aunt and mother:

> As far as I am concerned, my yearning was at all times directed toward an economically independent and practical effectiveness, which was denied me by circum-

stances. In my experience, the most useful *new* scientific ideas always came to me when I lay on the sofa with the cigar in my mouth and thought *con amore*, and thus not as the result of actual work; and I view this actual intellectual production in the narrowest sense only as the product of free time, as the accompaniment of life. Even now, my joy in the scholarly vocation would lie only on the practical-pedagogic, not on the actual "learned" side . . . Nothing is more abominable to me than the arrogance of the "intellectual" and learned vocations.*

But more important to Weber than either pedagogy or pure scholarship as a vehicle of liberation was politics. The final goal of Weber's scholarship in the decade after 1887 was a change in the balance of political forces in Germany that was in some sense a projection of the changes he wanted to achieve in his own family.

UNTIL 1892, when Weber's report on the East Elbian land workers appeared, the only clear traces Weber left of his political ideas were in his letters, primarily in his letters to Hermann Baumgarten. His views of current affairs were for the most part those of a gloomy liberal of pre-imperial vintage, i.e., he often sounded like his uncle, particularly in the earlier period.† Certainly his close view of national liberal politicians in his father's drawing room had not increased his appreciation of that breed; but he also detested the "pettiness" of the anti-Bismarckian liberals. In a letter of April 1888,

---

* *Lebensb.*, p. 217. For the influence of his aunt and mother on his attitude toward the scholarly vocation, see *Lebensb.*, p. 99, and *Baumg.*, pp. 621–3. See also *Lebensb.*, pp. 212, 215, 216.

† As, for example, in the often-cited passage where he discusses the "Greek gift" of universal suffrage, which permitted the socialists to endanger the regime and so placed German society before the unappetizing alternatives of exceptional laws against the socialists or a general curb on free speech, free assembly, and the right of association. (Weber thought the latter would be fairer.) *Jb.*, H.B., Nov. 8, 1884, p. 143.

he saw German liberalism as compromised by its split into "blind Bismarckians" on the one side and "stereotyped fanatical demagogues" on the other.[42] But the most significant passages in these letters are Weber's critique of the anti-Bismarckian liberals on the budget question, his varying assessment of Bismarck's treatment of the Catholics, and his remarks on the significance of East Elbian conservatism. When put together, the points that Weber evokes in these passages add up to a new program for German liberalism, a program which brings into a strange baroque harmony both his personal values and his early contributions to pure scholarship.

In Weber's letter to his uncle of June 29, 1887, he bitterly criticized the left-liberals (*Freisinnige*), primarily for their attitude toward the imperial budget. Out of spite for Bismarck, they had consistently opposed his budget proposals; the result of "this repulsive haggling" had been that nine tenths of the politics of the last decade had centered around the regime's continual anxious "straining at the money belt of the taxpayer."[43] Recently, the Prussian parliament had passed a tax on brandy and sugar, which affected the profits of the Eastern landlords, and as usual, the *Freisinnige* had demanded changes, despite the fact that their proposed changes, if implemented, would have increased the profits of their political enemies, the brewers and large estate owners. Apparently the real aim of the *Freisinnige* was to injure the Reich, and this attitude, according to Weber, seriously compromised German liberalism. In their pessimistic speculation that the worse the general situation became the better were the prospects for their faction, they showed a complete lack of "loyalty and trust." Moreover, with all their hopes pinned on the imminent succession to the imperial throne of the Crown Prince, they displayed a ridiculous servility toward the latter.

In this same letter, Weber's attitude toward Bismarck's treatment of the Catholics in East Prussia was quite favorable. For, unlike the *Freisinnige*, Bismarck did not permit traditional party or social shibboleths to take precedence over the welfare of the German nation as a whole. Bismarck had apparently convinced the Roman Curia that the interest of the German state coincided with that of the Catholic Church in East Prussia: the containment of Russian (Orthodox) power. The means to this end was the Germanization of those Catholic Poles who lived in Prussian territory, and the Church had shown its willingness to cooperate with Bismarck in this effort by gagging the anti-Bismarckian journalists of the Center Party in Posen, sending German priests to pastoral positions in the East, and deciding many issues in its ecclesiastical courts in favor of the state's interests; all of which was "directly contrary to all traditions of the indigenous clergy."

But Weber's view of Bismarck was really ambivalent,* and we see the other side of this ambivalence in remarks made to his uncle only a few months earlier on the same subject of Bismarck and the Catholics.

Bismarck finally ended the *Kulturkampf* against German Catholicism—that ideological foundation of his alliance with liberalism in the 1870's—only through a number of reconciliatory speeches and proposals in early 1887. Weber was not disappointed to see it ended, but he was depressed by Bismarck's tacit admission that his motives had always been political:

> If in fact it was not a question of conscience for us, but only one of opportunism, then, just as the Catholics assert, we have really violated the conscience of the Catholic people from motives which were of an external [N.B.!] nature—for to the mass of Catholics it was indeed a question of *conscience* . . . We have, then, acted unscrupulously and are also morally the losers, and that is the hardest part of the defeat, for it prevents us from ever resuming the struggle as it must be resumed if it is to lead to victory.[44]

---

* See above, pp. 35-7, 66-7.

The struggle that Weber would have liked to see resumed was certainly not the fight against Catholicism as a religion, but rather that against the conservative traditionalism represented by the Catholic spirit, which stood opposed, from Weber's standpoint, to liberalism and cultural progress. Still, the accusation that Bismarck and the liberals had committed an injustice in violating "conscience . . . from motives which were of an external nature" brought Bismarck and his father's own party under the same moral law by which he condemned his father's treatment of his mother. And the following sentences, which present the alleged and the real motives for the liberals' abandonment of the struggle, fully support this interpretation:

> Nonetheless, people are at present very cool in this respect [of resuming the struggle], *allegedly* because nothing more is to be done and they finally want peace—*in fact* only because the idea of what the future holds for us in this question is very uncomfortable and unattractive, and people would like very much to keep, or pump into themselves, a good untroubled confidence and a sense of happiness in what "we have" that is as quietistic as possible.

It is striking how closely Weber was approximating, in parts of this critique, not only his mother's spiritual values but his uncle's as well. In an early stage of the *Kulturkampf*, Hermann Baumgarten had written: "I am worried; I fear we are spiritually weaker than we have been for a long time. . . . Protestantism in Prussia must first become Protestantism again, before it can drive Rome from the field. . . . Sometimes one thinks perhaps, the great labor is now done, for the most part, and one can comfortably spend the rest of one's life in society of one's choosing. But then come *warnings to the contrary,* which drive one forcefully *to keep the old ranks firmly closed.*"[45]

Thus, Weber's misgivings represent, whether consciously or unconsciously, an echo of his uncle's liberal protestant intransigeance; and his father's desire to enjoy without emotional involvement the pleasures of his bourgeois household finds its political counterpart (and justification?) in the refusal of the older generation of liberals to allow the social and cultural needs of national life to disturb their complacency.

As early as 1884, Weber pinpointed the general issue which he later used both to turn the flank of German conservative power and to rouse the liberals from their complacency: the entrenched power of East Prussian conservatism. Alarmed over the fact that in the recent elections the voters of the Eastern provinces had not elected a single National Liberal deputy, he wrote:

> Apart from the fact that one has always conceded a certain pace-setting position to the [Eastern provinces] and that, for example, East Prussia has been a remarkably good political thermometer since 1847, it is cause for thought if the [National Liberal] Party, which hopefully may someday play another role than its present one, would become a merely West and Southwest German one. We already have a party division by religion, by social levels, and interest groups, and if now we were to receive yet another, by provinces and territories, it seems in fact most regrettable.[46]

This concern over the power of East Prussian conservatism was somewhat mitigated in 1887 by Bismarck's magical ability to entice the Church into an alliance against Russia and so to unify a part of the fractured political scene, but when Weber went to Posen the following year for his reserve-training period, he received a vivid, and disturbing, personal impression of the nationalities problem in the East:

> The Germans keep very much, and it seems, exclusively, together . . . On Sundays, one sees dense mobs of peasants streaming out of the cathedral, who come by foot and cart to the grave of Saint Adalbert. Some with the maddest haircuts, like straw roofs, and infinitely long frock coats, partly sheepskin, inherited for generations and therefore definitely not cut to any

particular body, and faces such that one thinks one is among Tartars.[47]

Through District Magistrate Nollau, Weber also had the chance to visit some of the estates of the Prussian colonization commission, where the regime was trying to settle German peasants.

About a year later, Weber accepted the offer of the *Verein für Sozialpolitik* to supervise their inquiry into the conditions of East Elbian land workers. His letter to Hermann Baumgarten of January 3, 1891, shows how crucial the East Elbian question had become for him, as a lever for the revival of German liberalism.

Weber was at this point discovering that the economic foundation of Prussian conservatism, i.e., the large estates of the German East, were becoming economically unviable because of competition from American and Russian grain. The results of insolvency were twofold. First, the Junkers could only survive behind increasingly high tariff walls, which imposed unnecessarily high bread and cereal prices on the nation. Secondly, the Junkers were slowly changing the economic character of their domains from a patriarchal feudal model with a permanent population of settled but half-serf peasants, to a more efficient capitalist one with migratory workers doing most of the work; in consequence the German peasantry was emigrating westward and its place was being taken by a Polish rural proletariat. The only way to halt this peaceful invasion of the East by Slavic masses was to close East Elbian borders to migratory workers, a measure which Bismarck had supported but which the Junkers now opposed because it would further weaken their already unstable economic position.

This latter point was the more important for Weber. Not only had the Junkers become an economic liability: since their economic interests were diametrically opposed to the political interests of the nation, they had lost the capacity for political leadership as well.

Through the letter of January 1891 we find that Weber, by bringing the political obsolescence of the Junkers to light in this way, hoped to produce a major reorientation in German politics. In particular, he wanted to bring liberals and enlightened conservatives together around a state social policy which would recognize the political, social, and economic bankruptcy of the Junkers and fight their influence over the national destiny. Only in such a commitment to a state social reform, which the liberals had hitherto evaded, did he see any future for them. But he was convinced that this alliance with the more intelligent conservatives was possible; for "if there occurs a more lively conflict [over the agrarian question], the enlightened bureaucratic conservatism shared by a great number of younger politicians, with whom discussion is possible, will cut itself off from the representation of the big landholding interests to which it is now bound—and, among my peers, in seven out of ten cases unconsciously bound."

Thus, Weber was using the results of the scholarly study he was writing for the *Verein für Sozialpolitik* to lay the foundation for a new political alignment. This alignment would bring together, in the interests of the nation as a whole, two segments of the body politic which had previously been separated by an abyss, against a third, which had formerly been the dominant guiding force in national politics, but whose own personal needs were now shown to run contrary to those of the German people. We have already seen Weber's disgust with the left-liberal *Freisinnige* for putting their own petty political advantages over the requirements of national politics, and with German liberalism as a whole for abandoning—out of decadent complacency—the *Kulturkampf*, the struggle against the spirit of Catholic conservatism; and we have also seen how in both cases he was projecting onto national politics the values and resentments, acquired in part through his mother and uncle, that he had accumulated against his own father because of the way the *pater familias*

tyrannized his family. We have also seen Weber's admiration
for the way Bismarck was able to make an ally out of a
former enemy, the Catholic Church, for the sake of national
self-preservation against the Slavic menace. The conclusion
seems inescapable that Weber had come to identify the cohesion of the German nation with the cohesion of his own
family, and himself with the man who would rescue this
nation from the divisive self-interest and complacency of
entrenched traditional interest groups—with in fact, a kind
of bourgeois Bismarck, who would take over where the
aristocratic Bismarck had left off when Wilhelm II dismissed him from office (an event which preceded Weber's
letter of 1891 by less than a year). A crucial indication of
Weber's desire, probably unconscious, to take Bismarck's
place—and therefore, in a sense, his father's—emerges from
his very first sentence following on the suggestion of an anti-
Junker front:

> The chief worry for the future is naturally what fur-
> ther personal development the Kaiser will take, and
> whether finally collaborators will grow up to him [*sic!*:
> *"ob ihm endlich Mitarbeiter erwachsen werden"*] who
> influence him; whether in particular Miquel will re-
> main such a one.

Through the medium of German politics, then, Weber
transformed his mother's intense Christian compassion for the
downtrodden, which his intellect rejected in its religious form,
into a concern for the cultural and social vitality of the nation
as a whole. To give objective support to this concern, he
worked out a philosophy of history, in which historical correlates of his own desire for personal independence from
his father's household (*"sein eigenes Brot"*) were seen as the
key factor liberating men from the despotic paternalism of
the Roman slave plantations, the closed medieval trade associations, and the Junker estates. There should be nothing
surprising about his transference of this theme from his per-

sonal fate to the history of mankind, since he had already made the connection, quite consciously, in the letter to Emmy of 1887, cited above:

> I am also incapable of convincing myself that the feeling [of frustration in his father's house] is unjustified, because *one's own bread, for the man,* is the foundation of happiness, the lifelong goal of the majority of men. It was for centuries the point around which the history of the world turned.

Superimposed, then, on Weber's personal struggle for liberation was a tendency to view historical change in terms of his own predicament, and particularly the changes then occurring in the economic and political position of the East Elbian landlords; superimposed in turn on both of these was an active political career in which he attempted to use the Protestant social reform movement of Friedrich Naumann and Paul Göhre as a catalytic agent to split the intelligent and courageous *Sozialpolitiker* from both the conservative and the liberal camp. The goal of this tactic was the implementation of Weber's political strategy for the defeat of agrarian conservatism and the rejuvenation of liberalism, a strategy which emerges gradually through his scholarly work from 1892 to 1895: closing the borders to Polish seasonal labor, expropriation with compensation of some of the large landowners, settlement of self-sufficient and independent peasantry on their land, and finally—completing the shift of power to the liberal bourgeois intellectuals—a program for overseas imperalism. All of these together would enable his own generation to grasp and wield the power which his father's generation had relinquished to Bismarck.

Assault on the
Junker Hegemony

HAMLET: *Has this fellow no feeling of his business,
that he sings at grave-making?*

Hamlet, *Act V, Sc. i*

To GRASP the nature of Weber's intellectual creativity one
must keep in mind some such metaphor as the archaeological
one that Freud used, with some reservations, in *Civilization
and Its Discontents*. There the metaphor served to illuminate
the various layers of buried memories, consciousness, and
perception in the human mind. Similarly, I would suggest
that we can best comprehend Weber's work of 1892-5 on the
land question if we think of it in terms of three congruent
realms of consciousness, partly buried and partly open, superimposed on a fourth realm, quite hidden, whose existence we
know only by inference from the contours of the realms
above and by documents that we find elsewhere.

The most superficial of these realms of consciousness is
Weber's broad, scholarly analysis of the social and economic
changes occuring in the relationship between Junker landlord
and peasant in the German East. In the framework that
Weber builds around this changing relationship, he also

reveals the contours of a semiburied realm of historical and philosophical presuppositions which underlies and supports the more exposed and empirical realm of economic analysis; this stratum of presuppositions, taken as a whole, constitutes Weber's initial philosophy of history, in which he implies that the real driving force of historical progress is the rise of the free individual from the shackles of earlier, patriarchal forms of social organization. Both of these more scholarly realms in turn rest on and are shaped by a third realm of consciousness, generally more buried but sometimes quite visible, a genuinely political realm in which Weber sees the German people as attempting to rid itself of a decadent Junker hegemony: at first for the sake of national self-preservation, but then with the additional purpose of national greatness and self-assertion.

At the same time, through all of these strata, and through the apparent earthquakes that continually alter their contours in these years, Weber reveals a great subsurface transformation in the oldest and most primitive city of his mind, his personality, composed of conscious and unconscious attitudes toward his family, his society, and himself. In revealing, however indirectly, this turbulent fourth stratum, Weber is surely—if without intent—writing an autobiography, and it is this autobiography which provides the key to untangling the confused relationships between the scholarly, philosophical, and political strata of his mind and work.*

---

* Cushing Strout, in a most interesting essay on "Ego Psychology and the Historian," supplies a general framework for the applicability of psychoanalysis to history which roughly approximates the distinctions made above: "For some purposes of historical analysis we want to know a man's self-conscious ideas, opinions and values; for others we want to know his conscious feelings, often demonstrated in his actions; for still others we want to know his deep-rooted biases. In none of them are we *compelled* to appeal to psychoanalytic categories. . . . The historian may be forced by his evidence, however, to consider problems and raise questions that he cannot treat intelligently without benefit of the psychoanalyst's experience. The historical subject may have experienced bouts of depression, suicidal inclinations, inorganic illness, inability to work, intense phobias, bizarre visions, inappropriate effects,

Though these underground upheavals in the most fundamental regions of Weber's mind resulted in a strengthening and clarifying of his ideas and values between 1892 and 1895, they reached such an intensity in the latter part of 1897 that all the realms hitherto created by his soul and intellect crumbled into ruins. For five years, a near-total psychic collapse paralyzed the creativity of this man of genius, and when he did again begin to design new realms of intellect in the years after 1902, it was with the wariness of the master builder who has already seen his creations destroyed by the defects of his own hubris; it was with the hopeless courage of the prophet who has seen freedom—both his own and his nation's—transformed by some inescapable destiny into slavery, and whose only hope and only liberation rest paradoxically in his knowledge and articulation of his—and the world's—enslavement.

[1]

WEBER'S PERSPECTIVES ON THE EAST ELBIAN QUESTION (1892-1895)

Four summaries of his approach to the East Elbian land question punctuate Weber's development, both public and private, in the years 1892 through 1895. In this section I will

---

or paradoxical behavior—all signs of deep internal conflict. Such material has invited psychoanalytic probing of figures like Luther, Darwin, Mill, Schopenhauer, Goethe, Johnson, Boswell, Swedenborg, William James, Henry James, and Freud himself. With these men psychic disturbance is intimately connected with the development of their work and ideas. . . . For many creative men, whose willingness to probe reality may lead them to be open to deeper conflicts than most people dare to let themselves in for, the depths of their lives call out for an analysis that common sense cannot make. Such people make more evident and intense the conflicts which in ordinary psychic growth are more blandly resolved." *History and Theory*, Vol. 7, 1968, No. 3, pp. 283-4.

broadly sketch out those themes which are similar in all of these summaries and also indicate why any such attempt at a unified presentation of these studies breaks down in the light of gross contradictions between them.[1]

A part of the problem Weber was dealing with in these studies had been discussed in the *Verein für Sozialpolitik* in 1886 and 1890: the exodus of German peasants from the East Elbian region. But Weber's analysis, based on the inquiry of 1890, also explored the economic demise of the traditional domainal form of agriculture in this area.

The bankruptcy of the older system had occurred, according to Weber, in part from economic causes, themselves results of the absorption of the German East into the world market, but more importantly through psychological causes: the Junker's need to compete socially with the rising living standards of the urban bourgeoisie and the farm worker's need to free himself from the landlord's despotism.

Although Weber hardly mentioned the impact on German agriculture in the late nineteenth century of competition from Russian and American grain, he traced with some subtlety the effect of this impact on traditional forms of economic activity. Since the 1870's and '80's, absorption into the world market had created sharp annual fluctuations in grain prices. Given the semifeudal domainal system of East Elbia, if grain prices rose, the landlords had a powerful incentive and would do everything they could to seize part of their peasants' land and abolish their share of the threshing. On the other hand, if grain prices dropped, then the semi-serf peasants had a strong motive for converting their share in the lord's harvest to a straight money wage. The result was the rapid conversion, after 1870, of many landed estates, particularly in the north, from the traditional semifeudal labor system to one based on wage contracts.[2] A second consequence of absorption in the world market was the use of machinery, especially the threshing machine, and of intensive agriculture (e.g., sugar beets) as more efficient ways of cultivating the land. While the machinery made superfluous many of the semi-serf peasants who had long been essential at harvest time, the effect of intensive agriculture was "the diminution of the permanent settled workers lastingly bound to the land in favor of seasonal workers, and quite generally the capitalist transformation of the old labor relationship into purely contractual wage labor."[3]

Apart from these strictly economic pressures, a psychological need drove the Junkers to exploit their enterprises more efficiently and so to undermine the patriarchal social order: keeping up with the rising standard of living "of the urban bourgeois population . . . principally that of the upper bourgeoisie, i.e., of the hitherto chief competitor of the landed aristocracy for political power."[4]

But for the most part, the psychological motives for destroying the patriarchal social system came from the land workers themselves, the best of whom were obsessed by the desire for personal independence. This is the key unifying theme of Weber's early work: "Separation at any price from the patriarchal domestic and economic community . . ."[5]

On the basis of the changes he had observed in the social framework of East Elbian agriculture, Weber drew both universal-historical and political conclusions.

He interpreted what he had seen in the German East as part of an historical process, away from traditional patriarchal institutions and toward rational capitalist ones. Furthermore, the key forces in bringing about this change were not, as Marx might have put it, the development of the forces of production, but psychological motives among both rulers and ruled.

Weber saw the Junker's need to keep up with the urban bourgeois as a "disaster which must endanger their economic foundation even without all the influences of foreign competition."[6] At least as significant in undermining the older ways was the growing desire of the worker for independence, which as I have made clear above, Weber saw even in 1887 as "for centuries the point around which the history of the world turned."[7] The destruction of the Roman slave plantation and the creation of the relatively greater freedom of the medieval peasant was a result of the slave's refusal to reproduce himself when deprived of his own land and family. When the period of Roman conquest ended, the market for cheap slaves vanished, and slaves became so expensive that the landowners could only obtain the manpower to till their fields by converting their slaves into serfs.[8] This was, of course, one of the main themes of Weber's inaugural dissertation of 1891, *Die römische Agrargeschichte*.[9] The individual's desire for greater independence had also been for Weber a crucial factor in the dissolution of the medieval trading houses, built as they were around the enlarged family, a principal theme of his doctoral thesis of 1889.[10] Indeed, in contrast to the medieval tolerance for the enlarged family as the basic economic unit, Weber saw as "characteristic of the modern world" and "the product of a psychological development of a general character," the land worker's demand "to be creator of his own happiness—or unhappiness."[11] These changes in men's minds were the driving forces of contemporary history: "The work hands no longer want to tolerate the patriarchal disposition over the fate of the laborer . . . *Psychological* motives of overwhelming power bring on both the flight to the cities and the disorganization of this form of labor."[12] Weber was, of course, analyzing the same social processes that Ferdinand Tönnies had dealt with in terms of the evolution from *Gemeinschaft* to *Gesellschaft*.[13] But Weber's approach differed from Tonnies's in two important respects.

One was that Tönnies offered no explanation to account for the change. Weber offered both economic and psychological reasons. The other was that Tönnies's values were completely on the side of *Gemeinschaft* : *Gesellschaft* he saw as representing not merely the victory of commercialism but of arbitrary power (*Willkür*) over the intimate community based on family ties of love. Weber, contrariwise, viewed arbitrary power as the characteristic of the patriarchal overlord in the traditional society—i.e., in what Tönnies had called *Gemeinschaft*—and one of the most powerful agents undermining this traditionalism was the desire of the sons to free themselves from it. Despite such sharp differences of approach, however, at a certain political level, the aims of Tönnies and Weber coincided: both opposed the Prussian conservative dominion in Germany. Neither could tolerate the hypocrisy of the social monarchists, who were, in effect, arguing that a political extension of the patriarchal system of the East to all the subjects of the Emperor could tie Germany together in one "organic," or "harmonious," *Gemeinschaft*. For Tönnies the idea was absurd, because the essential nature of Prussian state and society was a primitive authoritarian variety of *Gesellschaft;* for Weber, because the proposed basis of the national community, the patriarchal system of the East, was economically bankrupt, socially despotic, and, as a result of its metamorphosis into capitalism, politically a danger to the national existence.*

For the Junkers were solving their economic problems by the massive importation of Polish labor. The need to lower overhead expenses dictated the replacement, wherever feasible, of German semi-serf labor by Polish migrant workers. The Poles were accustomed to a lower standard of living and therefore consumed less of the landlord's food. They were aliens who could be deported at the landlord's whim and so were obedient to his discipline. Moreover, as seasonal laborers they made no claims on the lord's food and shelter during the winter months. Thus, Weber's political program arose directly from his analysis of the way the economic reflexes of the Junkers were imperiling the future of the nation they had helped to create. The practical solutions he advocated were

---

* On Tönnies, see the author's "Anti-Progress, a Study in the Romantic Roots of German Sociology," *Social Research,* Spring 1966, pp. 65–85. Weber later wrote that at the time he gave his inaugural address, "the great majority of my colleagues ran after the swindle of the so-called social monarchy." Wolfgang Mommsen: *Max Weber und die deutsche Politik* (Tübingen, 1959) (hereafter cited as *Mommsen: Max Weber*), p. 43.

clear and sharp. To insure that the Poles did not obtain an ethnic majority in the East the Reich had to close its borders, as Bismarck had done from 1886 to 1890.[14] To keep the territory from becoming depopulated, the Imperial regime had to expropriate, with compensation, at least a part of the Junker estates for division among independent peasants.

Now Weber had pinpointed the political dangers of continued Junker rule and the need for an alternative to it as early as 1892, though at that time it was their new needs as rural capitalists rather than their traditional character that caused the trouble. And one part or another of his solutions to the more immediate problems appeared in each of his four approaches to the question. It was, however, only in the last of these, Weber's inaugural address at Freiburg, that he investigated the more deeply rooted problem of how one was to find a political force to replace the Junker hegemony. And here, in 1895, Weber encapsulated his whole previous argument in a radically different framework. The outstanding theme of the earlier work had been the desire for liberation from traditional servitude as the moving force of historical progress. But in the *Freiburger Antrittsrede,* this theme was subordinated to another: the inescapable struggle for survival—between nationalities, between economic classes, and between nation-states. And the first and last of these were for Weber the crucial ones to a German political economist.

Reduced to its simplest terms, Weber's argument was that the Germans were losing the struggle between Polish and German nationalities in the East because the state had permitted the Junkers' economic struggle for existence to govern its policies. The determining point of view which should have regulated this economic struggle was *Staatsraison:*

> With this slogan we want to raise the demand that in questions of German economic policy—even, for example, the question of whether, and to what extent, the state should intervene in economic life or whether and when it should rather unleash the economic forces of the nation to their own free development and tear

down their barriers—in the individual case, the last and decisive vote should go to the economic and political power interests of our nation and of their bearer, the German national state.

Weber made no bones about it: "The science of national economic policy is a *political* science. It is a servant of politics: not of the daily politics of the momentary power holders and classes, but of the permanent, power-political interests of the nation." Again and again, Weber hammered home the point that the state must regulate the economic struggle in the interests of "the *eternal struggle* for the preservation and the higher breeding (*Emporzüchtung*) of our national character." "Our descendants will make us responsible before history *not* primarily for the kind of economic organization we bequeath them, but for the amount of elbow room we achieve and leave for them," etc. Any illusions the political economist might have that he could escape his "own conscious value judgment," based on this situation, or that he could establish other criteria based on the interests of either the existing power holders or of rising economic classes, led only to lack of "conscious self-control" and to the dominance of "uncontrolled instincts, sympathies, and antipathies."[15]

The Junkers had earlier formed a political elite which embodied this *Staatsraison*. They had done so by virtue of their political and social organizations,[16] which formed the basis of their "political instincts." The problem Weber faced was that while the economic decline of the Junkers was sufficient to disqualify them from their former position of leadership, the mere economic *rise* of the bourgeoisie and the proletariat was in no way sufficient to qualify either of them to replace the Junkers politically, for they lacked the Junkers' hard schooling in political realities. The only way they could obtain this schooling was by a militant effort to make Germany a world power, which would place the entire nation, even the lower classes—like the French lower classes during the Convention and the English working classes in the nineteenth century—before the continual problems of national destiny. Indeed, Weber seemed to have more confidence in the ultimate political potentialities of the working class than he did in the bourgeoisie.[17]

Now the whole approach of the *Antrittsrede* is so different from Weber's previous framework, and particularly from the first general discussion of the East Elbian situation in 1892, that some explanation of the changes is imperative. Indeed, careful analysis also reveals marked shifts of emphasis in each of the first three studies (1892, 1893, and 1894). In particular, we find Weber repeatedly altering his perceptions of the following social groups and relationships: the land workers, with whose striving for independence he clearly identifies, and, more generally, the working class; the Junkers, in whom, as I shall show, he sees his father's vices writ large; the older generation of bourgeois liberals, of which his father was a prominent member; the relationships between the first three groups; his own relationship to the older generation of scholars of the historical school. Biographical evidence suggests that the source of Weber's kaleidoscopic vision of German society may be discerned in his rapidly changing personal situation in these years.

[2]

THE PERSONAL FRAMEWORK: MOVES TOWARD INDEPENDENCE

ACCORDING TO Gustav Schmoller, chairman of the *Verein für Sozialpolitik's* meeting of March 1893, most of the studies on the land problem then under discussion were written under great pressure before September 1892, because they were all supposed to be completed before the session of the *Verein's* General Assembly scheduled in Posen for that time. Unfortunately, a cholera epidemic in Eastern Europe had forced a six-month's postponement of that assembly,[18] but we can reasonably assume that Weber wrote the concluding "*Ausblick*" to his study of East Elbian agriculture over the summer of 1892. And he probably wrote the *Referat* that he gave on March 20, 1893, some time during the first two months of that year.*

In the summer of 1892, Weber was twenty-eight years old, living, as he had for most of the previous six years, in his father's house. He was completing his first semester of teaching as a *Privatdozent*† and, with his legal apprenticeship behind him, was still considering law as a profession: in the spring, apart from his work on the *Verein's enquête* and his teaching, he was also representing a Berlin attorney at the Supreme Court (*Kammergericht*) "daily from nine until about seven in the evening."[19] The result of undertaking three jobs at once was "that I had to suffer recently from the aftereffects of an overestimation of my capacity to work."[20]

But there was yet a fourth job. Weber was also very active at this time in the *Evangelisch-Soziale Verein* (Protestant Social Union), whose meetings he had begun attending in 1890, together with his mother.[21] He published articles on the land worker question in the April, June, and July issues of their *Mitteilungen* and defended his friend Paul Göhre—whose *Drei Monate Fabrikarbeiter* had evoked the wrath of the higher clergy—in the pages of *Christliche Welt*.[22] Indeed, his wife tells us that in early 1892 he was more interested in a political career than a scholarly one: "*Der Willensmensch in ihm sehnt sich nach grossen Verantwortungen, nach 'Lebensfluten und Tatensturm.'*"** It was

---

* Weber seems to have been working on the *Referat* at the time of his letter to Lujo Brentano of February 20, 1893, *Jb.*, p. 364; *Baumg.*, p. 84.

† The lowest rung of the German academic stepladder, in which the instructor received only his students' tuition (a nominal sum) as payment.

** The man of will in him yearns for great responsibilities, for the flood of life and the storm of deeds"; *Lebensb.*, p. 188.

because of this impulse for a more active life that Weber had in 1891 tried, unsuccessfully, to obtain the position of *Syndicus* in the Bremen adminstration that Sombart had just left.

Despite this appearance of moving in several directions at once, Weber was by September 1892 only months away from his two permanent lifetime commitments: to Marianne Schnitger and to a career of scholarship. Added together, they would grant him his long-yearned-for release from his father's house.

In the winter semester of 1892, his former thesis adviser, Goldschmidt, gave him the decisive push into the world of scholarship. Ailing, Goldschmidt asked Weber to take over his own courses at the University of Berlin, a great honor to the young *Dozent,* which led a year later to his appointment as *Extraordinarius.*[23] And in March 1893, Weber became engaged to Marianne Schnitger,[24] with whom he had been dilatorily keeping company for about a year. He had had to make up his mind about her during the month of January, for at the beginning of January he discovered that his casual manner toward her had encouraged a close friend to ask for her hand.[25] Helene Weber, who apparently could think of no other match for her son than his cousin Emmy[26] —a safe choice for the indefinite postponement of his departure from her side, since Max's most recent report on the condition of the sickly Emmy was that she was an invalid and her recovery would take years[27]—strongly favored Marianne's match with Max's friend, whom she also held in maternal affection. For this reason and for others yet more profound, these months formed a tense and crucial period in Weber's life, in which an oppressive sense of guilt alternated feverishly with passionate exaltation.

Weber's letter of proposal to Marianne, written probably in January 1893,* hinges on precisely this alternation

---

* Marianne gives no date for the letter which she reproduces in the *Lebensbild,* pp. 204–7, but she does say that the engagement followed the letter by "some months" (*"einige Monate"*); *Lebensb.* p. 207. In the *Jugendbriefe,* she says that the engagement was in March

of guilt and passion. Its second sentence contains a beautiful metaphor, which occurs again later at a much higher level of intensity and which here anticipates the desperate lunge from guilt and resignation to passionate involvement that is the conclusion and real meaning of the letter: "You believe —I think—that we are at the end of our relationship and that I would banish you to the still and cool harbor of resignation, in which I myself have laid at anchor for years. But that is not so." The following paragraph assures Marianne of the absolute seriousness with which he conceives the idea of offering his hand in marriage: ". . . only under the divine compulsion of complete, unconditional devotion . . ." The next five paragraphs, the bulk of the letter, are comprehensible only as a prolonged admission of guilt, the casting off of which through confession, like the casting off of an anchor, is the indispensable preliminary to Weber's departure from the "harbor of resignation."

After suggesting that he has only come to understand her in the past few days, he tells Marianne that *she* does not really know him at all. "You do not see how I try, with difficulty and varying success, to tame the elementary passions that Nature has placed in me; but ask my mother; I know well that her love for me, which forces me to silence because I cannot repay it [*"die mir den Mund schliesst, weil ich sie nicht entgelten Kann*], is rooted in the fact that, morally, I was her problem child. For years, the idea that the rich heart of a girl could come close to my sober nature never touched me; therefore I was blind, and with you too, certain of my opinion."

Precisely why, after discussing his enduring struggle to tame his "elementary passions," he should speak of his "sober nature" as an obstacle to love is not clear, but the apparently random sequence from the next-to-last sentence

---

(p. 367) and that the secret Max hinted at in his letter to Klara Weber of January 9, 1893, was "the expected engagement of Marianne with a friend of Max Weber." Only if the letter of proposal was written in January, then, would the interval *"einige Monate"* be accurate.

to the last has a perfectly clear psycho-logic, if we simply start with the casually inserted dependent clause to the effect that his mother's love prevents him from speaking because he cannot repay it. While Weber probably intended this to mean nothing more than that he could not speak of loving his mother because his own love was unequal to hers, neither this meaning nor the larger sentence of which it forms a part have any connection to the sentence that follows. On the other hand, by taking Weber's language literally, we can discern a most interesting connection indeed. "Her love . . . closes my mouth because I cannot repay it," is another way of saying two different things: (1) because his mouth remains closed (i.e., in the presence of his father's bullying), he cannot repay her love and this has put a moral claim on him, a burden of guilt, which has for years prevented him from getting close to another woman than his mother; (2) this burden of guilt inhibits his present expression of his love for Marianne, but since the guilt and the silence are interdependent, perhaps by openly voicing his guilt he can overcome it to the point of expressing his passion for Marianne. This interpretation would, of course, be nothing more than idle conjecture were it not for the fact that in the very next paragraph he himself makes an explicit connection between certain other of his guilt feelings and his inability to speak of his love for Marianne, and ends the paragraph by candidly confessing to a need to speak about them despite the fact that *"Du weisst von beiden"* ("You know about both").* To put it simply, she knows, he says, how he feels toward her, but he cannot say

---

* In this paragraph he explains why, though he felt sorrow at the prospect of Marianne spending her life with someone else, he did not immediately recognize his sentiment as love: *"Ich hielt es für die selbstische Empfindung dessen, der resigniert hat, beim Anblick fremden Glückes und unterdrückte es. Aber es war etwas anderes. Du weisst was. Über meine Lippe darf das Wort nicht, denn ich habe eine doppelte Schuld an die Vergangenheit zu zahlen und weiss nicht, ob ich es kann. Du weisst von beiden, aber trotzdem muss ich davon sprechen." Lebensb,* p. 205.

the word because of the double guilt he has to pay to the past. And she knows all about the guilt, too, but on that presumably painful subject he *must* speak.

The guilt of which he is conscious is the guilt he has incurred in his relationship both to his friend who had proposed to Marianne, and to his cousin Emmy. Through his procrastination, his failure to speak up in time, he has injured his friend. Similarly, through his failure to tell Emmy, during his visit to her the previous fall, that he no longer loved her, he may have aroused false hopes in her. In both cases, he cannot be free of the burden of guilt unless they accept his match with Marianne "*without* the feeling of renunciation," without "a cool renunciation, resignation." The facts that in these two terribly important cases, he incurred his "*Schuld*" by silence when he should have spoken up bravely, that he cannot go ahead with his desire to wed Marianne unless Emmy and his friend, like his mother, forgive and love him, and that the immediate effect of this guilt is to prevent him from expressing to Marianne the same emotion that his guilt toward his mother prevented him from expressing to *her*, constitute either an amazing coincidence or strong evidence that the guilt he has accepted toward Emmy and his friend is modeled on the guilt he so casually mentions toward his mother.

In any case, after a page and a half of agonized purgation, Weber, in the accents of an Ahab seeking comrades to hunt the white whale, finally proposes:

And now I ask you: have you inwardly separated from me in these days? Or resolved to do it? Or do you do it *now? If not, then it is too late,* we are bound to one another, and I will be hard toward you and not spare you. I say to you: I go the course that I must, and which you now know.—And you will go it with me.—Where it will lead, how far it is, whether it leads us together on this earth, I know not. . . . But I believe I know how you decide. High goes the tidal wave of passions, and it is dark around us—come with me, my high-souled comrade, out of the quiet harbor of resignation, out onto the high seas, where men grow in the struggling of souls and the past falls away from them.

At just this moment, when Weber is sailing out of the harbor and into the storm with his *"hochherziger Kamerad"* and the burdensome anchor of the past is disappearing behind him, he stops and insists upon dragging it aboard after all:

> But *reflect:* in the head and heart of the mariner there must be clarity, when all is burning beneath him. We may tolerate no fantastical surrender to unclear and mystical moods in our souls. For when feeling rises high, you must fetter it, to be able to steer with sobriety.

Marianne, completely caught up in the ecstatic fervor of Weber's letter, was shaken to her roots by "the unnameable, the eternal."[28] But the ecstasy waned during the long months that it took her future husband to ship anchor;[29] only in March was he willing to make their engagement public—that is, only after an exchange of letters between his mother and his Aunt Ida, and, more importantly, after he himself had had a long and emotionally exhausting visit with his aunt, as he told Marianne in a letter from Strassburg written shortly after that encounter:

> I did nothing but sit quietly, so as to discuss past, present, and future with my aunt . . . more from the standpoint of sentiment than with any practical goal. That goes strongly against my grain, and you have surely noticed in my letter the great exhaustion that it brought me. Nonetheless, it has benefited both me and her, and if I still feel as if I have emerged from a kind of soul and bone grinder, you will, my darling, when I take you again in my arms, surely remark that I have taken a step forward in the assimilation of all that the past has laid upon me.[30]

At this point in his letter, in the midst of describing his feverish efforts to expose and thereby heal all the sources of his guilt to Emmy, Weber makes a curious reference to Marianne's fear that something remains concealed:

> Then you will also not think, my child, as you wrote in your last letter, "I had something to hide from you." What should that be? You know well the past and my inner relationship to it and know that my concern is directed exclusively at producing the most sincere and natural relationship possible between past and present and thus at sparing us any possibility that our happiness might be built on the silent and painful resignation of others.

Now Marianne was a girl of uncommon powers of perception; she may well have intuited that behind the resigned Emmy—indeed, behind herself and her future husband, who were only then moving jointly out of the "harbor of resignation"—stood the implacably resigned figure of Helene Weber. For the concealment was, after all, rather thin. Somewhat earlier in the letter Marianne received from Strassburg, Max spoke of his "feeling of responsibility" as being unweakened and a permanent possession: ". . . but rest easy my child, I have assimilated it long since, and it is no longer a source of irritation for me, [as] it was under the pressure of the recent situation." Nine years earlier, in Weber's first open admission of gratitude to his mother, he had acknowledged her influence as having awakened this feeling of responsibility, as having rescued him from "quite eccentric paths" to "a calmer mode of perception," and as having enabled him "to observe the ideas and personalities of other men without prejudice and to learn from them."[31] In the shadow passage in his letter to Marianne, he wrote immediately after the sentence quoted above, "I am conscious of having committed serious mistakes, but nothing of which I should have to be ashamed." In the *Urconfession* to his mother of 1884: "In my earlier university days, I of course did many very frivolous things, as I now note, but no bad follies, and if that has not occurred—young as I was and am, the temptation was often great—then it has been because I thought of you."

If Weber's confession of his sins to Marianne parallels the much earlier confession to his mother, the casual connection he made in his letter of proposal between his unpayable debt to his mother and his incapacity to believe that a girl could love him echoes eerily through a letter he wrote to Emmy shortly before his marriage:

> The belief that I could never belong to a woman, nor be capable of coming close to a girl, was, you know it, the consequence of my unresolved doubt of many years over how you stood to me and would stand, and I would never have emerged from this deep resignation without certainty over our relationship. . . . Next to the picture of my mother, it is yours which, in the past barren and almost always prospectless years, gave me that degree of strength which I possessed and have retained.[32]

Clearly, at a certain level of Weber's mind, his mother, his cousin, and his future bride became one person. And the fugal alternation between guilt-ridden resignation and passionate boldness could not finally cease until Weber repayed his guilt-debt to that one person by ending his silence before his father.

Nonetheless, the period when Weber was trying so desperately to cast off the anchor of his guilt also offered him the glorious vision of a new life, outside the prison of his father's home. His letter to Emmy, written shortly after the announcement of his engagement, is suffused with a hope that forms a sharp contrast to the "joyless emptiness" and "resignation" in which he admits he had been immersed for years:

> The world looks very differently to me now than it did last autumn; for I now go forth to hard and great tasks of a purely human nature and for which it is worthwhile to exert one's strength, even if they appear externally to be less impressive than what the masculine profession,

which goes on in the market place of life, otherwise can offer us for goals. . . . And since I have never, apart from the obligation "to make the most of one's talent," had more than external respect for the value of the masculine profession, I have a deep yearning that such daily, purely human tasks may be placed before me.[33]

Again, a subordinate phrase, "apart from the obligation to make the most of one's talent," forms the background of his yearning and illuminates the sources of his guilt and resignation. For the Puritans he later wrote about and for his grandmother Emilia Souchay, whose Calvinist morality remained firm even when her theology had become heterodox, the parable of the entrusted talent was of crucial significance in giving a transcendent importance to worldly activity—in making such activity pleasing in the eyes of God and a sign of God's grace. In Weber's case the theology had evaporated, but the morality, inherited through his mother and still phrased in the words of the Biblical parable, governed his adult life until his breakdown. Indeed, although the divine sanction for making the most of one's talent had vanished in these years, an even more compelling deity subjected him to this morality: his mother—whose (paradoxically) paternalistic, authoritarian code dominated his soul through his harsh and demanding superego. And here lay the paradox that almost drove Weber mad: the horror of his early adult life was that no amount of worldly asceticism could procure him the grace and forgiveness of his Lord, for Helene Weber represented to her son a feminine as well as a masculine Godhead. As a masculine Godhead, she demanded of him a life of unsparing dedication to his work, and only through such unsparing dedication to his work, such ascetic subjection to the condition of son-hood, could he attain her grace. But at the same time, she was also the injured Mother-God, incapable of defending herself against her own subjection to her tyrannical spouse except by calling to her aid the rebelliousness of her child, i.e., by demanding that he grow up, speak up, leave his condition of son-hood, transcend, abolish, lift himself up, *sich aufheben*. Apart from the disorienting suppression and evocation of sexual impulses that these two roles must have meant for her son, Helene was in general requiring that he be simultaneously two completely different and antithetical persons.*

To sum up: the *"Ausblick"* at the end of the study of 1892 took shape at a moment in Weber's life when, through his new jobs as lawyer and *Privatdozent,* he had finally come within sight of the promised land, i.e., any land at all outside of his father's house. And he probably wrote the *Referat* of 1893 at a time of great inner agitation, when he was steeling himself to take that step toward marriage which meant not only a severe strain with a close friend but also the final severance of his ties to his faithful, long-suffering cousin—and mother: in short, at a time of renunciations as well as new responsibilities.

[3]

THE *"AUSBLICK"* OF 1892

THE *"Ausblick"* OF 1892, in keeping with Weber's insecure position as a young *Dozent* and lawyer, still dependent on his father's domestic grace and the good will of his teachers, is by far the most moderate in tone of the four studies under consideration. Weber traverses the difficult terrain of the

---

* On the parable of the talent as used by the Puritans, cf. Weber's *Die Protestantische Ethik* (München, 1965), pp. 172, 256–7; as used by Helene Weber's mother, *Lebensb.,* p. 9. The interpretation I have set out above also explains why, when Weber rejected Emmy's pressure to spend more time helping his mother—a pressure which almost surely originated in Helene Weber herself—he evaded it by referring to "a kind of dogma that certain things which one has firmly resolved to finish may not be left undone, and I cannot conceive that my mother could find that improper." See *Jb,* E.B., Oct. 21, 1887, p. 275. On the two sides of the Calvinist attitude toward authority, see Franz Neumann: *Behemoth* (New York, London, Toronto, 1944), pp. 89–92.

Junker estates as though it were made of eggshells rather than poor soil.

He makes it so clear that the Junkers are not to blame for the metamorphosis of the patriarchal estates into capitalist agriculture that the conservatives consider him their friend.[34] He does not even mention closing the borders as a solution, and barely mentions colonization. The one point on which he is unequivocal is the significance of the growing desire for liberation from the patriarchal relationship among the farm workers: "The most striking tendency among precisely the best elements of the workingmen, is separation from the patriarchal house and economic community at any price, even that of passing into the homeless proletariat."[35] In many cases, the consequence of breaking loose is material hardship. Nonetheless, the servant flees his master; the thresher tries to separate his piece of land from the lord's estate; the relatively well-off and secure, though servile, *"Instmann"* voluntarily relinquishes his place on the estate to become an impoverished but free wage-hand (though the man who owns a scrap of property would rather starve than look for wage-work); workers buy land, again, "at any price," because to own land means to be independent, even though they spend the rest of their lives wretchedly paying off the interest. Still, Weber is clearly ambivalent about the effectiveness af cutting loose. It is noteworthy that in all these examples, Weber sees workers as satisfying their underlying desires for independence primarily by individual ownership of land large enough to support a peasant family, rather than by either emigration or by an organized struggle of the rural proletariat against the landlords.[36] And in the passage that follows these examples, he is simultaneously doubtful about the results of those desires and quite clear about their crucial significance in the German East, in the modern world, and—to anyone who knows him—in himself:

> It is the powerful and purely psychological enchantment of "freedom" [N.B.: *"Zauber der 'Freiheit' "*]

which finds expression there. In large measure, it is a question of a grand illusion, but, as we know, man, and thus the land worker too, does not live "from bread alone." . . . In the first place, he demands to be the creator of his own happiness—or unhappiness. This characteristic of the modern world is the product of a psychological development of a general character, and we experience it in ourselves . . . Today we are driven to our own hearth, we strive to earn our own bread abroad, away from the table of the parents' house, and from the circle of our own; and the difficulty in the situation is that the evolution of the general conditions of life denies the desired economic independence until an ever-later age.

So here we find a young *Privatdozent* who is both enthused at finding the *"Zauber der Freiheit"*—like some proletarian cunning of reason—in the land worker, and despondent at the frequency with which *"Freiheit"* turns into the "grand illusion"—wage slavery. He seems to be a careful young man, and perhaps we should amend the proposition about the Promised Land being "any land at all outside of his father's house" to "any land large enough to support him."

The same carefulness conceals to all but the searching eye his true attitude towards the Junkers, which in several respects proves to be a hypostatization of his attitude toward his father. Thus, a number of sentences of this conclusion to the study of 1892, if taken out of context, sound like panegyrics to the Prussian aristocracy:

Regardless of any reservations to be made, the great landowners of the east are correctly valued as "pillars of the monarchy." They had the capacity to be this and it was safe to put into the hands of the much-decried Junkers far-reaching rights of dominion, not yet completely set aside, because they disdainfully refused to become an estate of profit-consuming magnates—which is to their honor— . . . and because the labor constitution was such that the landlord was in fact to a certain extent the born representative of the interests of his people.

Moreover, the old Prussian agrarian regime was the perfect breeding ground for "the psychological presuppositions of military discipline." Drawing on his own military experience, Weber argued that "the sons of the Northeast" were exemplary for their discipline, honor, and sense of duty: " '. . . *verdammte Pflicht und Schuldigkeit.*' "[37] Thus, he says, "It surely does not lie in the interest of the state to sacrifice frivolously an estate whose sons led the defensive power of the nation to unparalleled military successes, risked their lives more than all others, and linked their names inseparably to memories that will make our hearts beat faster for all time."[38]

Nonetheless, Weber's eulogies for the Junker ethos, on closer examination, bear all the earmarks of the toasts at a Borgia feast, by means of which the family enemies are coaxed into a spirit of cheerful reconciliation before they are served the poisoned dessert. For despite the high praise which these passages in his study of 1892 brought to Weber from the conservative press,* each of them was literally surrounded by what amounted to obituary notices for the feudal agrarians. The last of these is particularly noteworthy, since it resonates with other things Weber said and felt, both about the political fate of Germany and about his own personal lot as well:

> It is the tragic destiny of the German East that through its powerful achievements for the nation it has dug the grave of its own social organization. The creation of the political greatness of the nation is above all *its* merit. "Bright from the North, the light of freedom came," sang the poet eighty years ago. The German East, with its tight political and military organization,

---

* In the letter to Brentano of February 1893 referred to above (see p. 85), he singled out the praise of the conservative *Kreuzzeitung*, as "impertinence"; *Jb.*, p. 365.

was also the half-reluctant tool through which the nation achieved its desired unity. It was not narrowness of vision, but the vague presentiment of what must come, when leading men in Prussia, up to the highest position, strove against absorption into the greater unity of the Empire. The Eastern marches of the state, only meagerly supplied by nature, bore from the beginning and now, too, the economic and military costs of Prussian hegemony. With the unity of the Empire, the metropolitan and industrial development has experienced a strong boom. The South and West, with their overpowering capital, compel the East to accept their industrial products and send back the bread which the agriculture of the East wrings from its native soil with hardship and expense. Just as the East was the chief supplier of human material for the military foundation of the nation's political greatness, so now it delivers to the industry of the West the labor power for the foundation of the economic power position of Germany. Through the brilliant development of German industry and of the large cities, its life's blood, the new generation of labor power, is sucked from its veins.

Weber could just as well have applied, and three years later did apply, the principle in this passage—the idea that the conservatives were destroyed by their own successes—to his father's generation too, which he saw as having created the Reich and then become decadent in the (illusory) security it provided: *"Die deutsche Geschichte schien zu Ende,"* etc.[39] Indeed, the earlier linking, in this *"Ausblick,"* of the Junkers' honor to their disdainful refusal "to become an estate of profit-consuming magnates" was an oblique and probably unconscious cuff at his father, who, measured by this standard, must have lost both honor and independence ever since he began living primarily from the income of his wife's inheritance in 1885. Finally, the notion that the conservative agrarians were being bled dry by the departure of their own "life's blood, the new generation," applied directly to his relationship to his own father. At the time he wrote the conclusion to the East Elbian study, Weber had just begun teaching as a *Privatdozent* in Berlin, may have been considering marriage with Marianne Schnitger, and was certainly yearning to remove his father's "life's blood" from his father's house.

[4]

THE *REFERAT* OF 1893

WEBER'S CAREFULNESS in the *"Ausblick"* of 1892 served its purpose too well. No one noticed the poison. Weber admitted in a letter to Lujo Brentano that he had "perhaps gone rather too far" in concealing his position, but that he thought that it lay "in the interest of objectivity to have to suppress the naturally inherent aversion that we liberals have against the big Eastern landowners."

But the misinterpretation which really unleashed all of Weber's latent rebelliousness in the *Referat* of 1893 was not the foolish praise of the conservatives but the mistaken notion of a Silesian magnate that Weber's fears of a cultural regression in the East were the result of a "National Liberal miscalculation." Until this point, Weber's argument had retained much of the camouflage of the *"Ausblick."* Partly because he wanted to pay lip service to the standard conservative vocabulary of his day, partly because one side of him really believed it, Weber condemned the "unorganic and individualistic" ethos of the West German peasant:

> He is ignorant of the kind of work we in the East know, this stern, obligatory exertion of labor power that encompasses one's whole life. The characteristic Prussian concept of "damned duty" is lacking in these people. This often-overlooked psychological aspect is of considerable significance for the question: Is such a formation of the labor constitution as would be identical with

the radical shattering of all large holdings politically desirable as a goal? I think: No. It is no accident that the areas of Germany where this constitution prevails have been unable to attain that political organization and that shaping of the political consciousness which have created the unity of the Reich.[40]

Weber then meanders through several paragraphs which would not have offended a Romanov, much less a Hohenzollern, until he begins to discuss the harmful inroads that the erosion of the old rural labor constitution have had on the workers' living standards. Halfway through this somber diagnosis, he mentions the accusation that the Silesian magnate has only a few days ago made in the Reichstag: that his analysis must have been based on a National Liberal miscalculation.[41] At this he is doubly roused to fury: not only has his carefully preserved objectivity been questioned, but he has been stuck in the detestable pigeonhole of a National Liberal—i.e., the magnate has called attention to the fact that he is his father's son. In the next seven pages, Weber does everything but burn the old man in effigy to disprove this notion.

The Silesian landowner had argued against Weber's notion that the new rural capitalism had led to a cultural decline by pointing out that he himself had undergone no cultural decline whatever. Weber retorted before the *Verein*: "Gentlemen, naturally *he* has not, but certainly his workers have, for whom he is responsible." At the very beginning of this passage, then, Weber centers his ire on the fact that the landowner is no longer what he used to be: "the born representative of the interests of his people," in the words of the 1892 *"Ausblick."* This anticipates the theme of this section, that the Junker of his own day has let his new material interests destroy his traditional sense of social responsibility while, conversely, his workers, driven primarily by the ideal of personal freedom, are all too happy to escape his tyranny.

The thinly veiled illogic of Weber's argument betrays his personal passion. In his initial response to the Silesian magnate, he points out that the capitalist transformation of Eastern agriculture has indeed resulted in a major decline in the quality of the workers' diet, from cereal and milk to potatoes. Though he is quick to deny that he is attributing any personal guilt to the landowners for their wanting to alter the traditional mode of labor and, therefore, the living standards of the laborer, it is perfectly clear that he does find them morally culpable, for in his following explanation of the land workers' parallel desire to escape the old labor system, he sees no significance in the falling standard of living he has just mentioned, but stresses only the ideal of liberation. Indeed, this ideal appears among the best-situated of the semi-serf workers, the *Instleute,* who gladly move into the rural proletariat despite the fact that they thereby surrender "an extraordinarily secure material position in favor of an insecure existence. Nothing," Weber goes on, "bespeaks a more crushing judgment on the future of the *Inst*-relationship than just this factor. The hands will no longer tolerate precisely that patriarchal disposition of the lord over the fate of his worker that the old *Inst*-constitution contains. *Psychological* factors of overwhelming power lead both to the flight into the cities and to the disorganization of this labor constitution."

Ockham's razor or any other rule of intellectual parsimony would suggest that the material factor of a declining living standard had destroyed the *Instmann's* "extraordinarily secure economic position" and thus might alone be sufficient to explain the land worker's flight from the Junker estates. But Weber does not even make the connection. When the fuses of logical connection blow in the mind of a man of genius, one can only assume an emotional overload. Certainly, on the basis of what we already know about Weber, it is reasonable to assume that he was himself obsessed by the same "psychological factors of overwhelming force" that he attributed (projected?) to the land workers.

This is not to say that ideal motives played no role whatever in the land worker's flight from the estates. Indeed, they may have been, as Weber contended, the most significant ones. But how could Weber, dependent as he was on the landowners' reports of purely objective data such as demographic stratification, emoluments, and food intake, have been so certain about the land workers' state of mind? And surely he could only have reasonably expected his listeners to accept the significance of the workers' ideals after first situating the importance of the poorer material conditions, which he had just described. That he failed, at this point in the *Referat,* even to consider these material conditions, strongly supports the argument that he was predisposed to identify his own ideal of liberation—already half-realized in his passionate letter of proposal to Marianne—with the land workers and to project his contempt for his father's smug, self-interested materialism onto the Junkers. Surely the following paragraphs of the *Referat* bear this out.

For what is the reaction of the Junker to his workers' insubordinate drive for freedom? Betrayal. Just as Max Weber, Sr., a leading member of the Bennigsen faction of the National Liberals, has betrayed both class and nation by aligning himself politically in the '90's with the conservative agrarians in the Reichstag,[42] and just as he has similarly betrayed the unity of his family by selfishly arrogating to himself his wife's inheritance, so the Junkers, too, have sold out the nation on an even grander scale by calling in Slavic migrant workers from the East, again purely for selfish economic reasons. These Polish and Russian workers are causing a national crisis in the East: "And if in West Prussia the representatives of the large landowners are now making common cause with the national enemies, then these are just the beginnings, which show us where it can come to if the matter continues in this direction."

Moreover, the Junkers, while betraying the nation, wear the deceiving cloak of hypocrisy in Weber's account, and it is again clear that this descendant of generations of Westphalian weavers[43] has carefully tailored that garment to his father's dimensions. The Junkers are hypocritical because their Manchesterian insistence on their right to procure labor where it is cheapest is utterly inconsistent with their refusal to allow the nation to buy grain where it is cheapest.[44] His father displayed similar hypocrisy when he fell back on his Manchesterian ideology to reject all responsibility for the plight of the lower classes at the same time that he exploited his traditional patriarchal prerogatives by refusing to allow his wife access to her inheritance so that she could exercise that responsibility.

In view of the Junker's betrayal and hypocrisy, the land workers' migration (like Weber's coming departure from his parent's home) is more than justified, it almost assumes the character of an ethical obligation.*

Finally, Weber briefly mentions one other perspective for viewing the landowner's betrayal of the nation: that of class struggle. ". . . From the standpoint of the workers' interest, the employment of Poles means a most serious conceivable crippling of the German workers in the wage struggle with the big landowners."

IN THE AFTERMATH of his affair with Emmy Baumgarten, Weber had largely abandoned his passions and retired to his monastic cell in Charlottenburg; but by 1893, through Marianne, he has recovered them. In the *Referat* of that year, this re-found store of emotions functions like a set of prisms,

---

* "It is not only the difference in wage levels—that is not so important—which leads to migratory labor, but something quite different; it is the disinclination to bind oneself, particularly in the homeland, to lasting work. Precisely the well-known work bell of the neighboring big landlord has an especially sinister sound"; 1893, *S.W.G.*, p. 451. Weber later evoked the same feeling of leaving a moral plague spot in describing his own move of 1894 from Berlin to Freiburg: "I admit quite openly that, when I came, in due course, from the sphere of the Prussian educational administration into that of Baden, I had the feeling of coming into cleaner air"; quoted in *Lebensb.*, p. 471. On the relationship between the Prussian Minister of Education, Althoff, and Weber Sr., see below, pp. 109–19.

through which he refracts the deceptively neutral white light of his analyses of the rural proletariat and the Junker land-owner into its genuine colors. Through his fierce identification with all his nation's oppressed, sons who like himself struggle for liberation, his analysis of the land workers refracts on the left into a band of social-democratic red and on the right into a somewhat broader and sharper band of black, red, and gold, the colors of the revolutionary nationalists of 1848. Through his hatred for the authoritarian code of his father, his analysis of the Junkers refracts for the moment only toward the right, into the heavy gold and black of the Romanov standard, but dim traces of his father's National Liberal grayness extend out toward the left.

Given the predominance of revolutionary nationalism in Weber's empathic projections, his choice of an ultimate standard for judging the East Elbian land question, its implications and its solutions, is clear. Though he refuses to accept the workers' welfare as the most important question, "even less is it the question of how the big Eastern landowners are to obtain their labor power" that concerns him. The uniquely valid standpoint, he argues, is that of *Staatsraison*, in effect, a nationalism which, like that of his uncle's generation of forty-eighters, will demand, if necessary, a revolutionary transformation of the political order to secure the nation's safety and greatness. And it is necessary:

> The interest of the state in the Eastern land worker question is contained in the simple query: Are the foundations of the social organization firm enough so that the State can in the long run support itself on them for the sake of solving those political tasks which await it in the East? The answer to this question, in my opinion, is *no*. . . . Such a crumbling organization is incapable of helping to solve the most important political tasks of the state: in the first place the preservation of German culture in the East, the defense of our eastern boundaries, of German nationality, even in peace. The big landowners cannot solve this task. We

must give up the idea that in the long run, we can and may support ourselves in the East on them alone. They have become uprooted and worthless for the state— not through their fault [*Schuld*], I repeat, but through overpowering national changes of a material and psychological nature.[45]

With this final protest that it is not he, but history that has condemned the Junkers, Weber's volcanic passion cools, his rediscovered emotions slip once more away from him, and the initial theme of conformity, concealing, as we know from his letter of proposal to Marianne, guilt and resignation, returns. Instead of making specific demands for expropriation, which would have followed logically from his argument and which he *will* make the following year, he retreats to the less thorny position of demanding "at the present moment . . . the *absolute exclusion*" of Slavic workers from the East.[46] And in the very next sentence he moderates even this to propose the "immediate" exclusion only of those workers who enter Germany before the grain harvest.

Ten pages later, Weber's attitude has completed a 180-degree turn from his dark hint of revolutionary expropriation and his contemptuous dismissal of the landowners' problems in recruiting labor:

We neither *can* ruin the large Eastern landowners, nor *wish* to. There is nothing to be gained by destroying them; indeed, there is something to be gained by preserving these economic and, above all, social centers of intelligence, so that this spiritual capital should not be also monopolized by the cities and come exclusively into the possession of the urban bourgeoisie; so that political intelligence should not, in the future, leave the land as labor power is now doing.

Having penitentially returned to their eminence those very Junkers whom he had ten pages earlier declared "uprooted and valueless for the state," Weber now calmly attends to the question which, from the standpoint of *Staatsraison*, he had then declared trivial: "If the big landowners of the East are to continue to exist—and they will—where will they recruit their labor power?"[47] Weber has reflected, felt the passion rising high, and fettered it "to steer with sobriety." If, in his proposal to Marianne, it had been his aggressive eroticism which had required chaining down, here it was the obverse of that eroticism, his simmering rebellion against his father which had threatened to get out of hand.

Near the end of the *Referat* of 1893, Weber summarized his mood of the moment via an involuted, gloom-ridden confession of generational difference, in which a strange mixture of resignation, guilt, and rebellion shaped his every sentence:

> Gentlemen, I have reached the end of this necessarily unsystematic presentation. You will, perhaps, have not entirely lost the impression that I have spoken under the pressure of a certain resignation, and that those demands that I have posited here are likewise the product of such resignation—and that is in fact the case. Nonetheless—and I have the honor here to speak before predominantly older and more experienced gentlemen than myself—it is based on the difference between the situation of the older generation *vis-à-vis* the tasks of its epoch—yours, gentlemen—and the situation in which we, your followers, find ourselves today. I do not know whether all my peers feel it in the same strong degree as I in this moment: it is the heavy curse of epigonism which burdens the nation, from its broadest strata to its highest summits. We cannot again bring to life the naïve, enthusiastic energy which inspired the generation before us, because we are placed before other tasks than our fathers were in their time. They have built for us a secure house, and we are invited to sit down in it and let ourselves be at home in it. The tasks which are placed before us are of a different nature. We cannot use them to appeal to grand sentiments, common to the entire nation, as was the case when it was a question of creating the unity of the nation and a free constitution. But we also view these

tasks as men of a different nature. We are free of
innumerable illusions, which are required for the building of such enthusiasm. For the creation of the German
Reich, illusions of an enormous nature were necessary,
which have now flown away with the honeymoon period
of imperial unity, and which we are unable to reproduce
by means of reflection.

The traces of National Liberal grayness now become
considerably more distinct in the spectrum of Weber's ani-
mosities. *"Sie haben um uns ein festes Haus gebaut"* can also
mean "They [the fathers] have built a secure house around
us," though it is improbable that Weber meant to convey
that impression. But taken in this sense, it evokes the dismal
image of that rebuilding work on the Charlottenburg family
house that Weber Sr. had undertaken eight years before to
the detriment of his wife's inheritance and to the passive
disgust of his son, who resented his father's piracy of his
mother's fortune and who was trying to concentrate on his
studies while the racket was going on.* Again, this secure
house (*"festes Haus"*) that Weber rejects is probably intended as mere metaphor to signify the overorganized and
slackly uncreative social institutions bequeathed by the older
generation to his own; but it is striking that a decade later,
at a similar point near the end of his study of the *Protestant
Ethic*, Weber uses a very similar, though somewhat harsher
metaphor, to describe the reified institutional cosmos that
has evolved from the Puritan's voluntary asceticism and that
determines the psychic needs of modern man: ". . . *ein
stahlhartes Gehäuse"*—literally, a housing hard as steel, or,
in Talcott Parsons's translation, an "iron cage." And again,
the metaphor dissolves into its material reality when we keep
in mind that an iron cage is a way of describing a jail, and
that it was precisely like a prisoner in a jail that Weber felt
during his long years in Charlottenburg.

---

* *Jb.*, E.B., July 14, 1885, p. 162. The rebuilding is also mentioned in the letters to H.B. of the same date (*Jb.*, p. 175), and to
H.W., *Jb.*, March 29, 1885, p. 154.

Moreover, when Weber rejects the "secure house" of the "fathers," the generationally situated "tasks" which he chooses instead are clearly the professional and political correlates of the new personal responsibilities he feels at the time of his engagement to Marianne: ". . . I now go forth to hard and great tasks of a purely human nature and for which it is worthwhile to exert one's strength even if they appear externally to be less impressive than what the masculine profession, which goes on in the market place of life, otherwise can offer us for goals . . ."[48]

The guilt that Weber tried so hard to shake off after his letter of proposal to Marianne, echoes throughout this paragraph of the *Referat*, but most explicitly when he indirectly acknowledges that his challenge to the older generation will split the nation: "We cannot . . . appeal to grand sentiments, common to the entire nation, as was the case when it was a question of creating the unity of the nation and a free constitution." In this admission, Weber also makes it clear that the "curse of epigonism" falls on him not merely from the Junkers but from his father's generation of National Liberals as well, who alone have been responsible for "a free constitution."

Nonetheless, the struggle for liberation from "illusions," like the struggle against "unclear and mystical moods in our souls," amounts to a careful and strained hauling in of the anchor, so that Weber in his new freedom can sail confidently out into the storms of reality. Finally, just as Weber saw himself compelled to intervene in his friend's affair with Marianne before it was too late, so in his closing lines before the *Verein*, he conveys not only the earlier note of challenge, of revolutionary state intervention, but also the urgent necessity for an immediate response to the Eastern social problem, a response while there is still time: "We hope that we will some day be able to say in retrospect: At this point, the Prussian state perceived its social calling at the right time; it intervened in the spokes of the gears of social development from its own initiative and with success, and it had the courage to make this intervention for once *at the right time*."[49] Personal indeed are the traces of this bourgeois Bismarck.

[5]

ALTHOFF, WEBER SR., AND MARRIAGE

WEBER'S AMBIVALENCE in the *Referat* of 1893, between an ethic of "duty" and an ethic of freedom and rebellion, represented a profound split in his values, and this split in turn reflected the self-contradictory expectations of his mother. Weber decisively overcame this ambivalence—and, almost, his sanity—by standing up to his father in the summer of 1897. But four years prior to that catastrophic encounter, shortly before Weber's marriage in September 1893, there is some evidence that there was a dress rehearsal for it. Indeed, if we take seriously Weber's hints about the causal relationship between his silence *vis-à-vis* his father and his inability to feel the love of a woman, and about his determination not to enter marriage with the merely "resigned" consent of those near him (his mother being the nearest), some act of aggression against his father—real or symbolic—may have been the psychological prerequisite for his marriage. Such aggression, and the consequent partial liberation of Weber's superego from the ethos of ascetic labor and subjection to authority, may also explain the much more consistently rebellious tone of Weber's two approaches to the land question in 1894 and 1895.

The evidence that such aggression, at least in Weber's own mind, occurred in the summer of 1893, over the suspected connivance of Weber Sr. with the Prussian Minister of

Education for the purpose of keeping Max Jr. in Berlin, is circumstantial and complex, and can only be deduced from a discrepancy between Weber's account of the incident and some of the facts and documents as they were later brought to light.

On April 28, 1893, Weber wrote to his sister (then learning the household arts from a family in French Switzerland) an amusing and somewhat manic letter in French. He told her to tell his father, who was apparently visiting her at the time, that he was soon to become an *Extraordinarius* in commercial law at Berlin. Privy Councillors Althoff and Eck had told him that he might receive the appointment as early as May, would probably receive it in July, and certainly not later than the next winter. The faculty was in full accord and the appointment was in no way dependent on the health of Professor Goldschmidt, whose place he was taking during a prolonged illness.

In his next letter to Klara, dated July 15, 1893, he writes of an even better offer that he is expecting from Freiburg: *Ordinarius* in *Nationalökonomie*. He has just heard that the faculty have recommended him for the position on July 6 and have sent a delegate to Karlsruhe, capital of Baden, to urgently request his appointment. Of the five state officials who will have to approve it, four are in favor and the fifth, Nokk, the state Minister of Religion, is on vacation. Weber is expecting an official notification of appointment in a fortnight, and has agreed to accept it, provided he is not in the interim nominated or informed of a forthcoming nomination to the *Extraordinariat* in Berlin.

Two weeks later, Weber is much less sure of the Freiburg appointment:

> Probably nothing will become of it. There are too many false rumors (*"Die Sache ist zu sehr verklatscht"*). Still, tell the parents [who are apparently spending the summer with Klara] that I received a summons from Herr Althoff this morning. But I am only going the day after tomorrow.—Who knows what the old monster

has to say to me; I hardly think much news. I immediately telegraphed to Freiburg to discover until when the decision might come and to remark that if necessary I would ask for time to consider [from the Berlin authorities]. For if something comes of the call [from Freiburg] I will surely go there. Herr Geheimrat Eck said to me that the faculty here was agreed that I become a professor here—but they did not want to propose me, and were waiting for the ministry to do it so that they could say to the older *Privatdozenten* that they couldn't do anything about it.

A letter from Weber to his mother, probably written on July 29,* says that someone was ruining the Freiburg offer "through malicious gossip" (*"durch die Klatscherei"*):

> . . . I have only bound myself until the end of the semester . . . What may happen here, I don't know. I have told Eck how the matter stands. He considers it pure carelessness on Althoff's part, but said to me it would not be taken amiss if I went away, which I understand to mean: it would not be uncomfortable for the faculty if it should happen. They are thinking about seniority. I shall in any case let myself be registered as an attorney, for this whole business, in which essentially the fear of Laband's appointment plays to my favor, is too repulsive. As far as Althoff is concerned, it is certain that he (or Schmoller, which is the same

---

* The letter is dated July 26, 1893 in the *Jugendbriefe,* but it follows (p. 372) the letter to Klara of July 27 (p. 371). There are two reasons for assuming it was written on July 29: (1) In the letter to Klara of the 27th, Weber writes of a "summons" from Althoff to see him *"übermorgen,"* which would be Saturday, July 29 (he also says toward the end of the letter, *"nachdem ich Sonnabend Herrn Althoff genossen habe"*). In the letter to his mother, he refers to a meeting that has just occurred between himself and Eck, Althoff's colleague, who has probably been substituting for him. (2) In the letter to Klara of July 15, he writes: *"Der Kultusminister Nokk ist noch verreist, doch scheint es ziemlich sicher, dass ich in vierzehn Tagen berufen werde . . ."* In the letter to his mother, he writes: *"Nokk muss dieser Tage vom Urlaub kommen."* Fourteen days after July 15 is July 29.

thing) has claimed in Freiburg and Karlsruhe that I would only use Freiburg as a springboard, since a "magnificent" law career was awaiting me in Prussia, and therefore it would not pay with me . . .

The composite description of Weber's professional situation that emerges from the four letters cited—the only documentary source revealing Weber's immediate reactions to events—is as follows:

At the end of April, Eck and Althoff of the Prussian Ministry of Education assured Weber of an imminent appointment at Berlin as *Extraordinarius,* with the full support of the faculty, in commercial law. By July 15, Weber discovered that the faculty at Freiburg had nominated him on July 6 for an *Ordinariat* in *Nationalökonomie.* He was more eager to take this than the Berlin position, both because of its higher rank and because of its more interesting field of specialization (he was getting sick of law). Two weeks later, though, he found out to his disgust that Althoff, and perhaps Schmoller, were sabotaging his chances in Freiburg by spreading the story that he would only use a position there as a springboard for a law career in Prussia. He also found out that the faculty at Berlin was not at all as favorable as Althoff and Eck had pretended. The real situation, he had come to believe, was that the faculty at Berlin felt obliged, for reasons of seniority, to appoint someone named Laband, probably a *Privatdozent,* to the *Extraordinariat,* but that they were covertly supporting Weber because they did not really want the other man. Therefore, it would be necessary for the Prussian Ministry of Education, rather than the faculty, to appoint Weber.

The next, and last, piece of documentary evidence on this sordid comedy appears in a biography of Friedrich Althoff.[50] The biographer, sympathetic to his subject, reprints verbatim an exchange of letters between Weber and Althoff on the subject of Weber's employment in Berlin. The first, from Weber to Althoff, is dated August 5, 1893. It is a resumé of a discussion he has just had with Althoff, written, Weber says, at Althoff's request. It contains two main points: (1) that if Goldschmidt does not give his lectures in the winter semester, the ministry will inquire among the faculty about Weber's possible appointment as *Extraordinarius,* and, in the case of a favorable answer, will appoint him to this rank; (2) that Weber will not accept an appointment from Freiburg unless one is already "underway" to him. The letter from Althoff to Weber is dated August 6, and, in effect, repeals the second point:

> Allow me to add to our conversation of yesterday that you ought not to be bound to point #2 of the note received by me. Rather I wish to leave you a completely free hand in reference to Freiburg, and therefore ask you to make your decisions completely according to your own judgment. In any case, the prospect that I held out to you under #1 of the note remains.

Marianne Weber's account of Weber's dealings with Althoff is coherent with what her husband's letters to his sister and mother have to say about events up to the end of July, but it differs radically from what the exchange of letters between Weber and Althoff indicate about the way these men reached their final agreement on Weber's Berlin appointment.

Marianne says that Althoff, wanting to keep the extremely gifted young scholar in Prussia, decided before consulting the Berlin faculty that Weber would be Goldschmidt's successor and sought to keep him in Berlin by a combination of extravagant promises (such as the one that Weber's *Extraordinariat* would go through regardless of Goldschmidt's state of health) and defamatory rumors (such as the one he spread in Baden about Weber's exclusive concern with a law career in Prussia).[51] But Marianne also adds some extremely interesting detail to the summary of the early August negotiations contained in the Althoff-Weber exchange, and this detail is significant not because of any certainty of its empirical truth, but rather insofar as she is representing in this passage what her husband recalled of the incident (she herself was away in

Altmorschen at the time, taking her future sister-in-law Klara's place in the prosaic business of learning how to be a house-wife).[52] Marianne, almost certainly referring to the discussion of August 5, says that in accordance with Weber's request that he retain a free hand with regard to Freiburg, Althoff gave him a written promise to propose his candidacy to the Berlin faculty "without any obligation for the *Dozent*."[53] But when Weber arrived home and read the agreement, "he noticed a clause which obliged him to reject any other possible appointment offered to him. His immediate objection was answered by return post with a note that withdrew the clause as an error, and the pre-dating of the document made it seem as though it was prepared before Weber's objection. Weber remained always convinced of the opposite." It was almost twenty years before Weber committed his impressions of this incident to print, and it is likely that he recreated the circumstances of the incident partially from memory and partially from Althoff's note to him of August 6.[54] If so, he may simply have deduced from a hurried rereading of Althoff's note that it was not he but Althoff who had written up the agreement and that Althoff's withdrawal of the clause obliging him to reject the Freiburg appointment was not, as the documents themselves suggest, a sign of Althoff's "kid-glove" handling of an insecure young man who had com-mitted himself to more than he should have, but rather Althoff's Machiavellian response to Weber's perception of a trap.* The question then arises, if Weber's memory erred, was this sheer accident?

---

* Althoff was without doubt, a Machiavellian character hated by many scholars. Indeed, Tönnies too had his problems with Althoff, and in the same month of August 1893 that Weber felt so bedeviled, Tönnies quoted to Paulsen the *Aufwiedersehen* of the historian Schirren: "Until we meet again, may someone hang the ——— Althoff by his feet"; Ferdinand Tönnies and Friedrich Paulsen: *Briefwechsel, 1876–1908* (Kiel, 1961), Aug. 29, 1893, p. 304. Nonetheless, Althoff's view of Weber, probably gained either at or before the August 5 meeting, that "This Weber brings to view an exaggerated delicacy in personal matters" (*Lebensb.*, p. 229), would have held him back from trying precisely the trick of which Weber accused him.

From other comments Weber made about Althoff's relation to his father, we can probably conclude that it was not. Weber saw Althoff as attempting to use Max Weber, Sr., an important member of the Budget Commission in the Prussian House, as he had used Schmoller; i.e., to keep the young scholar in Berlin. According to Mommsen, who seems to rely exclusively on Weber's speech and articles of 1911, "Althoff had attempted to obtain the agreement of the National Liberals to a new chair in *Nationalökonomie* by casting into the scales for father Weber his son's prospects for an academic future. Which led Father Weber, perhaps under the pressure of Max Weber, to resign from the commission."*

Now Marianne Weber, in her scathing passage against Althoff, mentions as one of his evil deeds his approach to Weber Sr. in the Budget Commission with what smelled suspiciously both to father and son like a deal (*"kuhhandel"*); and Marianne also mentions, some pages earlier, that at the time she and Max were settling down in Berlin (i.e., the fall of 1893), "Weber Sr. was separated from his office, and the still fully vigorous man, barely half occupied, now remained a good part of his time at home." But Marianne nowhere mentions any official "resignation" from office or ties Weber Sr.'s "separation" from office to Althoff's maneuvering—a strange omission in view of her husband's assertion that his father had resigned as a matter of honor and her own recapitulation of so many other scandalous details of Althoff's behavior and their effects on the Weber household. But perhaps there was a reason for the omission, perhaps she was aware that though he may indeed have gone into retirement at this time, Weber Sr. had not, as his son later asserted, officially resigned his post. For Sachse[55] maintains unequivo-

---

* Mommsen: *Max Weber*, fn. p. 3. Arnold Sachse: *Althoff und sein Werk* (Berlin, 1928), pp. 113 ff., quotes Weber as saying: "It came to the point where my father, because of the tactless and impudent way that the head of the ministry of culture referred to these personal relationships, resigned from his mandate in the budget commission of the House of Deputies." (Sachse does not indicate his source.)

cally that Weber Sr., according to the official records of the National Liberal Party, belonged to the Budget Commission of the Prussian chamber from 1893 until his death in 1897. We are faced then with two questions: Why did Weber Sr. go into an unofficial semiretirement in the fall of 1893? and Why was his son so passionately (and wrongly) convinced, eighteen years later, that the retirement resulted from the older man's official resignation over an insult to his integrity that involved his son?

The source of Max Weber's conviction that his father had resigned his office because of Althoff's presumption could only have been Weber Sr. himself. But it is unlikely that the impression Weber Sr. conveyed had a grain of truth to it. To begin with, the story is out of character. From everything else we know about the father, he was hardly prone to quixotic sacrifices in affairs of honor. Furthermore, even assuming a change of character, it seems unlikely that if Weber Sr. had really gone into retirement for the reason he made known to his son, he would have failed to resign his position officially. But he did go into semi-retirement, and at the relatively early age of fifty-seven. Why then did he present his son with a false notion of his motives?

Perhaps he did so for two reasons: first, that he did not wish the real motive known; second, that he wanted to appease his son. And perhaps, too, there is some relation between the two.

Max Weber, Sr., died in 1897, apparently of a combined paralysis and hemorrhage of the stomach.[56] His daughter-in-law writes that at the time of his death "his powerful constitution had been hiding the germs of illness for some time."[57] The causes of death suggest either stomach cancer or an ulcerated colon. Either of these illnesses may have begun plaguing him four years before his demise and thus could have been the real cause for his retirement. Moreover, Weber Sr.'s travels in the spring and summer of 1893 may have been in part motivated by the desire to "take a cure" or to obtain an expert opinion about an ailment from a major diagnostic center. On April 28, he was visiting his daughter at Vevey in French Switzerland,[58] which, at about the turn of the century, was one of the principle Swiss centers for ailing foreigners seeking a cure. By July 15, he had taken his daughter somewhere else, probably to Heidelberg,* where he joined his wife. Heidelberg, where a famous medical school is located is not far from Stuttgart, where two of his nieces were in a sanatorium. If the real purpose of Weber Sr.'s visit to Switzerland and Baden was to find out what his illness was, or to take a cure, then perhaps the decision to retire in the fall of 1893 was motivated by the fear that he did not have long to live and by the desire to spend as much of his remaining time as possible with his family, particularly, one might guess, with his youngest children: Arthur, sixteen, and Lilli, thirteen. This was surely, however, not the kind of situation that an authoritarian, paternalistic figure like Weber Sr. would want to disclose to his children—and possibly not to his wife either. But why should he allow his son to believe a probably mythic account of his retirement?

Looked at from the son's standpoint, an altogether different set of interests may have been associated with his father's travels in 1893. Assume now, as seems likely, that his parents and sister were indeed visiting the Hausraths (his aunt and uncle) in Heidelberg. Heidelberg was only some thirty miles from Karlsruhe, the seat of the Baden government, where, in the second half of July, 1893, bureaucratic peers of his father were deciding whether or not to appoint him to an *Ordinariat* at Freiburg. Either Althoff or Schmoller was spreading the rumor that he would only use Freiburg as a springboard for a law career in Prussia. But his own

* *Jb.,* K.W., July 15 and July 27, 1893, pp. 370–2. The letter of July 15 reveals that both parents are now with Klara and they are no longer at Vevey, since Weber mentions receiving letters from Marianne *"aus Altmorschen"* (Vevey). The letter of July 27 consoles Klara over the lessened contact between her and himself that will result from his marriage by saying that "in the summer you could then come to us in Freiburg for a couple of months instead of to Heidelberg."

father, staying only an hour's trip from Karlsruhe, was in an excellent position to tell the bureaucrats there that he had no such intention, that, as he put it in the letter to his mother about this time, "I would regret it if I should remain fettered to the relatively barren jurisprudence."[51] He would never have thought of writing himself to his father at this time—no letters to Max Weber, Sr., appear in the *Jugendbriefe* after 1885—but in the three letters to Klara preceding the one to his mother, he tells her each time to inform his father (in the latter two, "*den Eltern*") of his employment prospects. Is it conceivable that Weber only thought of his father in these days as an immobile, unconscious *thing* sitting in Heidelberg, that he never once considered the possibility that his father might take a short trip to do some rumor mongering of his own, for—or against—his son's prospects? Or that his father's failure to do anything to dispel those false notions might be interpreted in Karlsruhe as indirect confirmation of Althoff's argument?

At any rate, he did not receive the Freiburg appointment that summer, and there is an excellent possibility that he held his father at least partially responsible: after all, he had already identified his father's politics, in his first analyses of the land question, with a conservative conspiracy against the national interest and had moreover viewed this conspiracy as totally antagonistic to the drive for freedom of the younger generation.

Now Weber Sr. must certainly have been aware that his political status put him in a position to affect his son's future, that his son knew it, and that his son's failure to obtain the coveted Freiburg position laid him open to the accusation of having either directly or indirectly harmed his son's cause. Whether or not Althoff did or did not discuss his son's tenure with Weber Sr. in terms of a "deal," the latter probably considered it politic simultaneously to appease his son's hostility and conceal the true reason for his retirement by letting Max Jr. think he had resigned his office because of Althoff's sinister attempt to keep the young scholar in Berlin. And at some

level of Max Weber's mind, his father's retirement surely signified a victory for youth and freedom, and a token offering
for his embattled, victimized, and depressingly resigned
mother. Just as surely, it gave an invaluable psychological
uplift to Weber at the time that he began his married life and
formulated his third and most radical attack on the Junker
hegemony. On September 20, 1893, Weber was joined in
wedlock to Marianne Schnitger, the daughter of a first cousin,
by another first cousin, Otto Baumgarten, brother of the
cousin Emmy with whom Max Weber had been in love six
years earlier.[60] At the beginning of the following year he published his first article in the journal whose editor he was to
become ten years later, Heinrich Braun's *Archiv für Soziale
Gesetzgebung und Statistik* (hereafter cited as *Archiv*):
*"Entwicklungstendenzen in der Lage der ostelbischen Lan-
darbeiter."* He apparently wrote it in the fall of 1893.*

[6]

FROM SOCIALISM
TO LIBERAL IMPERIALISM

WEBER's THIRD major study of the East Elbian land question
followed or accompanied four events of great significance for
him. His failure to obtain the Freiburg appointment in the
summer of 1893 must have sharpened his hostility to the older
generation, since he believed his chances had been sabotaged
by one of the leading representatives of that generation,
Geheimrat Althoff. On the other hand, barring a miraculous
recovery by Goldschmidt, he was certain he would receive an
Extraordinariat, with an adequate remuneration for the first

---

* Weber seems to have made no mention of it in detailed descrip-
tions of work in progress that he wrote to Marianne the summer before
their marriage. See *Lebensb.*, pp. 218 *ff.*

time in his life, at Berlin during the winter of 1893–4. He also had the pleasure of seeing his father, whose complicity in the events that kept him from Freiburg was vague but possible, accept retirement, rather (he thought) than conspire with Althoff to chain him to Berlin. And finally, two days before the autumnal equinox introduced the darker part of the year, he married Marianne Schnitger.

There are two versions of *"Entwicklungstendenzen in der Lage der ostelbischen Landarbeiter"* ("Developmental Tendencies in the Position of the East Elbian Land Workers). The first, probably written in the fall of 1893, appeared in the initial number of Braun's *Archiv*.[61] The second, which he may have written in the spring of 1894, appeared, with a number of minor changes and a few major ones in the *Preussische Jahrbücher*.[62] There is a noticeable difference of emphasis between the earlier and later versions.

In general, the revised effort betrays a sharper, more aggressive tone. While this is partly the result of stylistic changes, these changes themselves reflect a more fundamental alteration in Weber's perception of the problem. The first paragraph of the *Archiv* study is a meandering—and fruitless —search for a point of view from which to proceed. The *revised* first paragraph, after succinctly describing the background of empirical research on which he will draw to illuminate the historical development of the land-worker problem, posits just that concern for the larger political significance of his subject that had been so prominent in the more radical section of his *Referat*. But here, unlike the *Referat*, the main perspective from which he expresses this concern is not a revolutionary nationalist variety of *Staatsraison*, but rather a broadly social-democratic sympathy for the fate of the landworker *vis-à-vis* his Junker exploiter: "The most important question is not whether the *contemporary* workers have a sufficient wage and good housing, but rather, what is the direction of the over-all development of their position in the nation, what is their future?"

If this decisiveness of tone is stronger in the revised article, it nonetheless characterizes both versions when we compare them with the ambivalence of the *Referat*. From the second page on, Weber's clear hostility to the paternalistic, authoritarian Junker ethos and his partiality for the cause of the rebellious land worker sharply illuminate the fact that Weber's Rubicon was the property line of his father's house in Charlottenburg, and having moved across it, he too had raised the standard of rebellion.

Here there is no trace of that placid acceptance of the Prussian yoke which characterized the first half-dozen pages of the *Referat*. Where less than a year earlier he had praised "that kind of labor we know in the East, this austere, obligatory exertion of labor power, embracing one's whole life . . . the characteristically Prussian concept of 'damned duty,' "[63] and related this work ethic to an indispensable talent for political organization, in 1894 he condemned the Junkers' economic ethic as undeveloped and slovenly and called into question their contemporary political indispensability:

> ". . . they were economically "satisfied existences," with a relatively undeveloped profit motive and a correspondingly underaverage economic intelligence—therefore not [subjectively] inclined to a purely businesslike exploitation of their power position, and in any case not [objectively] directed to it. The rule over the eastern half of the state, socially and economically undeveloped and politically most important, was accomplished, with the support of this estate, cheaply and without danger of corruption. In a word, the domains of the East signified the decentralization of a political ruling class across the countryside. As the strong points within which the garrisons and officialdom of the district and even government capitals find an adequate social milieu, they form even now an uncommonly effective—actually decisive—counterweight against the monopolization of political intelligence by the urban bourgeoisie.[64]

Now Weber, as he was to reveal the following year,[65] had no trust at all in the political intelligence or competence of the urban bourgeoisie. But in the course of his own progress from dependent son to independent husband (or in socio-religious terms, from Calvinist work-slave to Calvinist tyrannicide), he was abandoning the submissiveness he had externally displayed to the representatives of authority;* and he showed this abandonment by removing the presumption of economic virtue and political indispensability that he had formerly, with the exception of that impetuous outburst in the *Referat,* granted the Junkers.

As other parts of the essay show, his preferred candidate for the Junker inheritance is not the urban bourgeois but rather some combination of enlightened conservatives—state socialists—and a working-class aristocracy. Nonetheless, in these first few pages he gives the superficial appearance of being a loyal bourgeois liberal. The earlier notion (of the *Referat*) that the economic and political virtues of the Prussian ethos justified one another is exploded as Weber now deprives the Junkers of any economic talents, and by implication transfers such talents to "the big bourgeoisie, the previous chief competitor of the rural aristocracy for political power,"[66] the emulation of whose opulent consumption patterns is driving the Junkers bankrupt. He thereby reduces the landowners to a caricature of their former selves, a caricature whose "demand for protection already assumes the tone of a dissatisfied receiver of charity."[67] And for Weber, this pretention to an opulence unattainable by their own efforts, this infection by what looks very much like a vulgar, petty-bourgeois spirit of conspicuous consumption, but unaccompanied by any of the acquisitive skills of the bourgeois, is what has

---

* *Cf.* the extreme deference, bordering on obsequiousness, in his letter to Althoff (Sachse: *Althoff und sein Werk,* p. 112). No doubt it was the custom to adopt such a servile tone toward powerful superiors, and it must have been a continually galling experience to a man as strong-willed as Weber. But the point is, he did adopt it, and swallowed his gall.

condemned the Junkers both economically and politically to decline. Once again though, if we scratch off the mask of this strange, petty-bourgeois Junker who lives in nervous apostasy of his ancestors' simple, precapitalist virtues, we find the face of the bureaucrat from Charlottenburg, child of a patriarchal linen merchant, who has rebuilt his house and enabled himself "to keep pace with this living standard"[68] only by pirating his wife's inheritance, in short, the scholar's father.

Despite this new decisiveness of tone, if one tries to follow the line of argument of the 1894 article, it becomes clear that, structurally, this is the least satisfying of Weber's analyses of the land worker problem, primarily because he is trying to do considerably more than he is aware of. Though a similar excess of libidinal energy over conscious intellectual precipitation probably was the source of the logical complications of the earlier studies, in this one the problem is even greater. The ostensible object of the 1894 work is clear: to trace the historical background of a situation Weber had previously discussed only in its immediacy. And he does this at a level of detail which is both enviable for its clarity and frustrating for the remoteness of its subject matter. But the nature of the frustration alters when we realize that in many passages, Weber's mind seems to be reaching for the answers to a whole series of questions which he never explicitly states, and of which in most cases he was probably not consciously aware.

In the passages analysed above, Weber seems to be raising the following series of questions: Suppose I use as my standard of value not that arbitrary, authoritarian Prussian dictum of doing one's damned duty but rather that magical yearning for freedom and independence that I certainly accept myself and which my research tells me is impelling the land workers to leave their masters' property, how then does my world look? what does Germany mean to me, and in particular what do the Junkers mean and how do I view their future economic and political role? And if I decide that their economic decline has ended their political hegemony, what effect does all this have on the aspirations of their estate workers for liberation? Does this—*can* this—desire for freedom signify any meaningful historical progress?

Now the key to comprehending the *Weltanschauung* that distinguishes Weber's approach to the Eastern question of 1894–5 from that of 1892–3 is that he is indeed posing this series of questions, and others as well that flow from his answers to them. Moreover, he is doing so consistently, not sporadically as had earlier been the case, for he has outgrown the abject dependence and much of the sense of guilt that had formerly bound him, restless though he was, to the Prussian-Calvinist work ethos.

And what distinguishes the vaguely socialist sentiments of 1894 from the brutal imperialism of the inaugural address at Freiburg a year later is that in 1894 he is trying out, with only the dimmest awareness of what he is doing, an idea similar to the one consciously formulated a decade later by Georges Sorel in his anarcho-syndicalist phase, the idea that perhaps the nation can best preserve its vitality, and the workers (with whom Weber identifies) best attain their freedom, through an open struggle against the entrenched, and decadent, enemy powers within the national frontiers; in Germany's case this means for Weber the Junker-capitalist alliance and the older generation of the academic and bureaucratic establishment—all incarnated, we may again recall, in the scholar's father.

This point of view, while consonant with the passionate outburst triggered in the *Referat* by the Silesian magnate's condescending criticism, leads Weber to jettison virtually all his past panegyrics of the Junker character and to view it in that clearly hostile tone which emerges in the first few pages of the *Archiv* study. The answers to Weber's unstated, perhaps unconscious questions, continue this tone.

When he had earlier accepted their ethos, Weber had read into the Junkers' heritage the qualities of courage, unceasing work, and iron self-discipline, therefore complete reliability in the defense of the eastern frontier, moreover a sense of responsibility to the needs of the estate workers. Only after the landowners became trapped by international capitalism did they lose their virtue, according to this earlier view.

But if Weber scrutinizes these traditional Prussian land-lords from the standpoint of their semi-serf dependents—with whose progeny Weber identifies his own new ethic of free-dom—rather than from the perspective of their military prowess against the Slavic hordes or their capacity for pre-serving an archaic authoritarian discipline, he finds a differ-ent creature. The Junker "was not an ordinary employer but rather a political autocrat who personally ruled the work-ers."[69] His character was a "mixture of naïve brutality and benevolence."[70] "The worker's *family* [was] subjected to the lord's authority and therefore obligated to work with all the power at their disposal as he will[ed]."[71] "The lord's lack of a specifically businesslike sense of profit and the worker's apathetic resignation complemented one another and were the psychological props of both the traditional mode of enter-prise and the traditional political hegemony of the landed aristocracy."[72] Note well: For the Weber of 1894 *these* were the good old days, *before* capitalism had turned Dr. Jekyll into Mr. Hyde.

For about half of this work of 1894, Weber writes only of the particular paths of degeneration into which this antique labor relationship has fallen in the modern era.* And here, more emphatically than in any of Weber's other surveys of the problem, the catalyst that explodes the inert, if stable,

---

* Max Weber: *Gesammelte Aufsätze zur Sozial und Wirtschafts-geschichte* (Tübingen, 1924) (hereafter cited as *S.W.G.*), pp. 480–90, deals primarily with the evolution of the Eastern landworkers' status from servile *"Instmann"* to *"Deputant"* to free contractual laborer in Silesia and in the Northeast. In pages 490–500, Weber argues that the pressure for more efficient use of resources compels the landlord to turn from extensive to intensive agriculture and that this in turn re-duces the need for a permanent labor supply and leads to the replace-ment of the secure, if dependent, worker and his family, by migratory labor during sowing and harvest seasons.

compound of brutal authority and apathetic resignation is in the psyche: the landlord's envy and greed which, through his economically unviable attempt to imitate the luxury of the *haute bourgeoisie,* condemns him to bankruptcy; and the land worker's dark yearning for freedom.[73] But the answers to his first, unstated, questions give rise to new ones that further clutter Weber's unconscious. Occasionally they emerge into consciousness, but again and again they prevent him from writing a straightforward economic history of the problem.

For it is perfectly evident that the former "apathetic resignation" of the land worker under the *ancien régime* corresponds precisely to his own prolonged dalliance in the "harbor of resignation," that magnificent simile for a sarcophagal womb that characterized, in his eyes, all the women who were important in his life up to his engagement in 1893: mother, cousin, and second cousin. And while he himself was emerging with his "high-souled comrade" onto the stormy seas of life, so too were his secret brothers, the land workers, deserting their autocratic masters for the enchantment of freedom. But in describing a situation that so intimately concerned him, Weber had to pose questions that transcended the empirical: not only "What has happened?" but "What *could* happen?" and also "What *should* happen?"

He sketches out what has happened with a fair degree of clarity: the metamorphosis of the despotic, decadent harmony of the traditional estate into, on the one hand, the convulsive, disruptive, exploitative energy of the capitalist-minded Junker and, on the other, the proletarian will to freedom.

But the usually unacknowledged presence of the other questions persistently befogs this clarity. For Weber, like a real child emerging to new life from a real womb, is extremely uncertain of the perspective he should use to view his new world. One thing, however, he seems to know intuitively: it was no simple force of external and capricious nature, no mere act of feminine grace that led him from his imprisoning womb, but the energy of his own free will—and he had expressed this intuition in the earlier stages of his emergence when he wrote into his *Referat*: "The work hands no longer want to tolerate the patriarchal disposition of the lord over the worker's destiny . . . Psychological impulses of overwhelming power lead both to the emigration into the cities and to the disorganization of this labor constitution." If this act of will, then, is so vital to the attainment of freedom and progress, and so widespread, then the question arises as to the optimal form which this vital will should take if it is to preserve and extend the freedom it has already created. In social and political terms, the following questions emerge: Should and can the land workers collectively consolidate their new freedom by organizing for a class struggle against the forces of exploitation and despotism, or should and can they develop an elite, which, like the English labor aristocracy, can guarantee a channel for upward mobility into the ranks of the peasantry? If neither perspective is really possible, should one accept and encourage the present trend towards emigration into the urban centers of western Germany, and thereby let the Junkers decay into their own little hell? Or are there broader political grounds— matters of national interest—for demanding state intervention to resettle the land workers on expropriated Junker colonies? and should Weber view these broader grounds in terms of the social well-being of the nation or in terms of the political interests of the German nation-state, struggling for its life in a hostile world and losing its ethnic majority in the Eastern regions to Slavic migrant workers whom the now traitorous Junkers have imported?

These are the questions which secretly obsess Weber in both versions of the article of 1894 and in his inaugural address at Freiburg. In the *Archiv* article, probably written just after Weber's return from his September honeymoon, he is overwhelmingly concerned with the answers to the first two questions, which focus exclusively on the preservation and extension of the land workers' freedom. He is aware of the third, which merges the problem of the workers' freedom with that of the national interest, but is not preoccupied with it; and he virtually ignores the fourth, in which he raises the possibility that the idea of freedom ought to be absorbed completely into a neo-Bismarckian *Staatsraison*. In the second version, which he probably worked out in the first three or four months of 1894, the concern with the first two questions persists, but it tends to be overshadowed in the altered conclusion by the third and fourth: a renewed awareness of the Polish problem dictates major revisions in the second half of the article. Finally, in the Freiburg inaugural address, he encapsulates all of his earlier work on the subject in the framework of a national struggle for survival that is ordained by nature; the fourth question alone remains significant, and the workers' demands for political and social power may only be granted when they develop the political consciousness to lead successfully this rational struggle. Thus, the inaugural address reintroduces the revolutionary-nationalist *Staatsraison* which Weber had momentarily posited as the only valid criterion for judgment in the rebellious outburst of the *Referat*, but presents it in the framework of a comprehensive *Weltanschauung* by means of which he largely transfers his identification with the struggling proletariat onto the fateful exertions of the struggling nation.

Again, these questions do not abruptly appear for the first time in the *Archiv* study, but where Weber had earlier brought them up—i.e., in the *Referat* of 1893—it was almost in the form of a momentary, irritated lapse from good taste and decorum; and the honorific posture in the rest of the *Referat* toward the Junkers' ethos and economic needs belied the radical tone of the center section. If we were to sustain the metaphor of rebirth that I have used to describe Weber at the time he was probably writing the *Archiv* study, it would be fair to describe those angry paragraphs in the *Referat* as a false labor.[74]

What are the answers, then, which Weber is offering

to those first two consistently troubling questions in the *Archiv* study?[75]

Weber apparently is testing the situation of the land workers against the situation of urban factory workers, to see if there is any prospect that a class struggle, with real chances of success, might arise in the rural East. What, given the example of the urban proletariat, are the preconditions for such an organized struggle? A set of uniform economic interests (as opposed to the fundamentally different statuses that had formerly characterized the land workers: *Instmann, Deputant*, etc.);[76] a system of formal legal equality *vis-à-vis* the landlords (subjection to a purely "businesslike exploitation" as opposed to "a brutal personal dominion"[77]), and finally, concentration of large numbers of permanent workers in production centers (as opposed to "workers broadly scattered across the land, incapable of organization").[78] Now Weber is firmly convinced that the change among the estate owners from a patriarchal to a capitalist ethos is creating the first two preconditions: a leveling of traditional status distinctions and the destruction of the old patriarchal relationship of political domination has given rise to a rural proletariat whose character does seem comparable to its urban counterpart.[79] Indeed, the historical inquiry into the changes that have brought about this transformation constitutes the bulk of the first half of the essay. But the second half of the *Archiv* study centers around Weber's examination of the last precondition for a meaningful class struggle: concentration of a permanent labor force. After a close look at the requirements of capitalist agriculture, he decides that this precondition does not exist, primarily because the developments associated with capitalist agriculture, such as stock breeding and intensive cultivation, require either a marked reduction in the labor force or migrant rather than permanent workers.[80]

Now it is most noteworthy that this rather pessimistic conclusion follows an analysis primarily of the objective, material conditions that mold the potentialities for struggle of the rural proletariat. When, contrariwise, Weber momentarily considers the subjective, psychological motives that impel the laborer himself to desire migratory work, a different, almost jubilant, tone emerges:

> Migration allows him to escape the necessity of seeking work from the neighboring, local ["heimatlichen"] landlords. But just this work in the locality ["Heimat"] is bound mentally and historically to the traditional relationship to authority: it is the obscure urge toward personal freedom that drives the laborers to labor elsewhere. They sacrifice their customary living conditions to the striving for emancipation from unfreedom: their dull resignation is broken through. The much lamented "moving around" of the land workers is at the same time the beginning of mobilization for the class struggle.[81]

This passage evokes two images. One of these is, of course, Weber himself, whose personal life about the time he was writing the *Archiv* study was completely centered around the long-desired separation from his father's household and the breaking through of his own "dull resignation" that accompanied his Berlin appointment and his marriage in the latter half of 1893. The other is that of a socialist of the chair flirting with thinly masked revisionist socialists who were seriously attempting to spread their ideas in academic circles. In fact, at the time he wrote the *Archiv* study, Weber's intellectual frame of reference seems to have been the group of young leftist intellectuals who clustered around the journals edited by Heinrich Braun, the *Archiv* and the *Socialpolitische Centralblatt.**

---

* The significance of the *Archiv* at this time may be gauged by the concatenation of authors being reviewed and authors doing reviewing in the same volume that Weber's study appeared in. A book of Karl Grünberg, later editor of the *Archiv für die Geschichte des Sozialismus und der Arbeiterbewegung,* was reviewed by Heinrich Herkner, a prominent pro-labor *Kathedersozialist.* Herkner's book *Die Arbeiter-*

One of the most prominent of these was Werner Sombart, and his circumspect ambitions and those of his friends were reflected in a letter he wrote to his friend Otto Lang, a Swiss Socialist leader, in 1893:

> We are all standing behind you, more than you think. And what keeps us at the lectern, is for one thing a matter of disposition—I, for example, would make a very poor party man—and partly, a healthy objective opportunism (. . . a matter of taste: it isn't true in my case), as I encountered it recently in the amiable Schulze-Gävernitz. . . . He said to me: what use would it be if you or Herkner or another of us . . . became "comrades," wrote in the *"Neue Zeit,"* and worked for the *"Vorwärts."* None at all. For the soc-dem. party has more than enough intelligence. But it can be of great use if the German universities by and by are filled with a new spirit. Still we don't all believe in miracles, but in a slow education and transformation, even of minds. . . . In a certain sense, we young writers and teachers are the most advanced posts of the great proletarian army, and the most suspicious ones to the enemy.[82]

Half a year later, Sombart, through the mediation of Heinrich Braun, obtained letters of introduction from August Bebel to Filippo Turati and other Italian Socialists.[83] Sombart's concerns in Italy were similar to Weber's in Germany: the implications of social and economic tendencies in agriculture for the socialist movement and socialist theory. And Sombart was even more gloomy than Weber; not only was there no sign in Italy of a rural socialist movement, there was

---

frage was reviewed by Bruno Schoenlank, a moderate socialist who had commented favorably on Weber's *Referat* at the 1893 meeting of the *Verein für Sozialpolitik.* Schoenlank's social history of the Reformation was in turn reviewed by Werner Sombart. No book of Sombart's was reviewed in this year, but he was otherwise represented in the *Archiv* by a forty-page critique of Marx's economics. Finally, Ferdinand Tönnies's review of a book by the neo-Kantian Paul Natorp also appeared in this volume.

also no evidence of any concentration of agrarian capital. As a result of his experience, Sombart raised the question of whether the socialist movement should not abandon its dogmas and make room within its ranks for "an individualist peasant movement." Further questions that he addressed to Lang about the attitude of Swiss land workers to the Socialist Party suggest that he and Weber were again thinking along parallel lines: "Do they want a socialized large estate or do they each want their own scrap of land? And how do you stand to them? Do you accept the individualism? Or do you want to cram socialism into the peasant's skull?"

Despite this similar line of inquiry, certain irreconcilable differences separated Weber's and Sombart's positions in 1894, differences incarnated in the personal and political circles in which the two men traveled. Sombart's circle at this time consisted of pro-labor academicians and international socialist *Stürmer und Dränger* like himself and his friend Lang, with whom he exchanged reminiscences of his student days for decades. Weber's milieu was the group of Protestant reformers around Friedrich Naumann, the *Evangelisch-soziale Verein,* to which he had been introduced by his mother. The one link between Sombart and Weber was Heinrich Braun, for whose publications both men wrote extensively. But Sombart must be placed in these years on the extreme left of the contributors to the *Archiv,* while Weber, in his study of 1894, had only momentarily assumed a position sympathetic to theirs—partly, as I have suggested, as a chance result of exploring the political correlates of his own recent independence; partly also at the prodding, during and after the *Verein für Sozialpolitik*'s meeting of 1893, of left-wing academicians who were regular contributors to Braun's journals.

There are two clear responses to such prodding in the *Archiv* study. Bruno Schoenlank, a contributor to the socialist *Vorwärts* as well as to Braun's *Archiv,* argued against Weber, in the debate period following his *Referat,* that as long as the land workers were forbidden to organize it would be impossible to keep out Polish laborers.[84] Much of the *Archiv* study is simply background material for a refutation of Schoenlank's point. Weber fully supported the land worker's right to organize but, he argued, considering the dislocation of the land workers over the countryside, no organizing effort could possibly be successful.[85] Another of Weber's opponents at the *Verein* meeting, however, Max Quarck, revealed the basic flaw in Weber's *Referat* when he noted that Weber, after denying that the satisfaction of the landlord's labor needs was any business of the *Verein's*, ended his paper by speaking essentially about how this need could best be satisfied.[86] And this objection, which Weber made no attempt to answer at the meeting, was apparently taken to heart: the *Archiv* study deals exclusively with the problems of the land workers; indeed it contains a paragraph, omitted from the later version, which specifically calls to task a conservative opponent of Weber for thinking "he can resolve the land-worker question into the 'question of how labor power can be provided for the big landowners.' "[87]

If we assume then that Weber's radical posture in the *Archiv* study is a result both of his own political inclinations and of the prodding given him by Schoenlank and Quarck, we now confront the problem of where Weber's political emotions could lead him once he had established the hopelessness of any organized class struggle on the East Elbian estates. His response in the conclusion of the *Archiv* study is to favor the land worker's emigration as the best means to freedom and to let the Junkers rot:

> Under these circumstances, [the workers] draw unconsciously but surely the appropriate conclusion: that given the predominating rule over the land of the big landowner and big business, homelessness and freedom are one and the same.

This reaction of flight, understandably prominent in Weber's mind about the time of his marriage, when he was finally moving out of his parents' house and looking forward to a permanent academic appointment, gives way in the closing paragraphs of the later version—probably written when he was already assured of the *Ordinariat* at Freiburg —to a more aggressive version of the *Staatsraison* he had championed in the *Referat*: "Only a foolish anxiety before the idea of an 'expropriation' prevents broad circles from saying what everyone quietly thinks: a large part of the large holdings in the East is no longer tenable in private hands."[88]

Thus, the concern for the future of the land proletariat that Weber expresses so sharply in the first paragraph of the revised essay has been merged by the end of this version into the broader concern for the nation and for the *Staatsraison* that formulates its needs. This switch is comprehensible in terms both of Weber's personal and political evolution. Personally, his marriage and departure from Charlottenburg had probably modified his powerful inclination to identify exclusively with the oppressed land proletariat, and his acceptance into the professional academic world very likely led him to contemplate more seriously the planful use of the powers of the establishment against Junker decadence. But supplementing these personal inclinations were the intellectual consequences of his earlier political positions. If the land proletariat was incapable of waging an organized struggle against the Junkers, and did indeed identify freedom with emigration, then Polish immigration was bound to lead to a complete deterioration of the German position in East Elbia, and only a radical state intervention to colonize German peasants on expropriated Junker estates could save the situation.

The shift in the revised conclusion from passive acceptance of the problem to an aggressive demand for state intervention is foreshadowed by two other changes in the latter half of the revised essay: a greater emphasis on the Polish danger, and a stronger attack on the landlord's responsibility both for this Slavic problem and for the earlier enclosures that wiped out the independent peasantry.

In the *Archiv* study, Weber had repeated his previous
critique of the Polish danger to German nationality, but only
near the end; and, just before a brief summary of his argument of 1893, he explicitly said that he would avoid precisely
such a repetition. His ambivalence on the Polish danger became more marked in a long and confused footnote at this
point, directed against critics of his study for the *Verein*,
where he said among other things:

> It seems that some . . . have wanted to find in my
> remarks a displaced appeal to national sentiments. But
> I am of the view that a Pole or Mongol as ruler of the
> East, if he took on the task of preserving the cultural
> level of the worker, could not act differently than a
> German.[89]

In the next sentence, he returned again to a more national-
istic posture. But he clearly had become uncertain, for the
moment, as to whether his position of more open and consistent sympathy for the land worker necessarily involved the
kind of intense pathos he earlier (and later) expressed on
the Polish question. This uncertainty has disappeared in the
later version, where four newly inserted references to the
Polish danger precede an unequivocal, expanded version of
his paragraph on the subject in the *Archiv*.[90]

Related to this increased concern with the Polish question is a heightened hostility to the landlords for creating it.
The landlords bring in the Poles as strikebreakers against the
latent strike represented by the emigration of the land workers.[91] Moreover, one of several added sentences at this point
in the study introduces a reference to the Prussian enclosure
movement which is remarkably hostile when compared with
a reference to the same phenomenon in his "summary" of
1892. At that time he had referred to the "land displacement
of the peasants [which] occurred mostly—not always—in all
respects legally."[92] But in 1894, in the *Preussische Jahrbücher*,
he says: "In the districts of the knights who have cleared out
the peasants, this robbery—for that it is, partly economically,

partly even juridically—is revenged through an anemia of labor forces."[*]

But Weber only reached the height of his political aggressiveness in his inaugural address at Freiburg, delivered at the beginning of May 1895.

THE *Freiburger Antrittsrede* is not only the culmination of Weber's early *Weltanschauung;* it merges this *Weltanschauung* into the demonic dynamism of German revolutionary nationalism. Midway between the first appearance of that nationalism in 1848 and its catastrophic climax in the years 1933 to 1945, the *Antrittsrede* represents a turning point in the relationship of German liberalism to nationalism comparable to the turning point represented by the Puritan ethic in the development of capitalism. Until this point, German liberalism's attitude towards the power state and imperial expansion was one of half-reluctant acquiescence in an unavoidable and mildly obscene fact of life. But the Freiburg speech, representing the first programmatic statement of what came to be called liberal imperialism, and written from an avowedly liberal and bourgeois standpoint, managed to formulate the ethos of German liberalism in such a way that a national program of world power politics and overseas imperialism was not merely tolerated but demanded of the German people.

The main themes of the *Antrittsrede* have been outlined before. Here they will be illuminated from four vantage points: first, how Weber's consideration of Germany's "objective" economic situation led him into this extremely sharp formulation of a liberal-imperialist ideology; second, how his ardent desire for a "political" nation, capable of throwing off and replacing the decadent Junker hegemony, also led inexorably to the demand for a German struggle

---

[*] Mommsen traces an increasing sharpness of tone through Weber's speeches and articles, primarily for the Protestant Social Union, in 1894: *Max Weber und die deutsche Politik*, pp. 35–8.

for world empire; third, how Weber's personal evolution brought him to the same conclusion; and last, how and why this imperialist credo came to be accepted by broad strata of the liberal intelligentsia.

WEBER's *Referat* OF 1893, in the paragraphs where he momentarily abandoned his self-imposed resignation and said what his rebellious self really meant, seemed to be pointing in two directions: a moderate, reformist socialism, marked by a clear identification with the rural proletariat's desire for liberation, and a revolutionary nationalist version of *Staatsraison*, dictated by identification with the broad political and economic needs of the *Volk*. Both of these identifications had as their obverse side an ill-concealed hatred for the Junkers, who, to satisfy their social pretensions, were oppressing the land workers and selling out the *Volk* to the Slavic hordes. In the *Archiv* study, Weber explored the possibilities of a rural class struggle and found them to be nil. In the *Antrittsrede*, and in several less important studies which preceded and followed it from 1894 to 1897, he worked through the economic and political implications for the national existence of both the Junker decline and the impossibility of a successful rural class struggle. Unless, he argued, the state intervened to buy up at least a part of the large domains and distribute them to German peasant-colonists, the East would become overwhelmingly Polish in character, since the German laborers would move out and the Junkers would cheerfully bring in Polish migrant workers to replace them. But if the state did establish a German peasantry in East Elbia, the consequent loss of economic efficiency would end all hope, not only that Germany could export grain, but that it could even supply itself with this basic food, since the small farms would produce little surplus for the rest of the nation. In that case, Germany would have to buy much of its food abroad, and would only be able to do so if it developed a large overseas market for its manufactured goods. And such markets would never be secure, unless protected by German power—in other words, by a German fleet and a German struggle for a share of the colonial world.*

In the *Antrittsrede* itself, however, the arguments for imperial expansion center more around the political than the economic needs of the German people. The Junker decline has left Germany leaderless, particularly in view of Bismarck's refusal to give any meaningful share of authority to the leaders of German liberalism. In effect, for all his Machiavellian wisdom, Bismarck, like the authoritarian despot of the Weber family, never allowed his people to develop their own power. Indeed, Weber strongly suggests at one point that traditional German liberalism is a dying creed.† And in the working class leadership, too, there is "no spark of that catalinarian energy of the Deed . . . no breath of the powerful *national* passion that prevailed in the rooms of the Convention." This example of the Jacobin Convention, in which the French nation received its education through a fiery struggle for existence against the forces of the old regime, merges with that of the English proletariat, which reached maturity not merely through economic struggle, but above all through the national struggle for empire— and the conclusion for Germany is inescapable:

---

* I have followed Mommsen's synthesis of Weber's ideas on this subject (*Max Weber und die deutsche Politik*, pp. 32–4, 77). Though there is a strong suggestion in the *Antrittsrede* (Max Weber: *Gesammelte Politische Schriften* [Tübingen, 1958] [hereafter cited as P.S.], p. 22) that a strong fleet is an economic necessity for German trade, he does not directly discuss the question until the following year (*Evangelisch-Sozialer Kongress*, 1896, *Bericht über die Verhandlungen*, p. 123).

† Speaking of the "enchantment of freedom," he writes, "In fact, its spirit rarely touches us today in the quiet of the study. Pale are the naïve, libertarian ideals of our early youth, and some of us have become prematurely old and think that one of the most deeply rooted impulses in the human heart has been carried to its grave with the slogans of a declining political and economic outlook." Only liberalism could be considered such an outlook that had "freedom" as its slogan.

the *resonance of the world power position* . . . places the state continually before great power-political tasks and puts the individual into a continual political education, which he only receives over here sharply if the borders are threatened.—The question of whether a politics of grandeur can again place before our eyes the significance of the great political power questions is decisive for *our* development too. We must grasp the fact that the unification of Germany was a juvenile prank which the nation committed in its old age and, because of its expense, would have better left undone, if it was to be the conclusion and not the starting point of German world power politics.

Again and again, Weber castigates the craven economic fears and desires of the philistine German bourgeois and juxtaposes against them a harsh political ethic of eternal struggle for power. The main pretender to the Junker's political inheritance, the bourgeois, thinks only in terms of a "soft eudaemonism," which leads part of it to a wildly exaggerated fright before the social and economic demands of the organized masses, and another part to base its social policy exclusively on an "unspeakably philistine softening of the spirit, which thinks it can substitute 'ethical' for 'political' ideals, and harmlessly identifies these again with optimistic hopes for happiness."*

For the new Freiburg *Ordinarius,* then:

> The ultimate meaning of the *social*-political problem is not a question of the *economic* situation of the ruled, but rather one of the *political* qualification of the *ruling and rising* classes. The goal of our social-political labor is not world happiness, but the *social unification,* for the harsh struggles of the future, of the nation, which has been rent apart by the modern economic development.

At this point in the text of the *Antrittsrede* appear two sentences which throw into sharp relief both Weber's ulti-

---

* *P.S.*, p. 24. Weber has in mind the German Ethical Culture Society.

mate choice for the political leadership of Germany and the relationship of his own personal development to that choice:

> If in fact a labor aristocracy should be successfully created, which would be the bearer of the political ethos that we today sorely miss in the labor movement, then only may the spear for which the arm of the bourgeoisie still does not seem to be strong enough, be placed on those broad shoulders. The road to that point appears to be a long one.

The imagery of the transmission of the spear must have had considerable significance for Weber. At his doctoral examination in 1889, Theodor Mommsen, after a prolonged disputation with Weber, concluded by saying that despite his differences, "when I have to go into my grave, I would gladly say to no other than the highly esteemed Max Weber: 'My son, here is my spear, it is becoming too heavy for my arm.' "[*] Thus, one can infer from Weber's use of this image, which, considering the source and time of its utterance, he was hardly likely to forget, his presumption that he now stood in the same position of authority *vis-à-vis* the proletariat that Mommsen had been in as against himself in 1889. And this inference enables us, perhaps, to gain a new perspective on the mighty pathos of the *Antrittsrede,* as well as to draw some final conclusions about Weber's personal, psychological development and its relationship to his plea for imperialism.

The closing paragraph of the Freiburg address places Weber in the position of a mediator between present and future generations. Again he elevates the political above the economic, when he says that the physical misery of the masses to which his generation's social conscience so readily responds, is less burdensome than "the consciousness of our responsibility before history." The crucial question is whether

---

[*] Walter Lotz, one of Weber's examiners, as quoted in *Lebensb.*, p. 132.

posterity will look to us as its ancestors. We will not
succeed in banning the curse under which we stand—
that of being the aftermath of a politically great epoch
—unless we are able to be something else: precursors
of a greater. Will that be our place in history? I know
not, and say only: it is the right of youth to stand to
itself and its ideals. And it is not years that make a man
old: he is young so long as he is capable of feeling the
great passions that nature has placed in us. And thus—
here let me close—it is not the millennia of a glorious
history under whose burden a great nation ages. It remains young, if it has the capacity and the courage
to remain true to the great instincts which are given
to it, and if its leading strata are able to rise up into the
hard and clear air in which the sober work of German
politics flourishes, but which is also permeated by the
serious splendor of national emotion.

In the *Referat* of 1893, Weber had displayed two fundamentally different ethoi: that of the loyal son and that of
the rebel son. As the loyal son, he seemed to accept the
Prussian-Calvinist virtues of military discipline and unremitting labor and confessed, in his conclusion, to feeling
burdened by the "curse of epigonism." As the rebel son, he
fulminated against the treacherous irresponsibility of the
Junkers—which stood condemned, he argued, by the very
Staatsraison they had once represented—and identified
wholeheartedly with the striving of the rural laborers for
emancipation. The *Archiv* study explored the historical possibilities of a real movement of social rebellion. In the
Antrittsrede Weber mounted a more sustained and open attack than ever before on all the objects of his hatred, but
now the rebel son was "able to rise up into the hard
and clear air, in which the sober work of German politics
flourishes, but which is also permeated by the serious splendor of national emotion." In other words, less than two
years after his marriage and departure from Charlottenburg,
Weber was at last able to create some kind of synthesis from
his earlier antithetical ethoi.

Does this mean that he was finally overcoming the hostility to his father that he had earlier expressed through his work? Not at all. He was simply substituting for its earlier capriciously explosive form a seemingly coherent nationalist ideology, couched in the framework of one of the commonplace presuppositions of late-nineteenth-century thought: the struggle for existence.

It is curious, though, how the focus of this ideology still shifts around nervously in the *Antrittsrede*. The subject that Weber discusses at the beginning is the Polish problem in the eastern provinces of the Reich, and his purpose in doing so is to show "the role that physical and psychological racial differences between nations play in the economic struggle for existence." And he makes it clear just how the Poles, because of their inferiority are destined to emerge demographically victorious in the German East as long as the struggle remains a purely economic one. Why then does the state not intervene to protect the German East? (*N.B.*: Already the focus shifts necessarily from the economic arena, as one of inevitable defeat, to the political.) Because the Junkers, once a healthy ruling class, have sunk into decadence, are mired in their exclusively economic problems, and have abandoned their political responsibilities and hence the nation. What group can represent the nation, rather than its own narrow economic desires? For the moment, neither the bourgeoisie, nor the proletariat, for both are politically immature. The bourgeois leadership have not created the state through their own power, and once Bismarck created it for them, they retreated from history, concerned only with lining their pockets and stomachs. The political leadership of the proletariat consists of a clique of journalists—de-classed bourgeois—with an overinflated sense of their importance and power.

What then can restore the political vitality of the nation? Only a determined policy of overseas expansion. But none of the apparent social powers in Germany have the will or the insight to demand this. Only Weber's younger generation of *Sozialpolitiker,* those who combine an iron will with the highest ideals, can rescue the German people from a tragic end.

Thus, by the end of the *Antrittsrede,* the culturally inferior Poles are replaced as the arch-enemy by virtually all of the older generation of political leadership within Germany; the economic struggle is replaced by a political one; and the demand for a defensive politics within Europe to ward off the Polish danger is replaced by the insistence on a militant overseas imperialism. The scene bears certain uncanny formal resemblances to the tragedy of Prince Hamlet. The brilliant but slightly mad hero begins his carnage with a wild lunge at the unwanted guest behind the curtain, the culturally subnormal peasant Polonius. Having demonstrated the force and accuracy of his sword arm, Weber-Hamlet shortly thereafter, in a furious effort to show his mastery of the total situation, carves up most of the remaining cast: the Junkers, the philistine bourgeois politicians, and the socialist leadership—all to be tossed on the scrap heap as politically ineffectual or worse. But the Hamlet of 1895 does not murder his false father until another two years have passed, and when he does, he has the misfortune to survive him.

Weber's *Antrittsrede* of 1895 appears to have been the most important single factor in deciding that marriage between liberalism and imperialism that was later to be consecrated by a millionfold human sacrifice in World War I. According to Wolfgang Mommsen, Weber's speech converted two of the most prominent publicists of Wilhelmian Germany to the cause of liberal imperialism: Weber's friend Friedrich Naumann, the editor of *Die Hilfe,* and Hans Delbrück, the historian and editor of the *Preussische Jahrbücher.*[93]

Both of their journals became organs, after Weber's speech, for an educated variety of imperialist ideology. Thus writes Mommsen:

The Freiburg inaugural address became the spark that set off liberal imperialism in Wilhelmian Germany. Only the liberal imperialists . . . made imperialism "socially acceptable" in Germany. Only with them was a broad imperialist movement formed, whereas the nationalists of the Pan-German League had found only a limited following.

Weber's importance in the development of German imperialism, as ideology and as a "socially acceptable" movement, was hardly accidental. For he incarnated all of the crucial psychological tensions that made broad strata of both the German intelligentsia and the populace at large receptive to a brutally aggressive imperial creed before and during World War I. And he also possessed the intellectual brilliance that could shape these tensions into a convincing and articulate ideology.

Talcott Parsons analyzes the basic social stresses of Prussianized Germany in his "Social Structure and Democracy in Pre-Nazi Germany."* Given the all-encompassing authority of a rigidly formalized, hierarchical social structure, sanctioned religiously by Luther and philosophically by Kant, the ongoing social structure, which functions as a monumentally oppressive cultural superego, simply affords the individual *no* opportunity to invest his emotional energies, aggressive or libidinal, within the given system. At the same time, since this rigidly authoritarian social structure tends to permeate the family as well as the state and the Church, youth's natural rebelliousness against external restraint grows into an extremely intense hostility, focused initially on the father but easily extendable to the social and political structure as a whole, a hostility which surely

---

* In Parsons: *Essays in Sociological Theory*, pp. 104–23. While Parsons acknowledges that his analysis refers primarily to Prussia, he also points out, correctly, in my opinion, that "the position of Prussia was sufficiently central to color the whole of Germany." I have in my own analysis drawn certain psychological inferences from Parsons's theory that may go beyond what he would accept.

is a major factor in the ubiquitousness of generational revolt in modern Germany.

Now a natural channel for this hostility, and one which functioned within the social framework of the state, was the socialist movement. But the strength of the formalized social structure was so great in Germany that even the labor movement tended to look increasingly like a mere petty-bourgeois and lower-class replica of the dominant authoritarian and bureaucratic machine. Several of the founders of German sociology looked to the socialist movement for salvation at one point or another in their careers. All except Ferdinand Tönnies turned from it in disgust, and he retained his interest only because, apart from the cooperative movement, he saw in it from the beginning of his career only a later stage of the *Gesellschaft* he detested. Indeed, Robert Michels acutely pointed out the disillusionment that eventually beset many of the bourgeois intellectuals who joined the Socialist Party in a quest for salvation, and carefully analyzed the motives that led most of them to remain in the party despite it all.*

It is not by chance that Michels, Weber, and Sombart, after an initial flirtation—of greater or lesser duration and intensity—with socialism, became, in later stages of their

---

* Robert Michels: *Political Parties* (Glencoe, Ill., 1949), pp. 205–14. It is of great significance that Michels himself, before his final exit from revolutionary politics, aligned himself with the French anarcho-syndicalists around Georges Sorel and that he attempted to awaken the interest of Sombart and Weber in this movement; the syndicalists, and Sorel in particular, were extremely sensitive and hostile to precisely that bureaucratic lifelessness that so repelled both Weber and Sombart in the German Socialist Party. But syndicalism never was a significant force in Germany, perhaps because it could never find any congenial environment in the extremely formalized German social structure, and both Weber and Sombart were by 1905 too thoroughly integrated, in their own ways, into German society, to identify emotionally with a product of a non-German culture. Thus, in the first decade of the twentieth century, when both men were developing world views based on the opposition of a heroic voluntarism to an increasingly mechanized world, neither of them could conceive of basing this antagonism, as Sorel did, on the primitive vitality of the proletariat.

development, either ideological predecessors or apologists of fascism. The emotional energies for which one could not find a rationally meaningful channel within German society thereafter sought and found an irrational channel, and the real enemy, the stultifying machinelike character of German state and society, i.e., paternal despotism writ large, which proved internally unassailable, was projected primarily onto the external enemies. This is true of the development of Sombart's thought between his socialist phase in the '90's and his proto-fascist mood before, during, and after World War I. But it is much more significantly true of Weber, because with his combination of overpowering intellect and volcanic passion he traversed a similar path between 1893 and 1895.*

Thus, if we examine the main tenets of liberal imperialism, as outlined by Ludwig Dehio in his excellent essay, "Thoughts on Germany's Mission, 1900–1918,"[94] we find that the later development of liberal-imperialist doctrine suggests the extremely broad presence in German society of the same tensions that made Weber a driven man. Far more explicitly than Weber, the imperial ideologists after 1900 gave to their main enemies, Russia and England, the same archetypical characteristics that Weber had opposed in his own, rather typical, German father—and feared in himself: the aggressive desire for universal domination (England) and the entropic impulse of universal bureaucratization (Russia). And the German nation, against these threats to the individuality and freedom of the other peoples of the world, identified itself with a neo-Rankean ideology of cultural pluralism. It seems rather clear that in the stark antagonism thus posited between, on the one hand, an alliance of self-consciously young and weak nations, and, on the other, the two hegemonic giants which threaten to destroy

---

* He was also one of the first to modify this view, in a direction clearly incompatible with later Fascist notions of *Realpolitik*, primarily as the result of his altered personal perspective after his breakdown. See below, pp. 167–71.

all the individuality of the lesser powers, we have a re-spectable ideological screen for the age-old struggle of sons against paternal despots, with the despots now projected into an international arena where it was not merely safe but highly patriotic to attack them.* Considering Max Weber's passionate involvement in this struggle on a personal level, and his ability to articulate and manipulate his passions through his powerful intelligence, it seems more than chance that he was the first to hypostatize the hopeless family struggle confronting so many young Germans into a global *Weltanschauung*.

---

* This theme of the relationship of politics to the conflicts of sons and fathers is discussed with great insight in Norman Brown's recent book, *Love's Body*.

4

Orestes
and the Furies

"*Die Propheten haben die Macht, durch ihr
Wort zu töten.*"

WEBER, R.S. III, *p.* 312

"*He that hath killed my king, and whored my mother;
Popped in between the election and my hopes;
Thrown out his angle for my proper life,
And with such coz'nage—is't not perfect conscience
To quit him with this arm? And is't not to be damned
To let this canker of our nature come
In further evil?*"

Hamlet, Act V, Sc. *ii*

"*Lasst mir so lange Ruh, ihr Unterirdischen,
Die nach dem Blut ihr, das von meinen Tritten
Herniedelträufelnd meinen Pfad bezeichnet,
Wie losgelassne Hunde spürend hetzt.*"

GOETHE, Iphigenie auf Tauris, Act II, Sc. *i*

WEBER'S PSYCHIC BREAKDOWN began, according to his
wife, in the late summer and fall of 1897, following shortly
after his father's death. Marianne Weber does not, in her
779-page biography of her husband, mention the date of

Max Weber, Sr.'s, death or burial except to say that his earthly
remains were last viewed by his family "on a brilliant August
day" and that that day followed by seven weeks an argument between son and father. Although she discusses for
three pages the character of this argument, and makes it
quite clear that she believes her husband's breakdown to
be related to the sequence of argument and death, she gives
no clear indication of when the altercation occurred either,
apart from the seven-week interval separating it from Weber
Sr.'s death, a curiously precise statistic for someone as con-
stitutionally vague on factual matters as Marianne Weber.

There would seem to be abundant cause for a nervous
breakdown simply in the fact of the dispute and its fatal
aftermath. Weber's meteoric rise in his profession was capped
in 1897 by an appointment as *Ordinarius* in Heidelberg, a
city to which he felt drawn by "happy childhood memories
and the first joyful student years."[1] He moved there in the
early months of 1897.[2] Some months later, Helene Weber
was making plans to spend a few quiet weeks with her son
and daughter-in-law, as she had done in previous years.
Her husband, however, "is unable to overcome the idea that
his now-aging wife still 'belongs' to him, that his interests
and desires take precedence over hers and all others, and
that he has the right to determine the time and duration
of her vacation." To complicate matters, Marianne adds,
Helene's Heidelberg "children" refuse to recognize the authority of Max Sr.; she herself would like to defy him but
lacks the strength. Apparently Max Sr. was insisting on his
right to accompany his wife, and the "children," meaning
primarily his son, bitterly opposed his coming.

Indeed, it is possible that Weber had a special reason
for not wanting to see his father at this time. Weber had
been obliged to accept a curb on his political activity with
Naumann's National Social Party as a condition for the
Heidelberg appointment. In a letter to his Heidelberg uncle,
Adolf Hausrath, he made clear his misgivings about this
curb while conceding that the greater responsibilities at

Heidelberg would require it anyway. But he refused to sever his personal ties with Naumann and expressed great concern lest any compromise make him appear a careerist.[3] The father, whose lack of purity had long made him an object of contempt in his son's eyes, may well have heard of Max's compromise, and his mocking presence could therefore have been especially objectionable at this time.

In any case, the upshot was that "Dates are not held to, irritated negotiations occur through the mails—finally the elder Weber accompanies his wife to Heidelberg, so that her undisturbed repose among her children appears shortened or completely spoiled."[4]

In 1887, at the time his father had dismissed his brother's tutor, Weber had suffered a serious blow to his sense of self and had probably forced himself to abandon the cousin he loved because he had been unable to accede to the pressure he felt, both from her and from his mother, to oppose his father. By 1897, Weber was four years removed from his Charlottenburg prison, had married and become economically independent as one of Germany's most successful young academicians. Sure of himself now, he was determined to show the manhood he had lacked ten years earlier. When the son saw his father arrive with his mother, the pent-up anger of a decade finally burst forth: such tyranny might still go on in Charlottenburg, but in Max Weber's own house, in his mother's childhood city, it must stop. If, in 1887, his father had forced Herr Voigt, a spiritual son of Helene Weber if there ever was one, out of his house, now, in excellent conscience, the son by blood would pay him back. It had, after all, always been the son's opinion that the best way to deal with despots was to oppose them openly, as his uncle had, Treitschke. In any case, the old man must leave.

The old man did leave, and his wife spent a few guilt-ridden weeks with her son and daughter-in-law. When Helene Weber returned to Berlin, she discovered that as a result of her son's action, her husband was totally closed to her. After a brief while, he left her to do some traveling with a friend. In the midst of his travels, something, perhaps a bleeding ulcer, hemorrhaged in Max Weber, Sr.'s, stomach, and he died.

One can never speak with certainty about psychic disasters nearly three quarters of a century old, but there is a certain possible significance in Weber Sr.'s insistence on accompanying his wife to Heidelberg, a significance only vaguely and indirectly suggested by Marianne Weber but which, if true, would go far toward explaining why her husband's burden of guilt became so great that he was unable to resume a normal professional life for two decades. I refer to the date which she implies by her very specific reference to a seven-week interval between the dispute and the viewing of the body in Berlin.

Seven weeks is a strange period to keep in one's mind for three decades. Given Marianne's looseness about dates, one would normally expect her to recall it as "two months" or "some months." The recollection of such a precise length of time suggests that there were very familiar dates marking the beginning and the end of this period. The end of the period is easy to establish. We know from other sources that Max Weber's father died in Riga on August 10; his body was probably shipped down to Berlin and viewed by the family on August 11. Seven weeks before August 11 was June 23. And June 23 was the wedding anniversary of Max and Helene Weber.*

Marianne may, of course, have erred slightly in her recollection of a seven-week interval; it is quite conceivable that Helene and her husband traveled to Heidelberg one,

---

* Marianne Weber is completely misleading about the anniversary date, saying merely that Max Jr.'s day of birth, April 21, 1864, was a year after his parents' marriage; *Lebensb.*, p. 37. A photocopy of the original inscription of the marriage notice from the Heidelberg *Standesamt* clearly gives the date of marriage as June 23, 1863. Döhner's genealogy (p. 317) gives the death date of Max Weber Sr., as August 10, 1897, "*Riga (auf der Reise)*"; the same information appears in the *Deutsches Geschlechterbuch*, p. 444.

two, or three days after the anniversary. Nonetheless, the proximity of the anniversary to the son's bold expulsion of the father from his house, a proximity which none of the members of this tightly knit family were ever likely to forget in view of the old man's subsequent death, probably haunted Max Weber as much as any other detail of that vitriolic final encounter. For what seems incontestable is that either on or shortly after his parents' wedding anniversary he ordered his father out of his house to permit his mother and himself the undisturbed enjoyment of one another's company. It was the first time that Weber had ever revealed to his father the full depths of his bitterness. And he never saw the old man alive again.

STANDING BY his father's coffin on that shining August day, Weber did not, according to his wife, show any sign of guilt or remorse. The argument that preceded it appeared unavoidable to him.[5] But shortly thereafter, on a vacation trip with Marianne at the end of summer, he displayed an unusual irritability over minor transportation difficulties, and "he himself interprets the restlessness with which he grasps after ever new impressions as a sign of nervous exhaustion. . . . On the return trip the strained organism reacts with an illness. Weber becomes feverish and feels threatened."

Weber seemed for a few months to have recovered from this illness without aftereffects. He taught a course in Karlsruhe for the Protestant Social Union and then made his way without incident through most of the winter semester at Heidelberg. But at the semester's end (January or February, 1898), when he was overloaded with work, "some evil thing from the unconscious underground of life stretches out its claws toward him. . . . total exhaustion, with headaches and strong feelings of tension overcome him." Again, "Weber feels threatened." This time he saw a doctor, who told him he had been overworking, and suggested a trip. A journey to Lake Geneva in the early spring of 1898, accompanied by long walks, seemed to have improved Weber's condition. A letter to his mother for her birthday, however, after discussing his renewed sense of well-being, retained a certain good-humored cautiousness: "Naturally, we all remain nervous Nellies ["*nervöse Käuze*"], we can't change that, but now, after everything capable of oppressing one has been assimilated, we are not in a mood to worry ourselves about it."

But a couple of weeks after resuming his scholarly work, Weber began to suffer from a new affliction, sleeplessness, and from what his wife vaguely refers to as "functional disturbances." During Whitsunweek, to avoid a visit from a friend, he took a long walk alone through a nearby forest. Suddenly: "the glory of May is veiled by a dark curtain. He is very exhausted, his robust frame weakens, tears well up. Weber feels himself at a turning point. Nature, so long violated, takes its revenge."

Again, Marianne Weber omits the dates of these two important stages in her husband's breakdown, though one of them at least can hardly be insignificant. Whitsunweek fell on May 30, May 31, and June 1 in 1898. May 31 was the birthday of Max Weber, Sr., the first that his son experienced since his death. The date on which sleeplessness commenced may also be significant. If Marianne means the "couple of weeks" interval, at the end of which Weber could not sleep, to have been literally fourteen days, and means it to have begun with the day he wrote the letter to his mother—April 14—then simple arithmetic would place the beginning of sleeplessness on April 28. April 28 was the birthday of Weber's departed uncle and ethical model, Hermann Baumgarten, whose difficulties had introduced *him* to the sleepless night in 1873, a quarter of a century earlier.*

---

* Erich Marcks wrote in his biography of Baumgarten: "From 1873 on, complaints emerge in his letters about month-long, painful sleeplessness, about the paralyzing effect it has on him, about the crickets that tormented him then in the long nights." Marcks's work appeared as a 130-page *Einleitung* to Baumgarten's *Historische und*

In any case, Weber's doctor recommended a stay in a sanatorium for the summer of 1898. Although Weber took all the customary treatments of that age which his doctors imposed on him, he was still unable to rest at night or shake off his tension, and he began to think seriously of taking a leave of absence from his work to recuperate. Nonetheless, he felt considerably stronger by the fall, and plunged once more into his academic responsibilities. After a few weeks his nerves gave way again, and his lectures became a torment.

Weber became aware, in this fall semester of 1898, that it would be a long time before he could free himself of whatever was plaguing him and that it must have been building up for years. Marianne, in describing his view of his misfortune at this time, writes:

> And was not this illness perhaps only a long-gathering cloud, whose final discharge could effect a liberation from a secretly threatening, hostile power. Would it not prepare the way for a greater *harmony* of his vital powers in the future?

Marianne then quotes from a letter Weber wrote to her, apparently from the sanatorium, in which he makes that reference quoted above about his feeling released from an icy hand, meaning his sense of release from his earlier compulsion to work.

Indeed, it may well be that in this respect the breakdown was a blessing for both Weber and his wife. When he recognized the utter seriousness of his position, he accepted the inevitability of a lesser work schedule and became much closer to his wife, who, because of her husband's total dependence on her, was able to overcome earlier fears of a purposeless existence.

Nonetheless, his wife tells us, his misery was only then

Politische Aufsätze und Reden (Strassburg, 1894). (The passage quoted above is on p. cviii.) It is quite probable that Weber had read it before his breakdown.

beginning. A temporary recovery in the fall of 1898 was
followed by renewed collapse at Christmastime, when his
back and arms felt so exhausted that he was unable to deco-
rate a Christmas tree. Despite his agony, he doggedly completed his work for the semester.

Various attempts at occupational therapy produced no
substantial improvement in the subsequent months: "the
hands shake . . . the back hurts." Moreover, Marianne tells
us, the sleeplessness became worse: "A soft sound in the
afternoon or morning now became a torment to the man who
earlier, after intense work, fell into deep sleep and was insensitive to noise."[6] Weber requested and received per-
mission to cancel the lectures he was scheduled to give in
the summer semester of 1899.

One of the numerous irritations that Weber seems to
have felt in this period was his mother's skepticism as to
the seriousness of his illness. Apparently she still retained
some residue of the Calvinist conviction that a grown man
who was not blasted with sin would be able to overcome
any merely psychological obstacles to the fulfillment of his
duties, and this residue, which had earlier driven her son
on to heroic feats of scholarship, now became simply unbearable to him. "I only wish," he wrote her, "you would
now believe that it is not psychic apathy, if I reject, in certain stages of exhaustion, all so-called 'suggestions,' and if I
have now gone on leave. The inability to speak is purely
physical, the nerves break down, and when I look at my
lecture notes I simply can't make sense of them."

Marianne comprehends her mother-in-law's ethic and
her confusion: "Her own heroic will, continually tensed for
merciless self-violation, has mastered all spiritual and physical strains. Cannot her son do the same?" But Marianne
also sees how her husband is tortured by Helene Weber's
tacit assumption that, since he does not *look* ill, his main
problem is a lagging will: "I am sorry," Marianne writes,
"that I reacted with such irritation to your well-intended
plan.—The real reason may well be that from time to time

I seem to feel that you think Max's condition must be improved by energy, by some act of self-transcendence ["*durch ein Über-sich-hinaus-Kommen*"]. And I cannot allow even the appearance of a weak will to rest on him . . ."

Though he had dropped his lectures, Weber continued his seminar and tutorial responsibilities in the summer of 1899.[7] A fall vacation in Italy permitted a temporary "deliverance from the nightmare of duties,"[8] but the attempt shortly after to resume a part of these duties resulted in the most serious breakdown of all.

At Christmastime, realizing he would not for some years be able to fulfill his professional obligations, Weber wanted to resign his office, but the Baden ministry, fearing the permanent loss of one of its academic luminaries, offered him an indefinite leave instead, which he accepted.

Weber's last professional activity before completely giving in to his illness was an attempt to persuade the faculty and the ministry to accept Werner Sombart as his successor, an attempt which took two weeks of agonized argument, ended in failure, and required a week in bed for recuperation.[*]

His indefinite leave was to begin in the fall of 1900; for the summer semester though, he was still obliged to continue some informal work with students. Despite his near-total release from responsibilities, Weber's condition became worse as the summer approached:

> He can neither read nor write nor talk nor walk nor sleep without torment. All mental functions and a part of the physical ones fail him. If he nonetheless forces them to work, chaos threatens him, a feeling as though he could fall into the vortex of an overexcitement that would throw his mind into darkness.

---

[*] *Lebensb.*, p. 277. Did Weber know of Sombart's envy, communicated to Otto Lang, when he first heard of Weber's appointment at Freiburg? (Letter to Lang dated *Pfingsten*, 1894, *International Institute for Social History*, Amsterdam.)

At the beginning of July, accompanied by Marianne, he again entered a sanatorium. In retrospect, she considered that summer of 1900 as the worst phase of his breakdown. That this institutionalization, and the previous one in the summer of 1898, occurred not long after the anniversary of his final dispute with his father may be more than accidental.

IN THE NEXT three years, marked by almost continual European traveling, Weber experienced repeated slow recuperations and sudden relapses. He gradually severed his ties with Heidelberg and retained only a purely titular professorship from 1903 on.[9] A detailed discussion of this period is unnecessary: in any case, Marianne Weber has covered it quite comprehensively.[10] Nonetheless, several aspects of her husband's breakdown strike such deep chords in the history of his life and personality, that some worthwhile hypotheses may emerge from a careful analysis of them.*

FROM 1886 TO 1897, Weber had imposed a harsh work discipline on his volcanic temperament and combined this discipline with a deep sense of political and social responsibility. But it is arguable that as the discipline and the responsibility increased, they fed feverishly on the flames of mutiny that, under his mother's prodding, he cultivated toward his father. With the sense of professional maturity gained through his work discipline and his active political responsibilities, Weber was confident enough, in his Freiburg inaugural address, to direct these flames against virtually the entire older generation of German politicians. Two years later, when he expelled his father from his house, he used the same fiery passion to deal with the one German politician whose des-

---

* Most unfortunately, Weber's own detailed description of his illness, which he prepared for a psychiatrist before World War I, was destroyed by his widow during World War II. See *Baumg.*, pp. 641–2. See also below, p. 285.

potism was etched more vividly in his memory than any other. If Weber's breakdown resulted from the totally unanticipated success of his aggression, then it is reasonable to assume that what broke down was the entire character structure he had for so long been building so proudly into himself, a character structure which in August 1897 was suddenly revealed to be a weapon for the commission of patricide.

Thus, Weber finds any discipline imposed by fixed responsibilities a torment and is forced to relinquish that prize so dearly bought with years of tedium: the ability to earn his own living.[11] But if he loses his self-discipline and his sense of personal maturity—the character he had developed after 1885, under his mother's influence—he assumes another character which markedly resembles his father's. The paternal demons Weber always felt obliged to fend off—an amoral selfish egoism, on the one hand, and a passive vegetating existence, on the other—seem strangely combined in the life Weber was forced into as a result of his breakdown: "His life was now confined to the smallest circle; every problematic had to be kept distant." Toward his mother, he seems to be assuming his father's attitude of irritation, or so one gathers from Marianne's apology for him: " 'Max's taciturnity ("Verschlossenheit") was only the instinctive defense against any irritation.' "[12] Marianne used a similar phrase to describe Max Sr.'s hostility to his wife in the few weeks between her return from Heidelberg and his death: ". . . he closed himself off against her" ("verschloss er sich gegen sie"). From Marianne herself, on the other hand, Weber received the kind of total devotion that his father had come to expect from his mother.

What seemed to justify Weber's falling into this pattern of behavior was the unbearable tension, accompanied by physical symptoms, that prevented him from doing or being anything else. But viewed from another angle, these very symptoms look like a self-imposed punishment for having assumed these detested paternal characteristics. And indeed, this very well may have been the circle of hell to which Weber sentenced himself for his transgression.

Freud, in describing the phenomenon of melancholia, seems to have had in mind something much like Weber's affliction:

> The patient represents his ego to us as worthless, incapable of any effort and morally despicable; he reproaches himself, vilifies himself, and expects to be cast out and chastised. . . . This picture of delusional belittling—which is predominantly moral—is completed by sleeplessness and refusal of nourishment, and by an overthrow, psychologically very remarkable, of that instinct which constrains every living thing to cling to life.[13]

Freud notes that for one who is professionally obliged to listen to them, the severe self-reproaches of the melancholiac often "are hardly at all applicable to the patient himself, but that with insignificant modifications they do fit someone else, some person whom the patient loves, has loved or ought to love."[14] In Weber's case, clearly, this person, whose characteristics were absorbed into his ego, was his father. The reason for such identification, according to Freud, is the inability to accept the loss of the former love object—an inability in fact strongly suggested by Weber's behavior at his father's bier and accountable in terms of Weber's understandable reluctance to accept the profound sense of guilt that a true reckoning with his father's departure must have awakened. The result of this secretion of his father's spirit in his own ego was, however, the pitiless mutilation of this ego by a superego that still incarnated his mother's standards of discipline and independence.

Even the physical pain that accompanied Weber's breakdown may be explicable in terms of this psychological framework. Frequently, the psyche chooses the physical symptoms that accompany severe psychological punishment from memories of real afflictions. Freud called this process "somatic compliance." Many of the physical and mental afflictions that plagued Weber were compatible with the meningitis he suffered as a child: the back pain, the trembling hands, the sleeplessness and irritability. Indeed, Helene herself in her complaints about her son's "apathy" may have been thinking back to that fearful childhood disease, which may also be marked by depression and partial stupor. Of course it is quite possible that these symptoms, all of which may occur in severe psychic depression, had nothing to do with the childhood illness, but if this "somatic compliance" actually was happening, then it must have added an additional circle to Weber's hell. For the result of the recurrence of these symptoms may well have been psychological regression to those years of devoted maternal protection between the ages of two and seven; in fact, such regression is plausible even without any "somatic compliance," when we consider Weber's general helplessness and need for maternal care during his breakdown. And while a side of him may have gloried in this childish dependence, what impotent curses and torments his still functioning superego must have flung at his useless ego!

JOHN STUART MILL, in his autobiography, mentions a similar, though less severe, depression that he experienced at the age of twenty. His father, James Mill, had raised him in a rigorous educational discipline, such that as a child he was taught Greek from age three, Latin from age eight, and mathematics, natural science, and political economy as early as possible. Introduced to utilitarian maxims as a young man, he was accustomed to judge his world in terms of what ought to create the maximum social felicity, but was rarely permitted to enjoy personally any existing opportunities for spontaneous pleasure.

It is difficult to conceive that such a sustained assault on all the more spontaneous characteristics of a child's nature should not have aroused vast floods of hatred against the father. And in a preliminary draft of the *Autobiography*,

Mill made clear the lack of love between his father and himself, the atmosphere of fear, and a resultant crippling in his "moral" development. The implantation of a dominating paternal superego has rarely been expressed more directly than when Mill wrote, "I acquired the habit of leaving my responsibility as a moral agent to rest on my father and my conscience never speaking to me except by his voice."[15] In the printed version, Mill also revealed such hostility. Although it appears in a highly sublimated form, it comes at a critical and liberating moment in his life.

In 1826, a severe melancholy settled over the young Mill, when the following question and answer occurred to him:

> "Suppose that all your objects in life were realized, that all the changes in institutions and opinions which you are looking forward to, could be completely effected at this very instant: would this be a great joy and happiness to you?" And an irrepressible self-consciousness distinctly answered, "No!" At this my heart sank within me . . . I seemed to have nothing left to live for.[16]

Mill, unlike Weber, was still capable of work during the six-months' depression precipitated by these thoughts but, he says, "I went on with them mechanically, by the mere force of habit. I had been so drilled in a certain sort of mental exercise, that I could still carry it on when all the spirit had gone out of it."[17] In his reflections on this depression, perhaps his most significant discovery was that: "I now saw or thought I saw, what I had always before received with incredulity—that the habit of analysis has a tendency to wear away the feelings."[18]

After about six months, Mill became aware that his feelings were not entirely paralyzed by chancing on the passage in Marmontel's *Mémoires* where that author discussed the death of his father—a death which naturally produced great insecurity in Marmontel's family, but also evoked a sudden inspiration in Marmontel that he would take his father's place and reorganize the family around him-self. Upon reading this, Mill writes,

> A vivid conception of the scene and its feelings came over me, and I was moved to tears. From this moment my burthen grew lighter. The oppression of the feeling that all feeling was dead within me, was gone. I was no longer a stock or a stone. I had still, it seemed, some of the material out of which all worth of character, and all capacity for happiness, are made. Relieved from my ever present sense of irremediable wretchedness, I grad-ually found that the ordinary incidents of life could again give me some pleasure. . . . Thus the cloud gradually drew off . . . I never again was as miserable as I had been.

Weber's breakdown appears to have been more com-plex, more severe, and of much longer duration than Mill's. But like Mill, Weber too seems to have evaded any clear awareness of his patricidal inclinations by nailing himself on the cross of his father's ego, and there is an incident during his phase of recovery in 1903 that sounds something like the emotional breakthrough Mill achieved when he projected himself into the death scene of Marmontel's father.

Weber played a great deal with trains as a small child. At the age of two and a half, he built his wooden blocks into a railroad station and placed a small set of trains within it. Probably somewhat later, he frequently played on the overpass above a raiload line and apparently enjoyed being enveloped by the white smoke of the locomotives speeding below. There is nothing unnatural in this: the steam loco-motive was for the children of Weber's day the same kind of symbol of technological omnipotence that the space rocket is for the current younger generation. But in letters to his uncle written in his mid-twenties, Weber twice used the metaphor of a locomotive racing along with an inexperienced switchman on the tracks ahead to express his anxieties about the reliability of Wilhelm II as Bismarck's successor.[19] Weber certainly seems to have coveted secret hopes of himself replacing Bismarck's iron rule, and, given the general argument above and the occasional blurring of the distinction in Weber's mind between Bismarck, the Junkers, and his father, it has seemed reasonable to base his political hostilities and fears on personal ones.

In this context, Weber's recollection in 1903 of a train accident that frightened him as a four-year-old may have represented a highly sublimated emotional awareness of his father's death—an awareness that freed him from a great deal of the self-torment he had inflicted by identifying with his father's ego:

> At Verviers I remembered the first "shattering" experience of my life: the train derailment of 35 years ago. The shattering thing was not only what happened, but the view of something as sublime to a child as a locomotive lying like a drunkard in a grave—the first experience of the transitory nature of the great and beautiful things of this earth.[20]

The fact that Weber experienced his original fright while traveling with his mother in Belgium during his "delicate" phase—i.e., during the period when Helene Weber's great concern for her son's health was angering her husband —may mean that in both cases his "experience of the transitory nature of the great and beautiful things of this earth" was based on a sudden perception of the merely mortal nature of Max Weber, Sr.

PART II

Estrangement and Eros

1903-1920

PART II

Estrangement and Eros

1908-1920

5

Recovery: The Yoke of History

As WEBER gradually recovered from his prolonged ordeal, he was in many ways a changed man. Earlier, by fusing together the disparate spirits of liberal and Jacobin nationalism, he had hoped to find a new source of political vitality to replace the decadent order of Prussian feudalism. An aggressive course of global *Realpolitik* could, he believed, inspire in the plebs the same sense of political responsibility that had earlier animated the Junkers. This belief disappears from Weber's political writing after 1900.

It is no doubt true that some of Weber's political assumptions remain the same after his breakdown. The vision of worldly activity as an arena of struggle does not change, and there is a certain constancy in his personal commitment to what he conceived to be the interests of the German nation. But these are only the forms, the flasks inside which the intoxicating spirits of defiant, late-liberal hope have degenerated into the gall and vinegar of twentieth-century pessimism.

From the studies of *The Protestant Ethic and the Spirit of Capitalism* to the Munich lectures of 1919 on science and politics as callings, the threat of inescapable decline darkens Weber's horizons. With the exception of a brief period after

the outbreak of World War I, he no longer views the German people (or the proletariat) as capable of being inspired by the "breath of the powerful national passion" that
permeated the Jacobin Convention. The *Leitmotiv* of Western history has changed from progress through self-liberation
to enslavement through rationalization.

In the darkness of this political despair, Weber becomes
intellectually introspective. Like Sombart,* the turn of the
century brings a retreat from political involvement. When
he resumes his scholarly work, Weber focuses for almost a
decade on the relation of religion—especially the Calvinism
from which he descends—to modern capitalism, and on the
methodological bases of social science.

I do not intend to discuss in any detail Weber's methodological preoccupations in the decade following the most
serious phase of his breakdown. To be sure, these writings,
many of them sharp polemics against his contemporaries,
cover questions considered then and now to be of prime
importance for the scientific foundation of the study of society: the nature of causal explanation, the use and misuse
of *"Verstehen"* (intuitive understanding), the ideal type as
the most appropriate form of conceptualization, and, probably most important of all, the separation of values and
science. But for one thing, there is an abundant literature on
them in English. And for another, they are written on a level
of abstraction which makes close analysis for the purpose of
biographical relevance unusually difficult.

---

* Werner Sombart's development from revisionist socialism to
cultural pessimism can be traced through his unpublished letters to
Otto Lang in the *International Institute for Social History*, Amsterdam,
as well as in his published work. By 1907, Sombart, who had been
considered a notorious academic radical in the '90's, was writing panegyrics to cultural stagnation and urging contempt for modernity and
politics in the journal *Morgen*. He emerged from this mood after 1910
to become one of Germany's principal celebrants of atavistic heroism
in politics and economics. The letters to Lang also reveal a personal
crisis accompanying these changes which was similar to Weber's, though
less obviously oedipal and less severe.

Nonetheless, there are two possible connections which these technical concerns may have had with Weber's inner development. They may represent a defense against the implication of his earlier naïve joining of science and values. And the attack on existing historical and methodological assumptions may, as Wolfgang Mommsen suggests, represent an attempt to clear the ground for his own, decidedly voluntarist conception of history and social action.[1]

Weber's scholarship, as we have seen, had always had a complex emotional significance for him. Before the breakdown, his scientific efforts were expressed through compulsive work habits, which apparently signified both subjection to his mother's asceticism and rebellion against his father's selfish hedonism. Although he never pretended that he could deduce ethical values from his work as a political economist, he did argue explicitly that the science of political economy had to serve the power interests of the nation-state, and the alliance thus created allowed his work to serve as a vehicle for the generational revolt that ended in his argument with his father, his father's death, and his own collapse.

In 1887, at the time of his affair with Emmy, Weber had implied that the basis for his refusal to take his mother's side against his father was that their personalities corresponded to categories of judgment—rational and moral—which defied comparison. Weber later raised himself from his timidity and guilt to the point where he could openly judge and condemn his father, but only by joining these categories—with the result that we know. Is it possible that in the course of his breakdown, he developed some awareness that mixing such a proud defiance into his "scientific" analysis had led to his personal catastrophe, and that to overcome this catastrophe, to resume work, and perhaps to do penance for his earlier hubris, he had to expunge from his scholarship any trace of the latent parricidal motive which his brutal espousal of imperialist *Realpolitik* had masked in the '90's.

Thus, the withdrawal from very specific passions—the manifest one of identification with the German people against its putative oppressors, and the latent one of parricide—may have underlain Weber's refusal to legitimize *any* particular subordination of science to values as objectively or logically necessary.

Of course, values could be *related* to scientific inquiry in a number of ways. The investigator's values might determine the object of inquiry and the degree of penetration into the chain of causality behind the object. And scientific method was indispensable for determining the relationship of an historical or social process to particular values. Weber would probably argue, for example, that the consequences of nationalization of industry would be to improve the security and comfort of individuals, but at the expense of their freedom and responsibility, which would be subordinated to the bureaucratic authority of the state. He would deny, however, that there was any objective criterion for favoring one value over the other; and he certainly rejected the idea he had advanced so insistently in his Freiburg inaugural address: that the discipline of political economy necessarily had to serve the power interests of the state. Still, in the very place that he did so, he vigorously criticized the bureaucratic spirit of his contemporaries, not as a "man of science" (*"Mann der Wissenschaft"*) but as a "human being" (*"Mensch"*).[2]

Indeed, neither his despairing political perspective nor his separation of science from values prevented Weber from expressing his opinions again and again—in scholarly as well as nonscholarly contexts—on the nature and future of his society. If anything, his criticism of German politics was more outspoken and more fundamental after the breakdown than before. Weber continued to be an imperialist in the sense that he wished Germany to succeed in the increasingly bitter prewar competition for world influence. But his emphasis shifted from demanding imperialist politics so as to advance the political education and domestic power of the German people to demanding domestic reform as a precondition for a responsible and therefore successful foreign policy. And his total lack of confidence that the left-liberals and trade union-

ists he sided with could exert the necessary pressure to produce these reforms transcended the immediate political
situation and went back to a global *Weltanschauung* of inescapable rationalization and bureaucratization.

The components of this *Weltanschauung*, the historical
and intellectual influences on its development, and its relation to Weber's earlier perspective will be one concern in the
following pages. Another will be Weber's gradual discovery,
in the last decade of his life, of a second world view, centered
around the explosive power of charisma.

[1]

THE PROTESTANT ETHIC:
THE NEW UNDERSTANDING
OF WORLDLY ASCETICISM

*Christian asceticism, at first fleeing from the world
into solitude, had already ruled the world which it had
renounced from the monastery and through the Church.
But it had, on the whole, left the naturally spontaneous
character of daily life in the world untouched. Now
it strode into the marketplace of life, slammed the
door of the monastery behind it, and undertook to
penetrate just that daily routine of life with its
methodicalness, to fashion it into a life in the world,
but neither of nor for this world.*
    The Protestant Ethic and the Spirit of Capitalism

WEBER BEGAN his work on Protestantism and capitalism in
1903, while he was still very close to the psychic catastrophe
that had almost destroyed him after his father's death. Given
the evidence of his compulsive work habits, and his own perception of these as a pathological symptom during his break-

down (above, pp. 50, 154), it is clear that an inquiry into worldly asceticism must have had a more than scholarly interest for him.

Weber was identifying his compulsiveness with the most important component of the spirit of capitalism and tracing both back to the Calvinist's psychological need for proof that he was in a state of grace and hence among the saved. What has happened to the idea of work asceticism, as Weber describes it, is a classic example of reification: a value developed by men expressly to satisfy a psychological need leads them unwittingly to create new institutions which then impose the value on their successors.

> The Puritan wanted to work in a calling; we are forced to do so. For when asceticism was carried out of monastic cells into everyday life, and began to dominate worldly morality, it did its part in building the tremendous cosmos of the modern economic order. This order is now bound to the technical and economic conditions of machine production which today determine the lives of all the individuals who are born into this mechanism, not only those directly concerned with economic acquisition, with irresistible force. Perhaps it will so determine them until the last ton of fossilized coal is burned. In Baxter's view the care for external goods should only lie on the shoulders of the saint like "a light cloak, which can be thrown aside at any moment." But fate decreed that the cloak should become a housing hard as steel.*

The "housing hard as steel," of course, recalls the "secure house" of his father's generation that Weber had publicly refused to enter in 1893. But Weber now recognized the ascetic mien of his mother as well as the bureaucratic spirit of his father as a threat to his autonomy.

---

* Max Weber: *The Protestant Ethic and the Spirit of Capitalism,* trans. Talcott Parsons (New York, 1948), p. 181. (This work will hereafter be cited as *Protestant Ethic.*) I have changed the phrase at the end of this paragraph to its literal meaning in the German, which has a significance beyond the phrase "iron cage" used by Parsons.

In a psychological sense, Weber's work compulsion in the '90's was by no means as functionless as the closing paragraphs of the *Protestant Ethic* might lead us to think. To be sure, Weber was no longer a believing Christian. But even when the projected father of traditional monotheism had lost his sway, there remained the introjected divinities of his own parents. In relation to these gods, Weber did indeed find uses for the ascetic work habits inherited from his mother. Apart from accelerating his career, they also served as a means of reducing his guilt feelings—toward his mother for not aiding her as much as she had wanted, and perhaps also toward his father for feeling so hostile to him.

When the guilt feelings got out of hand, in the first half of 1898, and overworking himself proved insufficient to exorcise them, it may have been some lingering unconscious hope for a free gift of grace, of redemption from sin that led Weber to take a walk in the Odenwald (a large forest near Heidelberg) about the time of his father's birthday. For his father's birthday occurred the day after Whitsunday in 1898, and Whitsunweek (*Pfingstwoche*), the time of Weber's total collapse, was, according to the Gospel of John, also the time when the crucified Jesus returned to his disciples and conferred on them the power to grant redemption from sin.

Whatever he may have been seeking in the Odenwald (Marianne merely says that he wanted to avoid the visit of a friend), he apparently discovered nothing but the abyss of guilt his father's death had created for him. Neither the "talisman" of compulsive work nor any other "ghost of dead religious beliefs" could any longer save Weber from this guilt. But surely the first step toward overcoming it occurred when Weber was able to gouge out of his superego and examine critically the commandment of unceasing labor that had been lodged there. Thus, by identifying the work ethic of his mother's Calvinist ancestry as a device which formerly gave evidence of divine grace but now served only as a "housing hard as steel," Weber was focusing his intellect on his own experience in order both to liberate himself from it and to interpret the history of the modern world; he was perceiving the historical dimension of his personal dilemma.[3]

Indeed, the standard image of Weber sees him as pitting the individualist ethic of his Calvinist forebears against the institutional entropy of the age of bureaucracy.[4] But in the light of this significance of Weber's studies of Puritanism it should be evident that this interpretation requires re-examination. Although he appears naïvely to have identified with the ascetic values of his Calvinist mother before his breakdown, his analysis of these values during his recovery shows a great reserve and distance toward them. Certainly his manner of life after 1900—retirement from his *"Beruf"* of teaching for nearly twenty years, punctuated by long vacations, renewed convalescences, and numerous angry feuds with other scholars—was as distant from the Puritan style as his rigid, sober work schedule before his father's death was a model of it.* Nor does the personal testimony of those who knew Weber best support the conception of him as a bourgeois Marx, exemplifying the virtues of Calvinist asceticism. Frau Heuss later referred to him as "a Kaiser whose scepter has been stolen." And Marianne writes several pages on his *"Ritterdienste"* (knightly services) to colleagues he believed unjustly attacked.† Even before his collapse he

---

* "The person who lives as a worldly ascetic is a rationalist, not only in the sense that he rationally systematizes his own personal patterning of life, but also in his rejection of everything that is ethically irrational, be it aesthetics or personal emotionalism within the world and its order." (I have slightly modified Fischoff's translation.) Max Weber: *The Sociology of Religion* (Boston, 1967), p. 168; hereafter cited as S.R. Max Weber: *Wirtschaft und Gesellschaft* (Köln, Berlin, 1964), p. 424; hereafter cited as W.u.G. In the new English translation of this work, edited by Guenther Roth and Claus Wittich (*Economy and Society* [Totowa, N.J.], 1968), p. 544; this work will hereafter be cited as E.S.; all quotes from it, however, are my translation from the German edition, since the English edition was not available at the time of writing.

† *Lebensb.*, pp. 482–9. See also *Lebensb.*, p. 675: "Weber sits like an old knight among them [sympathetic young friends in Munich, 1919] and speaks from the bottom of his heart about the bankruptcy of the

accompanied his ascetic labors with a most un-bourgeois posture in moments of relaxation: his wife writes that students, amazed by his unprofessional behavior at a student drinking party, compared him to ". . . a giant resurrected warrior from the forests of Germany, in whose hands an unwarlike age had pressed a pen instead of a spear . . . a duke who moved into battle at the head of his vassals."[5]

The work on the *Protestant Ethic,* then, constitutes a chapter in Weber's own "genealogy of morals." Apart from its genuine insight into the psyche of modern man, it represents a new and much more sophisticated act of self-liberation on Weber's part, in which he substitutes for the earlier naïve identifications with the struggles of oppressed rural workers against despotic paternalism a truly Nietzschean assault on his own superego. But in doing so, he has joined to the despised *"festes Haus"* of his father enough of his mother's values for the entire structure of modern civilization to appear as a vast and inescapable prison. Juxtaposed to Weber's liberated intellect is a harsh, diabolical sphere of coercive power, an antinomy which in *Wirtschaft und Gesellschaft* will take the form of charisma versus rationalization.

Kaiser." A doctor who knew Weber during the war described him as "a modern incarnation of Dürer's knight between death and the devil"; *Lebensb.,* p. 718. Gertrud Bäumer saw him as a blending of aristocratic heroism with the legacy of "bourgeois-protestant culture" and as "one of the few truly aristocratic types from the German history of the turn of the century"; *M.W.z.G,* p. 118.

[2]

THE SOCIOLOGY OF REIFICATION
AND THE PRAISE OF FOLLY

Whoever pushes rationality forward
also restores new strength to the opposite power,
mysticism and folly of all kinds.

NIETZSCHE, The Will to Power, *1012*

THE PESSIMISM revealed in Weber by the closing paragraphs of *The Protestant Ethic and the Spirit of Capitalism* was to remain predominant in his outlook until he died in 1920. He was, of course, not alone in his gloom. In France and Italy as well as in Germany, political events of the decade before World War I inspired the more sensitive intellectuals with a feeling of disgust at the decadence of both liberal and social-ist conviction. And this was as true among the supposedly more neutral acolytes of the new discipline of sociology as it was among the philosophical and literary exponents of cul-tural pessimism. Certainly Ferdinand Tönnies, Werner Som-bart, and Robert Michels, who stood in varying degrees of personal closeness to Weber, shared his despair. And another, very close friend, Georg Simmel, gave to Weber a concep-tion of the inevitable triumph of "objective" over "subjective" spirit, i.e., of man's creations over the man-the-creator, which Weber put to excellent use in his sociology. Indeed, Weber's work could in many places be interpreted as a detailed application of Simmel's insight to the history of political and religious ideas and institutions—a sociology of reification.*

Nonetheless, the further removed Weber was from those years when the conflict between his work compulsion and

---

* See footnote above, p. 4, and pp. 209–30 below.

his inability to work had prostrated him, the more the character of his cosmic prison altered from one created by the
capitalist spirit to one in which the capitalist spirit was itself
but a tool manipulated by all-powerful bureaucratic machines. From the meaninglessness of wealth for the sake of
wealth, the sickness of modern society became, in Weber's
eyes, power for the sake of power.[6]

One perceives this horror of the mindless bureaucratic
machine most dramatically in Weber's comments at the
meetings of the *Verein für Sozialpolitik* in 1905, 1907, and
1909 and in his wartime political polemics, particularly *Par-
lament und Regierung* and the lecture *"Der Sozialismus."*
It accounts for the odd mixture of what one might conven-
tionally consider contradictory conservative and radical
strains in these writings, where on the one hand can be found
attacks on the Social Democrats, polemics against nationalization of industry, and arguments for the superiority of the
private entrepreneur over the bureaucrat, and on the other,
ardent defense of trade unions and the most bitter attacks
on the German political system for its domestic authoritarianism and its irresponsible foreign policy.

Underlying these cases is a harsh dualism, which bears
a certain resemblance to the hero-merchant dichotomy of
Sombart; for Weber, though, the distinction is really one of
hero vs. bureaucrat. Usually a specialist in some field, and
holding an appointive office in a social organization, the
bureaucrat has no commitment outside it and has an abhorrence of change. Where, as in Germany, the nation was
dominated by an authoritarian bureaucracy, even independent capitalists were filled with a savage desire to inflict on
their underlings the daily humiliations imposed upon them.
Weber probably best summarized his abhorrence of the
bureaucratic machine when, protesting the equanimity of
his colleagues before it, he said:

> As terrible as the idea seems that the world might be
> full of nothing but professors—we would flee to the
> desert if that should happen—so much the more terrible

is the idea that the world should be filled with nothing but those cogs who cling to a little post and strive for a somewhat greater one—a condition which, as in the papyrii, you rediscover increasingly in the spirit of contemporary officialdom and above all of its next generation, our present students. This passion for bureaucratization, such as we have heard expressed here, is enough to drive one to despair. It is . . . as though we knowingly and willingly were *supposed* to become men who need "order" and nothing but order, who become nervous and cowardly if this order shakes for a moment and helpless when they are torn from their exclusive adaptation to this order. That the world knows nothing more than such men of order—we are in any case caught up in this development, and the central question is not how we further and accelerate it but what we have to *set against* this machinery, in order to preserve a remnant of humanity from this par-celling-out of the soul, from this exclusive rule of bureaucratic life ideals.[7]

The 1905 meeting of the *Verein für Sozialpolitik* was held at the height of the revolutionary wave of that year, and, largely under the illusion that the German labor strug-gles represented a trade union rebellion against the demean-ing authoritarianism of the state, the capitalists, and the Socialist Party, Weber indignantly defended the unions before the *Verein* against the attack of a Saarland industrial-ist. Though Weber was wrong about the anti-authoritarian-ism of the German trade unions at this time, the Russian revolution of 1905 seems to have inspired in him a lasting interest in Russian culture which contrasts sharply with his contempt for the Slavic masses before his breakdown. But what he saw in Tolstoy, Dostoevsky and the Russian revolu-tionary tradition can only be properly understood in the con-text of Weber's conception of history, as it matures in the period 1903 to 1920. And that theoretical outlook, just as in his earlier period, is so hemmed in between two inescapable spheres of experience that it cannot be properly understood without calling them to mind. Underlying his historical perception is the massive and frightening weight of his own past. Issuing from that perception is an unending series of judgments upon it.

The conceit that historical progress would come via the self-liberation of sons from paternal despotism had led Weber to a nervous breakdown, but through it he had discovered in his demonic compulsion to work a strange legacy of his mother's Calvinist inheritance. In the course of recovering, he separated himself from this inheritance, intellectually and psychologically, and thereby also put into question his relationship to his mother. His mature historical perception is, then, one in which the generative forces are not to be trusted. His father's characteristics—authoritarian despotism at home and bureaucratic subservience in his office—and the side of his mother's religious inheritance which he identifies with the capitalist spirit—the ascetic compulsion to labor—symbolize for him the forces that unite to rationalize society and destroy individual autonomy.

Juxtaposed against these blind forces are what Salomon calls "emotional life forces," partly but not entirely summarized in the word *charisma*. These heroic "life forces" may intervene momentarily in history, they may even take advantage of the tools of the modern bureaucratized social order to attempt to instill new life in it (Weber's political ideal), but in the long haul they are doomed.

Thus, in his very strong interest in the *George-Kreis* and in Russian culture, and in his personal "brotherliness" to the outsider and the persecuted wherever he found him, Weber reveals a hopeless but persistent defiance of certain powers whose objective inevitability he cannot deny. To be sure, Weber did frequently write like an ardent nationalist and imperialist, as Wolfgang Mommsen has made clear, but the dominant emphasis in his later political writing is the demand for political and social reform that will reduce the servility and machinelike inhumanity that he sees endemic in the German tradition. And, contrapuntally opposed to his acceptance of power and violence as the nature of politics is a personal ethic of brotherhood.

HIDDEN IN *Wirtschaft und Gesellschaft,* Weber's unfinished, posthumously published masterpiece, and in most of the other work of his last decade is a history of rationalization in the political, religious, economic, and legal institutions of man. This study will focus only on those aspects of Weber's historical sociology of religion and politics which have obvious relevance to the antinomy of rationalization and charisma. These are: (1) his distinction of asceticism and mysticism and his discussion of the worldly consequences of these positions; and (2) his discussion of the historical antagonism between the patrimonial state and the independent feudality, as well as the significance for his historical world view of the bureaucratic and aristocratic codes which epitomize them. Weber's analysis suggests not only the persistent influence of personal motives on his work, but also an ongoing dialogue throughout his later years with the ideas and values of Nietzsche, Marx, Tönnies, Simmel, and Sombart.

6

Marx, Nietzsche, and the Spirits of Defiance

The higher culture of the West—whose moral, aesthetic, and intellectual values industrial society still professes —was a pre-technological culture. . . . a feudal culture, even when the bourgeois period gave it some of its most lasting formulations. It was feudal not only because of its confinement to privileged minorities, not only because of its inherent romantic element . . . but also because its authentic works expressed a conscious, methodical alienation from the entire sphere of business and industry, and from its calculable and profitable order.

While this bourgeois order found its rich—and even affirmative—representation in art and literature . . . it remained an order which was overshadowed, broken, refuted by another dimension which was irreconcilably antagonistic to the order of business, indicting it and denying it. And in the literature, this other dimension is represented not by the religious, spiritual, moral heroes (who often sustain the established order) but rather by such disruptive characters as the artist, the prostitute, the adulteress, the great criminal and

outcast, the warrior, the rebel-poet, the devil, the fool
—those who don't earn a living, at least not in an
orderly and normal way.

HERBERT MARCUSE, One-Dimensional Man

THE ULTIMATE BASIS of Weber's cultural pessimism after his breakdown probably lay in his personal experience, dominated though that experience may have been by the history of his age. But the theoretical structures which rose from this basis can hardly be understood without some comprehension of Weber's confrontation with the two men around whose ideas much of twentieth-century European thought has revolved: Marx and Nietzsche. Indeed, near the end of his life, Weber candidly admitted their importance for himself and his epoch, when he said:

> One can measure the honesty of a contemporary scholar, and above all, of a contemporary philosopher, in his posture toward Nietzsche and Marx. Whoever does not admit that he could not perform the most important parts of his own work without the work that those two have done swindles himself and others. Our intellectual world has to a great extent been shaped by Marx and Nietzsche.[1]

Even before his breakdown, Weber had shown the influence of Marx's ideas when he juxtaposed, in a style reminiscent of the *Communist Manifesto,* the personal domination of the precapitalist social order to the impersonal class rule of the modern bourgeois.[2] But this use of Marx was almost casual. Both Sombart and Tönnies showed a far greater interest in Marx before the end of the century. After his breakdown, however, much of Weber's work, from the *Protestant Ethic* to the wartime political analyses, was based on a critical examination of Marx's historical materialism.[3]

The *Protestant Ethic,* as Weber himself says, is an attempt to establish the psychological and intellectual origins

of, if not modern capitalism, at least its unique characteristic, the capitalist spirit. As opposed to the Marxist notion
that ideas are a mere superstructure reflecting a base of
material interests, Weber proposes "a contribution to the
understanding of the manner in which ideas become effective
forces in history."[4] This is not, of course, to suggest that
Weber is insensitive to the capacity of modern capitalism for
reshaping the world. But he is surely more aware than Marx
of the role of ideas—even ideas no longer consciously held—
in governing human action.

Certainly he had revealed this awareness in the '90's,
when he had interpreted much of world history in terms
of filial strivings for liberation from paternalistic restraints.
But in his work on the *Protestant Ethic,* the role of ideal
motives in creating modernity changes in three crucial respects, all of which center on his discovery, similar to that
of Hegel and others, of a complex "cunning of reason" by
which people may intend one thing and attain something
entirely different.[5] In the first place, he is now aware of the
strange genealogy linking the main motive force of modern
capitalism to the theology of predestination. Second, he is
discovering how a set of motives that one believes to be
merely a tool, a servant, can actually be one's secret master.
Third, because of these discoveries, he is no longer naïvely
projecting his ideals onto world history, but is analyzing
them to distance himself from them. Thus, Weber rejects the
"materialistic conception of history" as a *"Weltanschauung"*
accepting only as one of many explanatory principles the
"economic interpretation of history."[6] Alongside this interpretation must stand others which reveal the genuinely
independent lines of development of legal, religious, political,
and scientific ideas and institutions. This is the aspect of
Weber's relation to Marx which commentators most often
mention; it needs no elaboration. What is not always recognized, however, is that for all his theoretical emphasis on
plural causation, Weber later came very close to what
amounted to a transposition of Marx's monistic explanation

from the economic to the political realm.[7] One sees this most graphically where Weber describes the ongoing process of centralization of power in all fields of human activity: war, education, economics, religion, and most crucial of all, politics.

> The relative independence of the artisan or cottage out-worker, of the landowning peasant, of the holder of a benefice, of the knight and the vassal depended on the fact that he himself owned the tools, supplies, financial means, or weapons with whose help he pursued his economic, military, or political function and from which he lived during his performance. Contrariwise, the hierarchical dependence of the worker, salesman, technician, academic assistant, *and* state official and soldier rests on the fact that those tools, supplies, and financial means which are indispensable for organization and economic existence are concentrated in the hands of either the entrepreneur or the political lord. . . . The "separation" of the worker from the material means to his activity takes many forms; he is separated from the means of production in the economy, from the means of war in the army, from the material means of administration in public administration, from the means of research in the university institute and laboratory, from the financial means in all of them. It is the decisive foundation common to the capitalist private enterprise and to the cultural, political, and military activities of the modern power state.[8]

In his late political essays, Weber called this phenomenon "inescapable universal bureaucratization," and "the housing of that bondage of the future."[9] Borrowing a phrase directly from Marx, he characterized the postwar German revolution facetiously as an "expropriation of this expropriator"[10]—but he knew perfectly well that changing the ownership of the firm did not alter its bureaucratic structure or the servile existence of those dominated by it.[11]

There are a number of reasons for Weber's total disbelief in the possibility of an egalitarian, genuinely revolutionary "expropriation." Much of the detailed critique has become common coin among social scientists.[12] But certain general presuppositions are worth recapitulating.

For Weber, as for Michels and Tönnies, the kind of democratic participation of the proletariat which Marx expected to result from the socialist revolution, was excluded by the conditions of mass society. Two factors in particular seem to converge to make the continued subjection of the masses to bureaucratic machines inescapable: the technical superiority of bureaucratic administration over any other kind, and the growth of population.

A great deal of Weber's political sociology delineates the gradual evolution of earlier forms of rule toward the establishment of professional bureaucracies. The greater technical rationality (what Weber calls "formal rationality") of specially trained bureaucracies acts as a principle of natural selection which allows them ultimately to triumph over direct rule by a patrimonial prince, rule by estates (*Ständestaat*), rule by local notables, or feudal rule. Only in isolated areas such as the Swiss cantons, where no strong and ambitious centralized state exists to develop the instruments of bureaucratic domination, can local self-government survive, and even here it becomes the property of a native aristocracy.[13] But apart from its greater efficiency, bureaucratic administration becomes utterly indispensable when a political and economic unit reaches a certain population level. In fact, only an efficient bureaucracy is capable of supporting the creation and continued existence of modern mass society,[14] and for that reason, Weber bitterly attacked, as hopeless, programs for radical alternatives to some combination of bureaucratic and parliamentary rule when they began to flourish during World War I. "Ink bottle Romantics" was his epithet for the proto-fascist conservatives who sought to re-create community (*"Gemeinschaft"*) through a corporate state and argued for a political representation by professions.[15] His few comments on the soldiers' and workers' councils that briefly flourished in Germany at the end of the war suggest a prognosis that was slightly more respectful but no less pessimistic (". . . surrogate for the direct democracy that is impossible in mass organizations."[16]). And before the armistice, he was convinced that even the most sophisticated Marxist revisionists were capable only of creating a "dictatorship of the official."[17]

Of course, Weber's political pessimism was not absolute. Hundreds of pages of analysis of the German political structure and demands for reform (written in World War I and published in the *Politische Schriften*) testify to the persistence of some measure of hope in Weber's outlook. But this hope seems barely compatible with the gloomy portrait of inevitable bureaucratization that is otherwise dominant in his political sociology.

Very broadly, what distinguishes Weber's pessimistic sociology of power as a whole from Marx's optimistic one is that Marx views the locus of domination, of the machinery that oppresses its creators, in economic relations, and he sees the agent that can bring this machinery in harmony with the subjective needs of its creators in the most exploited economic class, the proletariat. Weber, contrariwise, views the locus of domination as politics, and looks to the nation-state as the agent of redemption. But there are two ways in which political object can dominate political subject: through the inevitable (for Weber) struggle between nations and through the despotism *within* nations of bureaucratic machinery over individual autonomy. In the '90's, Weber was concerned primarily with the conflict between nations, and he argued for imperialism as a means both of strengthening the nation's international position and of educating the citizenry to political maturity; in the later period, the problem of internal domination was uppermost and only political reforms to strengthen parliament could educate the people and allow Germany to play a major role in world history.*

---

* This is particularly important to keep in mind, for some parts of Weber's wartime policies, if removed from this context, permit the interpretation of Weber simply as a glorifier of naked power and hence a precursor of fascism; for example, his argument with a pacifist in

Weber's altered response to the threat of overpopulation clearly illustrates this changed focus. Before the breakdown, increased population makes a national struggle for expansion —with all the pedagogic value of such struggle—absolutely necessary. Afterward, when Weber's perspective moves closer to Marx's, it is bureaucratic domination which population pressure makes necessary, and control over the bureaucracy, while morally desirable, is only possible within the framework of the historical logic of rationalization.

It is this logic of rationalization—Weber's undialectical, and ultimately political counterpart of Marx's theory of capital accumulation—which permits comparison not only with Marx but with Nietzsche as well. For Weber's fascination with the political, religious, and ethical antitheses of ascetic rationalization flowed from an aristocratic presentiment, shared by both of his predecessors, that such rationalization was the prelude to a human catastrophe. All three men saw it as leading to an unparalleled reification of institutions and values and a corresponding destruction of essential aspects of human personality: grace, dignity, personal creativity, spontaneity, ultimate meaningfulness.[18] But

---

"*Zwischen zwei Gesetzen,*" (*P.S.*, pp. 139–42) or his use of the term "*Herrenvolk*" (master race) in an article of 1917. The context of the latter makes it perfectly clear that Weber adopted that shibboleth of the Pan-German imperialists only as an opportunity to attack his own nation for its subservience before an incompetent emperor and his irresponsible bureaucracy. Only, Weber argued, when the German people had become master, *through parliament*, over its own destiny, when it had ceased "to tolerate" the antics of Wilhelm II and had put his officials in their place, could it aspire to the status of a "master race"—in the sense of England and America—in the world. This violent attack on Germany's leadership at the height of World War I led to the censorship of the journal that printed it (the *Frankfurter Zeitung*) and probably was one of the major reasons why Hitler's early protector, General Ludendorff, viewed Weber's wartime activities as treasonous. (See *Baumg.*, p. 512, for the text of this passage and Ludendorff's denunciation, and *Max Weber und die Soziologie Heute, Verhandlungen des fünfzehnten deutschen Soziologentages* (Tübingen, 1965), pp. 104–9 and 146–7 for a lively polemic on the subject between R. Aron and Baumgarten.)

they differed in their notions of how the transcendence of these reified structures related to the ongoing process of history. Marx saw a historical dialectic at work in the accumulation of capital which would prepare the material basis for a nonexploitative realm of freedom and insure the internal disintegration of capitalism. Nietzsche acknowledged no historical process except a kind of Gresham's Law of demography, according to which plebeian culture, by its resort to cunning, calculation and hypocrisy, by the sterilizing power of religions of the weak, had destroyed the noble culture of the strong. Transcending this process was possible only for he who paradoxically employed the plebeian's own weapon—Reason—which did reveal a dialectic: ultimately Reason would turn on its creator and demolish the whole moral and psychological basis of plebeian culture[19] Transcendence, the reconquest of aristocratic values, was thus attainable only by the intellectual aristocrat. Society as such was written off.

Weber, in his postbreakdown *Weltanschauung*, shared with Marx the perception of an ever-increasing rationalization and efficiency of social systems, but, for many reasons, he saw this as a dead-end progress, leading only to the "cage of bondage" (*"Gehäuse der Hörigkeit"*). Unable to accept this bondage in his inner life, he tended to divide his thought into a public, historical *Weltanschauung* (comparable to Marx, but without the utopian dialectic) and a private a-historical ethic (comparable to Nietzsche, but abandoning the sphere of reason and philosophy altogether to the Devil of rationalization). He was, however, too much the sociologist to view his private code as totally without historical and social foundations. Instead, alongside the series of ideal types which he used to typify the various aspects of the process of rationalization, Weber established a parallel series which exemplify a world of doomed and rejected historical alternatives.

This latter world only emerged late in his life. Although the tormenting question of human autonomy and creativity in the "iron cage" was posed in the *Protestant Ethic* in 1905, and formed the inescapable psychological response to his personal predicament, and though the question recurred in Weber's contributions to the scholarly debates of his bureau-cratically minded colleagues, only in the decade after 1910 did Weber elaborate the shadow typology that ultimately stood as the historical alternative and condemnation of the ideal types composing the process of rationalization.*

The key concept illuminating these alternative realms is charisma, which in Weber's usage connotes "grace," both in the theological sense of divine election and the psycholog-ical sense of inner assurance and magnetic attractiveness for others. The term has of course received abundant com-mentary. But in general, scholarship has focused primarily on Weber's concern with charisma in terms of his contem-porary political setting, i.e., as a certain kind of extraordinary political authority, interrupting the normal processes of government with the unpredictability of a thunderstorm and temporarily suspending or transfiguring all traditional or legal-rational authority.

It is of course true that even within Weber's nightmarish cosmos of sterile bureaucrats and disenchanted "parceled-out" souls[20] he endowed the "emotional life-force" of cha-risma with the potentiality to bring an occasional restoration of vitality. Responsible control over this cosmos of blind power was possible, given parliamentary checks and the rule of a charismatic leader. Indeed, even in the spiritual desert of modernity a meaningful life was conceivable

---

* Baumgarten indicates the historiographical significance of this interest in defeated historical alternatives when he writes: "The ortho-doxy of an historicizing ethic of success, the idea that it was always the better and truer which, in alliance with time and history, won out, met with stubborn disbelief in Weber. Although he certainly did not devote himself to 'nonconformist' viewpoints as dogmatically given, it is nonetheless true that rather than siding with the typical 'success-ethic' of the historians, he was drawn to sympathy with oppositions who were defeated . . . methodologically, he kept an equal distance from both inclinations." *Baumg.*, p. 582.

through a transposition into personal relations of the love-ethic of charismatic mysticism. In both cases, the force of charisma promised intrinsic meaning to lives which otherwise existed only as means to unknown and unknowable ends.

Because of the role that charisma—particularly the political variety—clearly could play within Weber's rationalized, disenchanted cosmos of modernity, its shadowy stature as an independent force in religious and political realms antithetical to modernity has been ignored. Yet logically, within the Weberian vision of the world, whose *Leitmotiv* is the birth and rise to world dominance of the capitalist spirit, whose catalyst is the ethic of Calvinism, and whose dreary outcome is the "iron cage" of total rationalization, charisma has no place whatever. Indeed, of all the religions Weber discusses, Calvinism, whose kinship with capitalism and rationalization is Weber's best-known argument, is among the least endowed with charismatic inspiration—hardly surprising when we consider that it was precisely the uncertainty about one's possession of grace (charisma = gift of grace) that characterized the Calvinist and inspired his compulsive habits. Thus, Weber himself directs us by implication to seek out the historical and social basis of charisma in realms antithetical both to the legal-rational social order and to its Calvinist counterpart. And, in fact, he does discuss at some length two additional historical schemata in which charisma appears as an essential force: a political schema, in which aristocratic charisma struggles to the death against bureaucratic centralization, and a religious schema in which mystical charisma is juxtaposed to ascetic rationalization.

The existence of these realms, their embodiment of total value structures, is the key to Weber's value polytheism, his repeated representation of competing value systems as warring gods. These gods are not infinite in number, nor do they represent the sheer caprice of those who believe in them. Basically, there are only four: the god of Luther—bureaucratic traditionalism; the god of Calvin—ascetic rationalization; the god of Tolstoy—mystical immanence; and the god of Nietzsche and George—aristocratic aestheticism and worldly heroism. As the sometime ideologist of modernity (for example, in most of his discussions of German politics), Weber pits ascetic rationalization against bureaucratic traditionalism.[21] But to the extent that he finds the world created by ascetic rationalization drained of meaning, he tends to lump together the gods of Calvin and Luther and war against both from the camps of mystical immanence and aristocratic virtue.

The following chapters will discuss this four-sided conflict between ultimate values through an examination of Weber's religious and political ideas in the last decade of his life.

7

Asceticism
and Mysticism

WEBER's WORK on the sociology of religion falls into three principal periods. In 1904 and 1905, he dealt with the relationship of the Protestant sects—especially Calvinism—to the origin of the Western capitalist spirit, and from then until 1910 most of his work on religion consisted of defending his thesis against its critics. In the latter part of 1910, a second phase began with his sharp distinction between asceticism and mysticism at the first German sociology congress. In 1911–13, Weber, incorporating the asceticism-mysticism dichotomy, wrote a systematic sociology of religion for his massive compendium, *Wirtschaft und Gesellschaft*, in which he attempted to pull together four themes into a study of some 170 pages: an explanation of the origin of the religious phenomenon; an extended polemic with the theses of Marx and Nietzsche regarding the relationship of ideas, psychology and material interests; the far-ranging use of historical examples from both Eastern and Western religions to give evidence for his arguments; and the use of the categories of ascetic and mystical religiosity as ideal types to give an appearance of organization to the whole. The richness induces intellectual exhaustion, and it is perfectly understandable that in his lifetime Weber never attempted to publish this material.

But in a third period of intense labor on the sociology of religion in 1914–17, he completely reworked this earlier material into a set of essays, most of which he printed in the *Archiv* and all of which he planned after the war to publish in book form. These essays comprise the three-volume *Religionssoziologie* (published 1920–1), the first volume of which he was revising for publication at the time of his death. In this volume he abandons the first of the four themes of his earlier work—on the origin of religion in general—and substitutes a *"Vorbemerkung"* in which he posits as the main purpose of his investigation the comparison of Western ascetic Christianity, whose inner logic somehow leads to the kind of rationalism embodied in the bourgeois capitalist spirit, with various forms of Eastern religion, whose inner logic does not.[1] The other three subjects covered in the effort of 1911–13 are dealt with in the following ways:

(1) The historical examples of Western and Eastern religions are organized into separate essays which form the bulk of the three volumes. Volume I contains the essays on the *Protestant Ethic* (1904–7) and the essay on Confucianism (1916); Volume II contains the *Archiv* studies on Hinduism and Buddhism (1916); and Volume III, the *Archiv* studies on ancient Judaism (1917) plus an unpublished study of Pharisaism dating from the same year.

(2) Discussion of the material factors which orient particular social groups or classes toward particular religious positions— Weber's confrontation with Nietzsche and Marx—is largely limited to the thirty-five page "Introduction" to "The Economic Ethics of the World Religions" (Volume I of the *Religionssoziologie*—this essay dates from 1914, and was first published in the 1916 volume of the *Archiv*).

(3) The comparison of asceticism and mysticism, which had been briefly interpolated in the "Introduction" just mentioned,

is discussed comprehensively in the framework of the rationalization of economic, political, aesthetic, erotic, and intellectual spheres of life in a separate thirty-five page essay (also dating from the 1916 volume of the *Archiv,* but with a few crucial revisions) at the end of the first volume of the *Religionssoziologie.* It is this last essay which is most important for an analysis of Weber's values near the end of his life and for a comparison both with corresponding passages in his earlier work and with broader themes in his scientific and political *Weltanschauung.*

[1]

FROM ASCETICISM
TO MYSTICISM (1904–1910)

IN THE EARLIEST work on the *Protestant Ethic* (1904), the main theme is the near-ineluctable "progress" of Western rationality, which seizes upon the historical accident of Protestant worldly asceticism to establish its hegemony over the mind and actions of economic man. (This process of rationalizing economic behavior was to be described in *Wirtschaft und Gesellschaft* as "formal rationality.") Weber recognizes that "one may rationalize life from fundamentally different basic points of view," but only in a revision during or after the war does he insert a parenthetical phrase emphasizing this point.* He mentions the mystical religiosity which later appears as precisely such an alternative form of rationalization, but his principal example of it appears to be Lutheranism, which he despises for its social conservatism and which he deals with primarily in terms of its idea of the calling— a primitive and weak stage in that development toward Eco-

---

* *Protestant Ethic,* pp. 77–8: "This simple proposition, which is often forgotten, should be placed at the beginning of every study which essays to deal with rationalism."

nomic Man so brilliantly expedited by the Calvinist doctrine of Predestination. In one passage he does sharply distinguish between the ascetic and mystical attitudes toward God and the world, in the sense of the fundamentally different and equally justifiable modes of rationality that appear in the work of his last decade; this passage is also a later addition:

> Fundamental differences in the most important criteria for salvation, which apply to the classification of all religious activity, appear here. The religious believer can make himself sure of his state of grace either in that he feels himself to be the vessel of the Holy Spirit or the tool of the divine will. In the former case, his religious life tends to mysticism and emotionalism, in the latter to ascetic action; Luther stood close to the former types, Calvinism belonged definitely to the latter.[2]

Thus, Weber's first serious consideration of the mystical phenomenon appears in his commentary on a paper of Ernst Troeltsch at a scholarly meeting in October 1910.[3] In the course of a twenty-five page paper Troeltsch had delineated three basic forms of the Christian social idea: church, sect, and mystical enthusiasm.[4] Weber's critique covered several aspects of Troeltsch's presentation, but the opportunity of discussing the significance of mysticism precipitated an intellectual *tour de force* that carried him well beyond the perspective of his studies on Calvinism and set the framework for some of his most important work in the next decade.

In his commentary Weber establishes two intellectual reference points for comprehension of the mystical phenomenon: Tönnies's conception of *Gemeinschaft* and the cultural ambience of Russian literature and religion, especially Tolstoy and Dostoevsky. In the way Weber uses them we sense a profound reserve, perhaps even hostility, to the mystic's ascetic antithesis.

Weber sees in the Orthodox Church "a specifically mystical belief, imperishable on the soil of the East, that brotherly love, love of one's fellow man—those basic human relationships which seem so pale to us, but which the great religions of salvation have transfigured—lead not just to some kind of social results (which are quite incidental) but to the perception of the meaning of the world, to a mystical relationship to God." In turn, this belief in the mystical power of love infuses, gives inner shape to, the great novels of Tolstoy and Dostoevsky. In reading these novels, Weber argues, the reader's initial sensation of a meaningless welter of events and passions

> has its basis in the [author's] secret conviction that the political, social, ethical and literary forms of ordinary life, are really meaningless in relation to the substratum which spreads out beneath them. This substratum is embodied in the most characteristic figures that Russian literature has produced, figures which are so extraordinarily difficult for us to grasp precisely because they rest on the simple and quite ancient Christian idea that what Baudelaire calls the "sacred prostitution of the soul"—love for one's fellow man, whoever he might be—that this amorphous, unformed love relationship is what leads to the gates of the eternal, the timeless, the divine.

Thus the aesthetic unity of these masterpieces is a derivative of Russian and Greek Orthodoxy; it lies in the reverse side of the surface plot, in "the spiritual antipodes of the men of action whose doings occur on the stage of the world." The same "acosmic fundament" of Russian religiosity issues in a law of nature, which is found both in Tolstoy and the Russian sects and which receives additional support from the survival of agrarian communism among the peasant. This law of nature also serves as the basis for the Slavic idealism of Vladimir Soloviev, especially his idea of the Church, "which rests—in Tönnies's sense—on 'Community,' not on 'Society.'"

Somewhat later in the debate on Troeltsch's paper, Weber discusses the psychological problem of how one finds reliable evidence of one's salvation; as antithetical methods, he opposes the acosmic* love he had earlier identified with mysticism to Calvinist asceticism, and here the *Gemein-schaft-Gesellschaft* antinomy serves as his principal focus. After repeating his argument that the Calvinist tended to find evidence of election in his ability to celebrate God's glory by laboring successfully in His world, Weber says that this tendency has led to the creation of characteristic social structures which are basically "egocentric," in the sense that individuals are conceived only for themselves rather than for the collectivities they presume to serve:

> To employ the antitheses which have been used in one of the basic books of our social-political method of observation—in Ferdinand Tönnies's work on *Gemein-schaft und Gesellschaft*—the form of human relationship which grows on this soil is always a *Gesellschaft*, a "socializing," a product of that "Civilization," exchange system, market, objective common-purpose association which strips away the "human," rather than personal brotherhood. On the other hand, that other [form of relationship], that acosmic love, is always *"Gemein-schaft,"* on the purely human basis of "brotherliness."

The primitive Christian communism to which Weber relates the *Gemeinshaft* of acosmic love arises, he believes, from the natural family community and its norms of brotherly relations. There is no haggling among brothers, and Weber traces the medieval prohibition on interest to the code of brotherly behavior, which excludes *"Herrenrecht"* (the right of the master) from economic relations among Christians.

---

* "Acosmic" is a term Weber frequently used to describe the mystical perspective. He apparently wished to distinguish mystical love from the "cosmic" world view of a Church like Roman Catholicism, in which the entire material and human world was ordered by and infused with divine reason, and love had a definite purpose within it. Acosmic love lacks this ordered environment and has no purpose compatible with the ends of the human cosmos. It exists for its own sake, like the social relationships in Tönnies's concept of *Gemeinschaft*. This implied distinction between "acosmic" and "cosmic" appears clearly in Max Weber: *Gesammelte Aufsätze zur Religionssoziologie* (Tübingen, 1922), Vol. 1 (hereafter cited as *R.S.I*), p. 551.

Taking these initial comments on mysticism as a whole, there would seem to be three latent discrepancies in Weber's description of acosmic love. In the first place, there is a tension within the motivational structure. Just as Weber identified the real basis of the Calvinist ethos in "egocentric" concern for one's own salvation, despite an appearance of working for the collectivity, he might also argue (he later did, in a passage that sounds remarkably like Freud)[5] that the "sacred prostitution of the soul" through universal love serves only the interest of the lover's salvation and in fact represents a form of libidinal imperialism; objective concern for the other may be completely absent. The concealment of this spiritual aggression behind the mask of humility is, of course, one of Friedrich Nietzsche's major points of attack on the Christian ethic of love. Paradoxically related to the aggressive character of mystical love is the phenomenon that the personality which attempts it can succeed only by committing suicide, by losing its own identity in the cosmic All. Indeed, Weber himself later perceives this problem when he elaborates on the notion of a mystical union of each individual with all others and implicitly condemns the loss of individuality, consciousness, and responsibility by all concerned. Yet he does acknowledge the power and attractiveness of mysticism as offering an alternative to the dry hyperrationality that resulted from the ethic of worldly asceticism, and his last work before his death was an effort to find a variety of the mystical alternative which ennobled rather than dissolved individual personality.

The third problem lies in the derivation of the mystical community of love from the natural, genetic community of family or clan. As Freud remarked in *Civilization and Its Discontents*, it is impossible to expand the libidinal ties that join the family to embrace all mankind.[6]

There are, of course, solutions to this limitation in the idea of the community of the faithful, which may take the form either of the universal Church or of the *ecclesia pura*, the pure church of the faithful, which rapidly becomes a sect. For the community of the faithful stems from the same primitive Christian community that Weber views as the basis of acosmic, mystical love, and he sees two aspects of this original Christianity as crucial in establishing its function as a countercommunity: first, its explicit antagonism to the various "natural" family communities from which its adherents come, expressed as Weber later pointed out in Jesus' insistence that only he who hates his father, mother, and other relatives can be His disciple*; second, its transformation of the family meal into the sacrament of communion.[7] Weber views the latter as a powerful lever for control by the religious community, especially in the Protestant sects which do away with virtually all other ritual means (confession, penance, etc.) of assuaging guilt.[8]

The problem remains, however, that mysticism, though it may appear within both Church and sect, is also clearly distinguishable from both as a sociological and psychological *Gestalt.* Indeed, the "typical" organization of the Church appears to be a priestly bureaucracy while the sect, at least in its Puritan archetype, is primarily an organization of ascetic individualists. Neither of these types is ultimately compatible with the universal love of the mystic, nor is *any* clearly defined form of social organization.†

Yet Weber does later argue that the mystical experience "despite the apparent demands of logic" does "favor the creation of communities."[9] As he himself acknowledges, the doctrinal logic, which tends to be wholly asocial, is outweighed in this case (as it is in the Calvinist doctrine of predestination) by the psychological consequences of the religious posture: acosmic love can create community, in

---

* *Cf. W.u.G.*, pp. 449, 450 (*E.S.*, pp. 579, 580); *R.S.I*, p. 542. Eduard Baumgarten cites the first of these references as evidence of Weber's unconscious hostility to his father, since in it he abbreviated the scriptural reference to include *only* hatred of the father as the condition of discipleship; *Baumg.*, p. 628.

† *Cf.* Martin Buber's remarks on the asocial character of the mystic in *Verhandlungen des I. deutschen Soziologentages* (Frankfurt/Main, 1910).

much the same way that Tönnies's *Wesenwille* (organic will) is the foundation of *Gemeinschaft*.

Indeed, Weber displays a fundamental ambivalence toward the notion of *Gemeinschaft* that arose from his conflicting passions in the years before his breakdown. The ambivalence centers on the difference between "community" conceived as a band of equal brothers and "community" as an authoritarian relationship between a despotic patriarch and his family. In Weber's early work on the East Elbian rural crisis, he was motivated at least in part by his experience of his own father's despotism and he was inclined to view natural community in terms of the traditional system of patriarchal domination on the Junker estate. Consequently, he saw every modern intrusion and disruption of this system— the advance of capitalism, the flight of farm workers to the cities, trade union organization—as a liberating progress. But after the breakdown, he lost his certainty about the meaningfulness of this progress, and when in 1910 he seems to have become most skeptical about it and most attracted by the mystical alternative, he tended to view even natural community in terms of love and brotherhood rather than despotic patriarchalism. In his later, more considered inquiries into the religious phenomenon, he is much more inclined to separate sharply the redemptive ethos of love and brotherhood from the despotic character of "traditionalist" societies.* But even in these later studies there is a wavering between this very cold view of primitive community and a more involved one, as, for example, where he discerns a close relationship between the communist community of warriors, matriarchal law (*"Mutterrecht"*) and, most interestingly in view of his penchant for falling in love with his cousins, endogamous promiscuity.[10]

---

* See *R.S.I*, p. 269, where he defines "traditionalism" in terms of paternalistic domination; *R.S.I*, pp. 522–3, where he juxtaposes the Confucian family ethic against the Puritan (!) ethic of abstract love of mankind; *W.u.G.*, pp. 449–50 (*E.S.*, pp. 579–80), where he depicts primitive Christianity's hostility to traditional family ties.

Finally, these passages from the commentary on Troeltsch reveal once more the centrality for Weber's entire work
of the interpretation of Russian literature in terms of "outer"
and "inner." As a young man of twenty-three, he had couched
his analysis of his parents in these terms, and the significance
of the mystical search for "inner" meaning in a disenchanted
world—a surrogate for the meaningfulness that Weber sees
as an integral part of pre-industrial peasant life—is to serve
as the framework for his most profound observations on the
limits of science in his last years.

[2]

RELIGION IN
WIRTSCHAFT UND GESELLSCHAFT
(1911–13)

BETWEEN 1911 AND 1913, Weber completed a draft of a systematic sociology of religion which was intended to be part of
Wirtschaft und Gesellschaft. The initial chapters of this work
give the appearance of an anthropology of primitive religion,
in terms of its evolution from purely magical efforts at con-
trolling the supernatural to increasingly rational attempts to
comprehend the relationship of the gods to the order of
nature. Weber's juxtaposition of "religion" against "sorcery,"
"gods" against "demons," "priests" against "magicians," and
"religious ethics" against "taboo" all reflect his effort to view
religious development in terms of the progress of Reason. In
Chapter 4, "The Prophet," this effort to examine the development of religion as a universal historical process (after one
more demonstration of "progress," this time from mystagogue
to prophet) collapses on the distinction between ethical and
exemplary prophecy, and world history as well as the history
of religion becomes bifurcated. The ethical prophet, Weber
says, is "primarily . . . an instrument for the proclamation of

a god and his will, be this a concrete command or an abstract norm." The exemplary prophets, of whom the Buddha is Weber's model, demonstrate the way to salvation by their conduct. In their preaching, the exemplary prophets talk neither of ethics nor of their divine mission, but simply exhort their listeners to follow their own course of action. Geographically, the ethical prophet has been exclusively a creature of the Near East; the exemplary prophet is typically Indian, though occasionally found in China and the Near East.

Weber traces ethical prophecy to the belief in "a personal transcendental and ethical god,"[11] a concept stemming ultimately from the transcendent power of the Near Eastern monarchs and of the natural forces they and they alone controlled. Because rainfall in these desert regions was totally insufficient as the basis for agriculture, only the irrigation systems from the great rivers—irrigation systems created and maintained by the monarchs—made the harvest possible. Thus, the monarchs seemed to rule over the basic forces of nature itself.

> In the desert and semiarid regions of the Near East this control of irrigation waters was indeed one source of the conception of a god who had created the earth and man out of nothing and not merely fashioned them, as was believed elsewhere. A riparian economy of this kind actually did produce a harvest out of nothing, from the desert sands. The monarch even created law by legislation and rationalization, a development the world experienced for the first time in Mesopotamia. It seems quite reasonable, therefore, that as a result of such experiences the ordering of the world should be conceived as the law of a freely acting, transcendental and personal god.

This all-powerful, essential role of the monarch, the basis of the commoner's belief in a transcendent deity, did not exist in China. Rather than substituting for meteorological processes, and thus cutting men off from any personal connection or appeal to the beneficent elements of nature, the rulers of India and China were at most given the status of moral brokers between man and the spirits that controlled the weather. In a sense, polytheism and even pantheism were built into the climate. In China the regularity of the rainfall, which remained the direct nutriment of the harvest, if sometimes controlled by dams and canals, was held dependent on the normal activity of the spirits, who were in turn affected by the moral conduct of the emperor:

> The emperor sought to avert meteorological disturbances through sacrifices, public atonement, and various virtuous practices; e.g., the termination of abuses in the administration, or the organization of a raid on unpunished malefactors. For it was always assumed that the reason for the excitation of the spirits and the disturbances of the cosmic order had to be sought either in the personal derelictions of the monarch or in some manifestation of social disorganization.

In a later work, Weber made explicit the ties between, on the one hand, ethical prophecy in the name of a transcendent active God and the resultant ascetic ethic of serving as a tool of divine will, and, on the other, exemplary prophecy in the name of a contemplative deity and the mystical goal of possessing god (or serving as a vessel of divine grace).[12]

Once Weber had broached the dichotomy of ethical vs. exemplary prophecy, it would have been logical for him to proceed to a thorough discussion of asceticism and mysticism, the forms of religiosity which appear so intimately related to those forms of prophecy. But he did not. The chapter following his daring bifurcation of ecologically based religious conceptions constitutes a return to his original theme that there is a line of development of religious forms *as a whole* characterized by rationalization and *Entzauberung* (disenchantment or de-magication). The spontaneous charismatic force of the prophet becomes institutionalized, objectified in the community of believers created by the prophet's lay disciples: an excellent example of the routinization of

charisma.[13] Weber then follows up this initial, brief exploration of the character of specifically religious communities
based on the laity with a lengthy, penetrating, and polemical
analysis of the religious behavior of various social classes
and castes.[14] Largely covertly, but occasionally quite openly,
he is arguing with the ideas of Marx and Nietzsche on the
relationship of material interest, human psychology, and
religious ideology. This argument, however, which tends to
settle around the differences between aristocratic and plebeian religion, is basically of less significance for Weber's
religious perspective than for his political *Weltanschauung*;
its discussion here would divert us from our central concern.

It is only in the latter part of the systematic sociology
of religion (written in 1912–13) that Weber undertakes a
close comparison of asceticism and mysticism and of the
effect of each on the economic, political, aesthetic, and erotic
spheres of life. Based on this earlier discussion, "Religious
Rejections of the World" (written in 1916 for the *Archiv* and
revised just before its author's death) contains important
changes and additions; and "Science as a Profession" (1919)
shows Weber's continued reflection on some of these problems. Thus a résumé of the principal arguments that appear
in the essays of 1912–13 and 1916 will reveal the significance
for Weber of the asceticism-mysticism dichotomy, and a detailed comparison of all three studies will show clearly the
direction of Weber's religious thought in the last decade of
his life. [15]

BENEATH THE SURFACE of his sociology of religion, Weber is
grappling with his own ethical and philosophical convictions—convictions whose intimate, often antagonistic relationship with the harsh Calvinist ethic in which his mother raised
him continually taint the surface objectivity of his sociological
analysis. Indeed, the convalescing scholar's profound sense,
in the decade after his breakdown, of disillusionment and
disenchantment with German society and politics is almost

surely rooted in his own guilt feelings. He himself gives us a theoretical framework for comprehending this personal disenchantment when he makes the distinction, eminently applicable to his own youthful dilemma, between the Puritan ascetic as revolutionary and as work-slave. In his discussion of worldly asceticism as an ethical code Weber delineates two ways of demonstrating that one is indeed a tool of God's will. The acceptance of a natural law that establishes the model for transforming God's world imposes on heroic Puritanism of the Cromwellian stamp the necessity of changing the world to fit the model. Contrariwise, viewing the material world as inevitably blasted with sin leads to a worldly asceticism that is politically passive but economically energetic: *within* this corrupt order every pious man has a "calling" in "the *rational*, ethically ordered economy, carried on in strict legality," the profits from which are a sign of God's blessing.[16]

The demands placed on the young Weber by his mother and by his own ambition and historical situation had led him to attempt both roles. The disaster of his father's death and the ensuing breakdown permanently enshrouded his earlier belief in his own—or anyone else's—capacity to emulate in Germany the victory of Cromwell and the Puritan revolutionaries.[17] As to Weber's supposed commitment to a *"Berufsethik,"* the conclusion of *The Protestant Ethic and the Spirit of Capitalism* and his acid comments at the meetings of the *Verein für Sozialpolitik* show his utter desolation at the prospect of a society dominated *in perpetuum* by the latter-day inheritors of the Puritan ethic. Even in his most strenuous effort at creating a value-free social typology, Weber's partisanship for the "man of culture" and against the mere "specialist" (*"Kulturmensch"* vs. *"Fachmensch"*) is unmistakable.[18]

Thus, Weber's personal experience of the hopelessness of reviving Puritan heroism and his revulsion from a future dominated by unheroic post-ascetic "specialists" shape his acute interest in the mystical antithesis of the ascetic ethos. Nonetheless, the steady flow of diplomatic disasters in pre-

World War I Germany inflames his liberal distemper at the failure of rational worldly asceticism to prevail against the conservative traditionalism of Wilhelm's bureaucracy. This belief that a heavy dose of worldly asceticism is just what Germany needs to shake it loose from the dangerous inanities of prestige politics,[19] at the same time that he sees a much-needed antidote to the sterility of bourgeois culture in the spiritual vitality of Russian mysticism, creates a striking ambivalence in his comparison of mysticism and asceticism.

Weber distinguishes between inner-worldly and other-worldly varieties of asceticism and mysticism, but this distinction does not play a cardinal role in his analysis.* The means to salvation even for the world-rejecting ascetic is activity: to behave like God's warrior in struggling against the temptations of a corrupt world. For the mystic the path to salvation is a spiritual condition (*Zustaendlichkeit*) of "illumination." The only activity is contemplation, which simply requires the exclusion of all everyday concerns, the "quest of 'repose' in the Divine."[20] Total withdrawal from all worldly activity and concern is the precondition for divine possession, the *unio mystica*. This union with God brings with it an esoteric knowledge, that insight into the world's meaning to which Weber had alluded during his digression on Russian literature in 1910. It is not a communicable knowledge, not a knowledge of facts or doctrines, but rather "the comprehension of a unified meaning of the world."

Weber, pursuing his some-time theme of rationalization, remarks that the methods of attaining mystical contemplation and union involve "a considerable degree of systematically rationalized conduct." But he also notes that in opposition to the behavioral ethic of worldly asceticism, "Buddhism recommends the avoidance of any rational goal-oriented activity ('action with a goal') as the most dangerous form of worldliness."[21] Thus, the contemplative activity of the mystic

---

* For a concise summary of Weber's four categories of worldly and other-worldly asceticism and mysticism, see Talcott Parsons's "Introduction" to *S.R.*, pp. li *ff*.

must be undertaken for its own sake—an excellent example
of what Tönnies meant by *Wesenwille*. In general, moreover,
the mystical outlook inhibits worldly activity as a distraction
from the desired *unio mystica*, while the ascetic finds in the
ethical content of such activity the only evidence of his state
of grace.[22]

From the standpoint of the ascetic, Weber argues,
mystical contemplation—this activity for its own sake—is
"reprehensible self-indulgence . . . idle and religiously sterile,
a self-deifying reveling in one's own feelings."[23] But to the
mystic, neither worldly nor world-rejecting asceticism offers
any alternative. Because of its active character all ascetic
religiosity, but especially rational worldly asceticism, becomes
burdened with "insoluble tensions between violence and
goodness, objectivity and love, and thereby is continually
moved further from unity with God and is forced into unholy
contradictions and compromises."[24]

The sharpest opposition between the mystic and the ascetic appears in the mutually exclusive answer they give
to the question of ultimate meaning. The ascetic, and especially the worldly ascetic "must be afflicted with a kind
of cheerful stupidity toward any question about a 'meaning'
of the world and not concern himself with it." So it is hardly
accidental that worldly asceticism assumed its most consistent form in Calvinism, with its belief in a remote God whose
motives were impenetrable to mere human cognition. Weber's
interpretation of the social implications of this doctrine, insofar as it stresses the rational exploitation of the existing
order and omits the revolutionary, natural-law side of Calvinism, reveals clearly his reservations about the Calvinist
ethic:

> The worldly ascetic is thus the model *"Berufsmensch"*
> [man of a vocation] who neither asks nor needs to ask
> about the meaning of his objective exercise of a voca-
> tion within the *total* world—for which his God and not
> himself bears the responsibility—because for him the
> consciousness that he is fulfilling, in his personal rational

behavior, the ultimately unfathomable will of God is sufficient.[25]

The mystic on the other hand intuits the meaning of the world, but his insight necessarily lacks any "rational form" since "he grasps it [the meaning of the world] as a unity *beyond* all empirical reality."[26] Thus, Weber sees in the mystic's grasp of metaphysical meaning a "proud aristocratic feeling with respect to salvation,"[27] while his withdrawal from worldly concerns and activities leads to a passivity and humble "brokenness" in his everyday conduct.

It is most interesting that Weber makes no mention of the acosmic love he had associated pre-eminently with mysticism in 1910 until he discusses mysticism as the basis of chiliastic revolutionary movements and as a psychological force for the creation of community (*against*, he reminds us, the merely logical implications of the doctrine).[28] Since the ethic of acosmic love was the basis for his earlier enthusiastic discussion of mysticism in relation to Russian literature and Tönnies's *Gemeinschaft*, one could conclude either that a certain cooling had occurred in Weber's attitude toward the mystical phenomenon between 1910 and 1912 or that he was concealing his own values behind a mask of objectivity. Perhaps both were true.

But in the next chapter of *Wirtschaft und Gesellschaft* that deals with the ascetic-mystic antinomy, where Weber compares the relationship of each religious position to the autonomous development (*"Eigengesetzlichkeit"*) of the economic, political, aesthetic, and erotic spheres of life, his basic value choices become clearer. This clarity is increased in the reworked version of this passage in the study of 1916 entitled "Religious Rejections of the World."[29] The fact that the latter also contains some major additions which make clear just how far Weber has withdrawn from any naïve embrace of the ethic of worldly asceticism, and how seriously he considered the problems raised by the mystical quest for meaning, makes it desirable to focus our attention now on this later, more organized version.

[3]

RELIGION, RATIONALIZATION, AND EROS (1916)

THE FRAMEWORK of Weber's inquiry into the relationship of mysticism and asceticism to the various spheres of human activity is the process of reification that follows on the disintegration of the original harmony of these spheres in communal life.* Within primitive societies based on blood ties, magical religion, by providing rituals and norms for the sanctification of all accepted behavior, served as a bond between man's economic, political, aesthetic, and erotic activities. But as society becomes more complex, religion becomes rationalized in either an ascetic or a mystical direction, and religious communities based on prophets or saviors establish themselves independently of the tribal ones. The inner structure of these new religious communities often depends on their borrowing from the older, blood community the ethos of brotherhood; but since the same disintegration of the older ethnic community that led to the more rational religious ethic

---

* Weber was probably indebted to Georg Simmel, a close friend of the family, for this idea. Simmel's tragic notion of modern culture was largely based on it, and he expressed it clearly in a letter of 1913 to Marianne: ". . . the elements of life, as soon as conceptual formulation pries them out of the total harmony of life and objectifies them, obey a quite different logic and show quite different meanings than they had within the unity of life"; Kurt Gassen and Michael Landmann, eds.: *Buch des Dankes an Georg Simmel* (*Briefe, Erinnerungen, Bibliographie*) (Berlin, 1958), p. 133. Christoph Steding's remark that Weber's use of this concept reveals in him the "nominalist . . . puritan spirit of radical individualism and emancipation in its secularized form; it is the spirit of the liberal bourgeoisie culminating in Max Weber" misses Weber's considerable skepticism, after 1900, as to the value of such "emancipation" and his deep concern over the spiritually enervating loss of meaning that secularized Protestantism had brought with it. Christoph Steding: *Politik und Wissenschaft bei Max Weber* (Breslau, 1932), p. 83.

tended to lead to economic practices that were also divorced from tribal customs, and therefore more rational and less brotherly than before, conflicts arose between ethical religions of salvation and the increasing lovelessness of economic relations.

> Rational economics is an objective operation. It is oriented to the prices in money which originate in the struggle among men for their own interest at the market. Without estimates in money prices, and thus without that struggle no kind of calculation is possible. Money is the most abstract and impersonal element in human life. Consequently, the more the cosmos of the modern capitalist economy followed its own immanent lawfulness, the more inaccessible it became to any conceivable relation to an ethic of brotherhood. And so much the more so, the more impersonal and rational it became. . . . To be sure, the religions of salvation also displayed a tendency to a peculiar impersonalizing of love in the sense of acosmism. But they have observed with deep mistrust the development of economic powers that were impersonal in the quite different sense of specific hostility to the idea of brotherhood.[30]

This tension between religious ethics and commerce underlay the tangled efforts of all Western churches, and especially the Catholic, to regulate the taking of interest, and only the establishment of monastic orders whose members renounced possessions provided a consistent social form for those who would avoid the conflict. But Weber was inclined to see in Catholicism a confusing mixture of ascetic and mystical elements. The two archetypical (in the sense of logically consistent) solutions to the conflict were to be found in Calvinism's abandonment of the ethic of brotherhood, which permitted its ascetic rationalism to function without friction in the loveless realm of economic relations, and mysticism's abandonment of the world, which left its acosmic love ethic uncontaminated by the struggle for existence. Again citing the French poet, Weber describes the latter position as "a characteristic flight from the world in the shape of objectless devotion to any and all, not for the sake of humanity but purely for the sake of devotion as such—in Baudelaire's words, for the sake of the "sacred prostitution of the soul."

In the realm of politics, rational statecraft confronted religions of salvation with much the same challenge as did rational economics.

> Objectively, "without respect of person," *sine ira et studio*, the bureaucratic state apparatus and the homo politicus who is a part of it manage their affairs without hate and therefore without love. . . . Consequently it too, thanks to its impersonalism, is less accessible to a material code of ethics . . . than the patriarchal orders of the past, which rested on personal obligations of piety and concrete personal evaluation of the individual case, precisely "with respect to the person."

Puritan asceticism, believing itself to be the instrument of God's will in ruling the base world of matter by the laws of force and ethical barbarism, curtails the ethic of brotherhood in order to execute God's will: it is thus perfectly compatible with the impersonal rule of the legal-rational order. The mystical quest for salvation, however, is radically antipolitical, compelled by its principles of acosmic goodness and brotherhood to abstain from the inescapably violent game of politics.

But in contrast to his treatment of economic activity as wholly antagonistic to the ethic of brotherhood, Weber sees one aspect of politics, even in the modern world, as substituting for rather than negating the religious sense of brotherhood: the popular community created by war. The powerful impact of World War I on German society inspires in Weber a vision of a body politic without alienation and depersonalization—a vision which is absent from the earlier version of this argument in the manuscript of *Wirtschaft und Gesellschaft*.[31] Like the religious community of love,

> warfare releases a devotion and an unconditional community of sacrifice on the warring sides; moreover it

unleashes, as a mass phenomenon, a labor of compassion and a love for the needy which explodes the boundaries of natural associations. In general, religions can achieve similar results only in heroic communities based on an ethic of brotherhood.

Perhaps even more important than its ability to create communities transcending family ties is the function of war in providing ultimate meaning to the warrior communities—an ultimate meaning and sense of consecration in the final end of life, in death itself. Here Weber again broaches his concern about the desiccation of ultimate meaningfulness in modern society, a concern which at the end of this essay and at the end of "Science as a Vocation" will haunt his reflections on science and modernity.

> The community of the front-line soldiers today, as in the age of the warlord's following, feels itself to be a community to the death—the greatest of its kind. Death in the field is different from that death which is no more than the common lot of man, a destiny which hurries upon everyone, without it ever being possible to say "why just him and why now," which marks an end point [in an age] when the ever-increasing development and sublimation of cultural commodities makes only a beginning appear meaningful. From this merely unavoidable dying, death in the field is distinguished by the fact that here, and in this massiveness *only* here, the individual can *believe* that he knows he is dying "for" something. The reasons for his facing death can, as a rule, be so evident to him—and apart from him only for one who passes away in his "calling"— that there is no basis for the problem of the "meaning" of death, in that most general sense in which religions of salvation have felt compelled to come to grips with it.

Weber implies rather strongly, although he fails to make the point explicit, that the religious mode for which the experience of war provides a competitor is the mystical rather than the ascetic. To be sure, the ascetic style is compatible with the everyday impersonal use of force in the peacetime politics of preserving domestic order. But all the psychological features of the warrior community—the love and compassion it inspires, the discovery of meaning in death (and therefore in the life which leads to death), and in general "the extraordinary character of brotherhood and death in war, which is shared with the sacred Charisma and the experience of the Community with God"[32]—all of these imply an underlying similarity (and therefore a bitter tension) between the charisma of the aristocratic community of warriors and that of the mystical community of saints. Weber makes it additionally evident that he is juxtaposing the warrior community to mystical rather than ascetic religiosity when he specifies that the tension and hostility between the warrior and the saint stem from the saint's rejection of the brutality of the struggle waged by the warrior community and the warrior's rejection of the saint's pacifism. The ascetic position, to which Weber also attributes a "cheerful stupidity" about questions of ultimate meaning, has no qualms, in his view, about accepting worldly violence as part of the divine scheme.

Shortly after this passage, in a brief digression, Weber appears to submerge the polarities of mysticism and asceticism into the more general categories of rational action. In the course of this he again makes clear, by implication, the compatibility of worldly asceticism—and the incompatibility of mysticism—with the secularization and rationalization of life. In judging the ethical value of any action, he says, there is always a profound tension between evaluation by results and evaluation by some autonomous value of the action. On the one hand, "responsibility of the actor for the consequences consecrates the means"; on the other, "the value of the actor's state of mind is supposed to justify him in rejecting responsibility for the consequences, in transferring them to God or the corruption and stupidity of the world permitted by God." The person who rejects responsibility for the consequence of what seems to him to be good actions is thus condemned to a wholly irrational impact on the world: he is compelled to reject rationally purposeful[33] behavior and in general all behavior in which means are adapted to ends, as worldly and alien to God.

The revolutionary varieties of mysticism and asceticism reveal precisely this distinction between behavior which has a rational purpose and behavior which is immediately meaningful and gratifying. Worldly asceticism, where it is inspired by a belief in some divine law of nature, may set out, as an instrument of the Lord, to transform the world in accordance with this law (revolutionary Puritanism). The mystic, however, when he believes that the age of acosmic brotherhood is near, may become the prophet of a radical antinomianism. Possessed by God, he and his followers cease to recognize any law; from such beliefs arise chiliastic movements such as the Anabaptists.

In the next sections of this essay, Weber discusses the relation of religious ethics to those worldly powers which, unlike politics and economics are essentially not rationally purposeful, but arational, or rather capable of being rationalized only from the standpoint of creating some kind of immanent harmony which is inherent in them: art and eroticism. As one might expect, the general relationship of compatibility is reversed: asceticism is wholly antagonistic to the nonrational forces of life; its nonreligious kinsman, the spirit of rational accomplishment, profits by their demise.[34] Mysticism, on the other hand, stands in such a relationship of affinity to the irrational powers, especially eroticism, that it can easily change places with them.

Art, for example, "assumes the function, however it is interpreted, of a this-worldly *salvation* from everyday life and, above all, from the increasing pressure of theoretical and practical rationalism." Although Weber acknowledges a special antipathy of mysticism for any kind of formalized or rationalized art, such as music,[35] he makes it clear, at least in the earlier version of this discussion (*W.u.G.*, p. 470), that asceticism is "in principle more hostile to art" than mysticism.*

The affinity between eroticism and mystical experience is very clearly and elaborately defined, as is the function of both as refuges from the rationalization of life. In this section, as in the one dealing with the warrior community, there is a marked development over the prewar treatment of the same subject in the manuscript of *Wirtschaft und Gesellschaft;*[36] it is, however, highly unlikely that the heroic gore of world war can account for this development, and it is very probable that the sharpening of Weber's thought on the significance of eroticism goes back to the same basic shift in his views (away from the ascetic *Weltanschauung*) which underlay his first comments on mysticism in 1910.

In the early stages of Western culture, sexuality, like art, politics, and economics, was a part of religious experience: the ecstasy and intoxication of magical religiosity led to sexual orgies, and spirits and gods ruled in the sexual domain as in all others. The irrationality of such religions made them and the sexual practices associated with them a prime object of attack by the first prophets of redemption through ethical behavior. In general, Weber says, the prophets and the priesthoods that followed them, fearing the unfettered sexual impulse as demonic, tried to confine it to the utilitarian molds of marriage and the production of children. But a drive as profound as the sexual could not be subjugated to rational codes of everyday conduct, and the result was the rise of eroticism, in the more complex culture that followed "the sober naturalism of the peasant," as a consciously cultivated force outside the domain of normal existence. Weber describes several historical types of relationship between eroticism and society in which the social

---

* Although the material seems to point in this direction in the corresponding passage in "Religious Rejections," he merely says there that both forms of virtuoso religions—asceticism and mysticism—are opposed to aesthetics.

fabric—usually aristocratic and military—continues that integration of sexuality which religion early abandoned, but these need not concern us here.* What is of great significance, however, is the fact that Weber does perceive the gradual rise of eroticism as an autonomous force, independent in modern society of all social convention, and that he situates it in the context of the estrangment (*"Heraustreten"*) of human existence "from the organic cycle of peasant existence." Indeed:

> The last increase of emphasis on the erotic sphere occurred on the basis of intellectual cultures, where it collided with the unavoidably ascetic component of Vocational Man. Given this conflict with rational everyday life, sexual life, which had been removed from everyday concerns (and especially extramarital sexuality) could now appear as the only tie which still linked humanity, now completely separated from the old cycle of simple organic peasant existence, with the natural source of all life.

Sexuality is then, for modern man, "a this-worldly salvation from the Rational, a holy triumph over it."

Naturally, any religious ethic of redemption which preached the victory of spirit over matter had to reject the ethos of eroticism as corrupt and "animalic." But the tension was sharpest between an intellectualized eroticism which transfigured the physical relationship, and religions of salvation through love and brotherhood, precisely because of the psychological similarities. Unlimited devotion, the breakthrough of one soul to another—these highest attainments of religions of love were also the goals of the most profound and cultivated erotic experiences.

---

* R.S.I, pp. 558–60, and Hans Gerth and C. Wright Mills: *From Max Weber, Essays in Sociology* (London, 1952) (hereafter cited as *G & M*), pp. 344–6, where he sketches the significance of erotic experience in the culture of preclassical and classical Greece, the Middle Ages, the Renaissance, and the Enlightenment.

Opposed as radically as possible to everything objective, rational, and general, the limitlessness of devotion stems here from the unique meaning which this single personality, in its irrationality, has for this and only this other personality. But from the standpoint of eroticism this meaning, and thus the value of the relation itself, lies in the possibility of a community which is felt as complete unification, as a disappearance of the "thou," and which is so overpowering that it is interpreted "symbolically":—*sacramentally.* The undefinable and inexhaustible experience of the lover is in no way communicable and in this way is like the mystical sense of "possession." Precisely for this reason, not just by virtue of the intensity of his experience but according to the directly possessed reality, he knows that he is rooted in the core of the truly living, eternally inaccessible to any rational striving, completely removed both from the cold, skeletal hands of the rational orders and the hollowness of everyday life. For him who knows how to bind himself to "the most living," the *objectless* experiences of the mystic appear as a pale underworld realm. The mortal seriousness of this intellectualized eroticism compares with the chivalric troubadour as the knowing love of the mature man does to the passionate sentimentality of youth. As opposed to the troubadour, it [modern eroticism] affirms precisely the natural quality of the sexual sphere, albeit consciously, as the creative power incarnate.

Any religion which sees the highest power in another world must of course oppose unshackled eroticism. But, as Weber suggests in the passage above, the most intense conflict is that between mysticism and eroticism, because of the close similarity of the psychological and physical conditions they create. Rational asceticism unqualifiedly condemns eroticism as an irrational glorification of the flesh, and in its otherworldly, monastic form, it rejects all sexuality as "a diabolic power which jeopardizes salvation." But between *Mystik* and *Erotik* there is a peculiar kind of "interchangeability" ("*Vertretbarkeit*"), which puts the mystic in constant danger of a "revenge of the animal," a "collapse into the orgiastic."[37]

Shortly before his death in 1920, Weber made some very significant additions to this passage, originally written in 1916.[38] In one of them, he inserted a sentence in the section on the ascetic antipathy for sexuality, giving as an example Luther's view of the sexual aspect of marriage as a residue of the Fall, in which "God 'sees through his fingers' in order to avoid worse things."[39] Weber had always detested Lutheranism for the servility it inspired toward the bureaucratic state. But when he had first discussed it in *Die Protestantische Ethik* (1904), he used Lutheranism as the chief example of the *unio mystica* that contrasted so sharply with the active, ascetic posture. Now, near his death, he unambiguously associates Luther, the symbolic exponent of bureaucratic despotism, with the ascetic hostility to Eros—an example of Weber's sporadic tendency to link together bureaucratic and ascetic modes of life and to oppose both from mystical and aristocratic perspectives.

In this connection, Baumgarten has printed a scrap of conversation between Max and Marianne in which the aging sociologist suggests that his self-image was anything but that of an ascetic:

> MAX: Tell me, can you think of yourself as a mystic?
> MARIANNE: That would certainly be the *last* thing
>   I could think of. Can you conceive of it for
>   yourself?
> MAX: It could even be that I *am* one. Just as I have
>   "dreamt" more in my life than one really ought to
>   be allowed, I am also not really *quite* securely
>   at home anywhere. It is as though I could (and
>   wanted) to pull myself back from everything, and
>   completely.[40]

But despite his growing distaste for the ascetic way of life, the side of Weber which had struggled for decades to develop some kind of autonomous sense of rational responsibility could not unconditionally accept the rejection of consequences, the ultimate irresponsibility, that both the purely erotic and the purely mystic positions entailed. He found in the ethic of Quakerism a sense of responsibility and respect for the personality which did not exclude modified forms of either the mystical or the erotic sense of communion and which moreover reproduced, for the individual if not the social order, that sense of a meaningful life cycle whose destruction at the hands of modernity was one of Weber's deepest concerns in his last years:

> It is the Quaker ethic (as it appears in William Penn's letters to his wife) which has best succeeded in going beyond the rather crude Lutheran sense of the meaning of marriage to a truly human interpretation of its inner religious value. From a purely worldly viewpoint, only the tie to the idea of ethical responsibility for one another—a heterogeneous kind of relationship compared with the *purely* erotic sphere—can provide the experience that in the development of a consciously responsible feeling of love, through all the nuances of the organic life process "up to the pianissimo of old age" . . . there may rest something unique and most high. Rarely does life grant this in a pure form! He who receives it should speak of fortune and the grace of destiny—not of his own "merit."

[4]

SCIENCE, MODERNITY,
MEANINGLESSNESS (1919)

THE LAST PAGES of "Religious Rejections" (largely unchanged from the 1916 version) and the second half of "Science as a Vocation" (1919) reveal Weber's most troubled reflections on the problems of meaninglessness in modern society and provide a conception of history within which the personal philosophy suggested above appears as the only meaningful solution.

These pages have a precedent in Weber's work: like the rest of the essay of 1916, they go back to a passage of *Wirtschaft und Gesellschaft* that was written before the war.[41] But Weber only broached the problem in this particular form—that of the meaninglessness of death in modern society, and therefore of the life which must lead to it—earlier in this essay, very briefly, in the section on the enhanced value of death in war. Of course, the broad perception of "meaning" as a major cultural problem does take us back to Weber's first discussion of mysticism and asceticism in 1910, where he juxtaposed the mystical understanding of the basic flow of life and passion found in Tolstoy and Russian culture as a whole to the trivial machinations of modern life. For it is also from the mystic, Tolstoy, that in these crucial late passages of "Religious Rejections" and "Science as a Vocation" Weber borrows the notion of a meaningful death as the necessary condition for a meaningful life—a notion which enshrouds with gloom his basic historical antithesis of an intellectualized, progressive modernity vs. a primitively religious, cyclical peasant culture: indeed, given the earlier identification of Tolstoy and peasant *Gemeinschaft* with mysticism, and of Western *Gesellschaft* with worldly asceticism,[42] it is only reasonable to view this historical antithesis as an attenuated form of the mystic-ascetic dichotomy. Nonetheless, the pessimistic meditation over scientific thought and the meaning of death is a completely new approach and merits close examination.

The relationship of the problem of "meaning" to the development of modern culture in Weber's thought is similar to the relation of estrangement to capitalism in Marx. Only in undeveloped cultures is meaning inherent in the life cycle (for Weber) and the productive process (for Marx). But what begins the development toward modern complexities is obscure in both men's work. In general, Weber seems to relate this development to the problem of theodicy, the justification of God's existence in the face of massive and frequently unmerited human suffering. Yet the very posing of the problem seems to presuppose that separation of man from God which Weber views as the hallmark of ethical prophecy (ascetic), as opposed to exemplary prophecy (mystical). And these distinctions in turn collapse into the geopolitical distinction between the transcendental political religious systems of the ancient Near East and the pantheistic systems of China and India. In any case, it is clear that in Weber's view the historical quest for a cosmic theological answer to the question of suffering is the beginning of philosophy and rational thought, and, like Nietzsche, Weber sees the end of this process not only in the emancipation of rational thought from all religious beliefs and ethics, but also in the abandonment of any notion of an inherent meaning in worldly affairs.

> Wherever . . . rational empirical knowledge has con-
> sistently carried out the disenchantment of the world
> and its transformation into a causal mechanism, there
> appears the ultimate challenge to the claims of the
> ethical postulate, that the world is a divinely ordered
> cosmos with some kind of ethically *meaningful* direc-
> tion.[43]

Thus, in the course of mastering the world through empirical thought and of proudly creating a cosmos of art and philosophy, human culture lost all sense of its own ultimate meaning. For parallel to the direction of human thought toward emancipation from all concepts not susceptible to empirical proof ran the direction of human culture toward a life style in which men valued only the process of acquiring goods but not the experience of life as such. Since life could only end in death, the spending of it in acquisition—even acquisition of the most sublime artifacts and qualities of high culture—made death meaningless and cruel.

> The peasant could die "sated with life" like Abraham.
> The feudal landlord and warrior-hero too. For both

fulfilled a cycle of their Being beyond which they did not extend. They could thus, in their way, attain a this-worldly completion which followed from the naïve unambiguity of their lives. But the "educated" man, striving for self-perfection in the sense of the appropriation or creation of cultural values [*Kulturinhalte*] could not. He could of course become "tired of life," but not in the sense of the completion of a cycle. For his perfectibility was in principle just as limitless as that of the cultural goods. And the more the cultural goods and the goals of self-perfection differentiated and multiplied themselves, so much smaller did the fraction become which the individual, passively as a receiver or actively as a co-creator, could embrace in the course of a finite life. So much the less therefore could the entrapment in these external and internal worlds offer the probability: that an individual could absorb the total culture or what was in some sense the "essential" in it (for which there was moreover no definitive criterion). Equally unlikely was it that "culture" and the striving for it could have any kind of this-worldly meaning.[44]

To Weber, even the intellectualized mystical quest for salvation (which had become voguish in some German cultural circles after the turn of the century) was of no avail against the harsh conditions of modern society. For the intellectual elitism [*"Aristocratismus"*] of such efforts was contrary to the basic ethic of brotherhood which Weber associated with religions of salvation. And the material character of modern culture insured that "the cultivation of acosmic brotherhood" should remain at most an epiphenomenon confined to the leisured classes: "Under the technical and social conditions of rational culture, living the life of a Buddha, a Jesus, or a Francis seems condemned, from external considerations alone, to failure."[45]

Written some three years later (1919) the latter part of "Science as a Vocation" is primarily an embroidering on this theme of modernity and meaninglessness, but with a somewhat altered perspective. Rather than illustrating the desiccation of religious ethics by reason, Weber focuses on the decay of the metaphysic of Progress through science. The historical moment at which Weber wrote this piece enormously influenced its perspective. He prepared it for a lecture at the University of Munich only a few months after Germany's defeat and collapse. The disintegration of the old regime had brought about a mood of revolutionary chiliasm among great numbers of students, in which dreams of socialist utopias merged with the kind of antimodernist quest for mystical experience and charismatic leadership which had characterized the prewar youth movement. Part of the mood of the time was a demand which students have recently taken up once again: for the transformation of science and scholarship into instruments of relevance and personal meaning.

Although Weber could understand the students' needs and address himself to them with a brilliance matched by few of his contemporaries, the impact of the war on him had had the opposite effect. The outset of the war had induced a euphoria verging on ecstasy. For over a year, his mood seems to indicate some kind of fulfillment of his hopes of 1895, when he had searched in vain for a "spark of that Catalinarian energy of the *deed* . . . [a] breath of the powerful national passion that filled the chambers of the Convention," but had nonetheless looked expectantly to his own generation as the precursor of an epoch of German history that would be even greater than the then overshadowing period of the Reichsgründung. That earlier posture was, as I have tried to show above, almost certainly a projection of his suppressed hatred for his father and his desire to protect his mother from Max Sr.'s arbitrary wrath. Some of Weber's comments in 1914 and 1915 give strong support to this thesis concerning the personal basis of Weber's attachment to the nation. In a letter to Michels he defends his patriotism as an absolute duty, of the same nature as the "loyalty and thankfulness of a son toward his physical mother."[46] In another letter, complaining of the army's refusal to permit him active duty, he wrote:

> Finally, I have of all my mother's sons the strongest inborn warrior instincts—and sat first in an office, then at my desk, and now the troops march singing under my window—the devil take it.

Another letter of 1914 condoling his sister Lilli on the loss of her husband at the front shows a total abandonment of his usual (after 1900) insistence on an ethic of responsibility rather than immediate, experiential gratification:

> For whatever the outcome may be, this war is really great and wonderful beyond all expectation. Not the successes but the spirit of the soldiers that one could see here, (and daily in the infirmary), exceeds all expectations, and here at least, also the spirit of the populace, taken all in all. I would never have hoped for that, and whatever else may come, it will be unforgettable.[47]

Certainly this was the psychological framework for Weber's perceptions of 1916 (in "Religious Rejections") on death in war as an antidote to the meaninglessness of life in modernity. But the course of the war was evoking a growing disillusionment in Weber. As early as March 1916 he wrote a bitter memorandum against the advocates of unrestricted submarine warfare, the inauguration of which he correctly saw as provoking America's entry on the side of the Entente.[48] He hailed Hindenburg's appointment later that year, but only because he believed the General capable of concluding a peace that would be unassailable within Germany.[49]

In February 1917, there was a brief flicker of optimism, occasioned by the hope that America might after all remain out of the conflict.[50] But soon after, a growing despair colored all his thoughts on the outcome of the war and Germany's future.

Certainly for one who identified the future of his nation so closely with its political—and military—pre-eminence, this despair was inevitable in 1918. Yet if my thesis is correct that Weber projected his image of his mother onto the German nation, this despair need not have been unmitigated. For there were some rather satisfying conclusions that Weber may subconsciously have drawn from the collapse of 1918. The nation (mother image) may have been temporarily overcome, but the main source of its (her) undoing—the bumbling incompetence of the imperial regime (senescent paternal authoritarianism), which could not defend it (her) and could not properly direct the soldiers (sons) to do so—this incompetent authoritarianism had abdicated (in effect committed suicide). Thus the feeblemindedness of the old regime and the power of the external enemy war machine fully accounted for Germany's disaster. There could be no question of Weber's responsibility for the death of imperial paternalism (he had clearly established the credentials of his loyalty in 1914) and consequently no danger that his joyous martial excitement of 1914–15—a clear echo of his imperialist sentiments of 1894–7—might end in *his* renewed collapse. Yet in an intellectualized, spiritualized recapitulation of his earlier self-punishment for excessive hubris, he did return sharply to the sober disenchanted "lessons" he had drawn from his breakdown. Indeed, it was only natural that this man who had experienced the onset of the war with such naïve enthusiasm would see in its disastrous outcome proof of the correctness of his prewar pessimism, of his underlying conviction after his breakdown that the age of great beliefs and saviors, the age of enchantment and charisma, was dead, buried by bureaucratic domination and scientific thought.

Weber's mood then, in the 1919 lecture on "Science as a Vocation," was diametrically opposed to the apocalyptic enthusiasm of Germany's youth. After the prisonlike structure of imperial paternalism had disintegrated around them, the latter were in much the same position as those emancipated land workers with whose *Zauber der Freiheit* Weber had identified before 1898. Against their hopes, Weber, who clearly understood them, could bring only his philosophy of disenchantment.

For Weber, science and scientifically oriented technology are the driving forces of the historical process of intellectualization and rationalization. Although individual modern men may actually have less knowledge of the artifacts of daily life than a primitive savage, they believe that if they want to find something out about the world around them they can:

> There are in principle no mysterious incalculable powers that play a role. Rather we can *master* by *calculation* everything. But that means: the disenchantment of the world. No longer must we—like the savage for whom such powers existed—grasp at magical means to master or implore the spirits. But technical means and calculations accomplish that.

But the legacy of this process of rationalization is the loss of any sense that the world is ultimately meaningful, an abandonment of certain naïve hopes that science might lead to a greater and more precise understanding of the meaning of the world. These hopes were characteristically presented at the dawn of systematic philosophy, in Plato's cave allegory. The argument about the loss of meaning—the juxtaposition of scientific "progress" to the inherently meaningful life cycle of the peasant, the Tolstoian question about the meaning of death—is largely a recapitulation of similar passages in "Religious Rejections." But the use of the cave allegory is new and significant, for it brings into focus Weber's own development from the youthful naïveté of his early period, when the union of social science and nationalism was an unquestioned value (just as the union of social science and revolutionary messianism was an unquestioned goal for many German students after World War I), to the later dissociation of social science from any ultimate value in his postbreakdown period. Here Weber's frequent distinction between "inner" and "outer" is relevant.

Three decades earlier, Weber was in a somewhat similar quandary when Emmy Baumgarten asked him to do something to help his mother. He had answered by an allegory of his own, with similarities to Plato's. His father's public activity desensitized him to certain more profound kinds of understanding. Through his papers and documents, Weber Sr. saw people and their actions as though they were mere shadows, projected onto a curtain which cut the viewer off from the vivid reality. His mother had a more internal understanding of events: the implication was that she stood on the other side of the curtain.

For the time being, Weber was using his allegory to justify his retreat from Emmy's demands, his withdrawal from the parents' conflict. But implicit in Weber's response to Emmy was the suggestion that his father's posture was similar to that of the wretches chained to the wall of the cave, capable only of seeing the shadows of reality. His mother was like the one who, standing in the direct light of the sun, saw reality. Weber seems to have assumed the responsibility, before his breakdown, of transmitting the underlying spiritual content of his mother's vision to the trapped wretches on the other side of the curtain.

What was this vision? In Weber, it became transformed from its original spiritual substance into an ethos of ruthless nationalism. But in either case it simply meant an understanding of the *inner* meaning of the world. In 1919, Weber appeared to identify this understanding with the "gift of grace" (*Gnadengabe*) of seers and prophets,[51] and "gift of grace" is in "Politics as a Vocation" defined as "charisma."[52] It was precisely this "gift of grace" which, Weber insisted, science could in no way bring or further. Quite the contrary: the rationalization of conduct and perception which science created was the mortal antagonist of charisma.

Nonetheless, just as he had done so eloquently in his discussion of eroticism, Weber recognized the burning need felt by so many of his contemporaries for some kind of salvation from the harsh consequences of rationalization, and in the closing paragraphs of "Science as a Vocation" he addressed himself to that need.

For the "modern intellectuals" who sought to create substitute religions, prophets, disciples, and churches, who manufactured "mystical" experiences and built literary careers on them, for these impure souls Weber had only contempt: "It is simply swindle or self-deception." But he evinced a great deal of respect for the communities created by the German youth movement. Although mistrustful of their religious pretentions, he saw in them "something very serious and genuine."

Weber's personal credo appeared in the closing paragraph of "Science as a Vocation":

> It is the fate of our time, with its characteristic rationalization, intellectualization, and above all, disenchantment of the world, that precisely the ultimate and most sublime values have disappeared from public life, either into the shadow realm of mystical life or into the brotherliness of direct relationships between individuals. It is not accidental that our highest art is intimate rather than monumental, nor is it chance that today, only within the smallest circles of community, from man to man, in *pianissimo* [N.B.] does that Something pulsate which earlier, as prophetic *pneuma*,* went through the great communities like a fire storm and fused them together.[53]

No attempt at the artificial creation of monumental art, or of new religions, or of new communities, could possibly succeed in an age whose public life was so totally bereft of prophecy, *pneuma*, charisma. For whomever this fate was unbearable, Weber recommended—with only the faintest trace of irony—a return to the waiting arms of the established Church. For professorial prophets, who placed redemptive

---

* "Spirit" or "breath." The significance of the term is discussed in Rudolf Bultmann's *Primitive Christianity* (Cleveland, New York, 1966), pp. 203–5.

rhetoric above "simple intellectual honesty," he displayed total contempt. In his closing lines, he referred his auditors to the oracle of Isaiah, from the exile period of ancient Judaism. How much longer would the night of exile (the age without charisma) last? "Morning will come but yet is it still night. If you wish to ask, come again another time." Until the morning, Weber urged the students simply to fulfill the demands of the times, both humanly and professionally. And this task would be simple, he concluded, "if each finds and obeys the *Daemon* who holds the threads of *his* life."

Thus, in a public world that was thoroughly disenchanted (*"entzaubert"*), Weber twice directed his auditors into purely private and internal realms where concepts like *pneuma* and *Daemon*, relics of the dead world of *Zauber* and *Charisma*, were still meaningful. In these private realms, the quest for one's *Daemon*—for one's ultimate standard of values—suggested to some of his auditors an ethic of pure decisionism, dependent only on the *will* of the historical actor.[54] And indeed, one intellectual tendency in the Weimar Republic, that of Carl Schmitt, took up Weber's idea and built a political philosophy of decisionism on it. Schmitt became a leading spokesman for German fascism, and the fact that Weber's thought was subject to this interpretation has tended to tarnish his image as a champion of German liberalism. Yet, while Schmitt's decisionism laid the basis for a politics of total opportunism,* Weber's demanded high principle. Though he denied that he or anyone else could objectively justify value choices, the necessity of choice, of commitment to one's *Daemon*, was an ethical imperative. Furthermore, meaningful choice always involved accountability to the social and political forces of one's age.

As we have seen, the basic model on which Weber's

---

* Franz Neumann: *Behemoth* (New York, Toronto, London, 1944), p. 153, argues that Schmitt's justification for Germany's breaking the terms of the Versailles treaty "makes law a mere prostitute of politics." The theoretical basis of Schmitt's opportunism appears in his *Politische Romantik* (Berlin, 1968).

values centered, and from which he tried to distance himself after his breakdown, was that of Puritan asceticism. The countermodel discussed above, growing out of the polarity of asceticism and mysticism which he had developed in his sociology of religion, shaped the relationship between his scholarship and his inner life: public homage to an ascetic science drained of ultimate meaning, private cultivation in personal relationships of a quasi-mystical *"pneuma."* A second countermodel, which guided his *political* perspective in his last decade, related aristocratic charisma to his earlier ascetic code. To be sure, after 1914 this relationship changed dramatically. Before the war, he seems largely to have rejected, as a contradiction in terms, any marriage of charisma and asceticism, and to have celebrated the virtues of an aristocratic charisma which was firmly, if unhappily, locked into the feudal past; modernity might be a cultural catastrophe, but Weber never questioned its inevitability. During and after the war, he appeared to see no necessary incompatibility between political charisma and Puritan asceticism, and to consider their alliance as both possible and necessary for the future of his country. But in neither case did he consider, as either wise or feasible, that apocalyptic transformation of modern *Gesellschaft* through a charismatic hero for which major strata of the German people yearned in the postwar period and which National Socialism claimed to represent.

Thus, whatever its evolution in Weber's thought, political charisma was no more arbitrary in its historical appearance than religious charisma; specific social and political frameworks were its preconditions. We now turn to the examination of these preconditions.

8

Aristocracy and Charisma in Weber's Political Thought (1911-1919)

*Among the noble, mental acuteness always
tends slightly to suggest luxury and overrefinement.
The fact is that with them it is much less important
than is the perfect functioning of the ruling,
unconscious instincts or even a certain temerity
to follow sudden impulses, court danger,
or indulge spurts of violent rage, love,
worship, gratitude, or vengeance.*

NIETZSCHE, Genealogy of Morals,
First Essay, X

WEBER'S MOST OBVIOUS concern in his political sociology (*Herrschaftssoziologie*—literally, sociology of power) is the reason for the seemingly inexorable rise of the bureaucratic-legal order. The major historical antagonist (and, by virtue of its inevitable defeat, *victim*) of this order is that intricate network of intermediate and autonomous powers which constituted the feudal aristocracy. Interestingly, to the extent that Weber sees all-powerful bureaucracies as manipulating democratic principles of equality to "level" the ruled, to the extent that he views the principal accomplishment of the French Revolution and of Bonapartism as merely securing the omnipotence of the bureaucracy,[1] his perception parallels that of his French counterpart, the gloomy aristocratic liberal de Tocqueville. But where Weber had once asked, in helpless fury, "What have we to set against this machinery, in order to preserve a remnant of humanity from this parceling-out of the soul, from this exclusive rule of bureaucratic life ideals?" he was now, in the decade after 1910, finding a wide variety of answers.

The glorification of the warrior's death—an insight produced by the pathos of what Weber viewed as a national struggle for survival—was one. His personal retreat from asceticism, which will be the subject of Chapter 9, was another. The hopes for a political reform in Germany were yet another. But paralleling all of these went the scholarly inquiries of *Wirtschaft und Gesellschaft* and the *Religions-soziologie*. And the underlying *Motiv* of these studies was, as I have said, decidedly ambivalent. On the one hand, there was the sober, painful, and recondite examination of the historical sources of rationalization. On the other, half buried beneath the ponderous weight of Weber's scholarship, lay the inquiry into the cultural forces antagonistic to this "progress" that was almost more than Weber could endure.

AT THE CLOSE of his introductory chapter to the *Herrschafts-soziologie*[2] Weber outlines the basis for his "pure types of domination." There are fundamentally two legitimate foundations of government: rational principles and personal authority. In the first, which he finds embodied in bureaucratic systems of control, one obeys laws, not individuals; in the second, one obeys personalities. These latter receive their authority either from the sanctity of *tradition*, or, contrariwise, from the untraditional belief in the *charisma* of the ruler. Traditional forms of authority are typically represented by "Patriarchalism," while charismatic authority "rests on the authority of specific personalities, without either rational or traditional foundation." Thus, in the skeletal framework of his "pure" sociology, traditional and charismatic authority stand together as opponents of "impersonal" bureaucratic authority. Yet when Weber directs his attention to the historical evolution of these forms of domination, it becomes clear that "traditional" authority covers patriarchal-patrimonial systems, which can metamorphose into bureaucratic-legal ones without any great change in their basic ethos, and certain types of feudal systems based on the "free" aristocracy, whose ethos is utterly incompatible both with the patriarchal spirit and its rational descendant, the modern bureaucracy. Thus from the standpoint of its hostile posture toward an objective, well-ordered, and economically rational system, the code of the feudal aristocracy stands in the same general relationship of antagonism to the patriarchal type of traditionalism as the mystical variety of virtuoso religion does to the ascetic.

Weber handles the relationships of patriarchal traditionalism and feudalism to bureaucratic modernity in two chapters and on two levels. The first chapter deals simply with "patriarchal and patrimonial rule," and is somewhat less relevant for our purposes. The initial part of this chapter emphasizes the opposition between the rational spirit of modern bureaucracies and the irrational administration of the patrimonial prince. The latter part of it is largely devoted to comparisons of patrimonial systems of rule in various places and times—China, Russia, prerevolutionary France, etc. But the second chapter, on "Feudalism, Government by Estates and Patrimonialism" is highly important, for here the two levels of treatment appear with unmistakable clarity.

On one level, Weber examines the antinomy of patriarchalism and feudalism from the standpoint of their "external" historical devolution or nondevolution into bureaucratic forms of rule. On another, he examines them "internally" from the standpoint of the "*Gesinnung*" (mode of thought) they produce, and tests this attitude for its compatibility or incompatibility with the spirit of rationalization. *

From the external standpoint, feudal and patriarchal systems, although in somewhat different ways, both contributed to the development of rational bureaucracy. Weber delineates two paths from personal authority to bureaucratic. The implicit *Leitmotiv* of both developments is the compelling force of what he calls "formal rationality" over economic development. Formal rationality is "the degree of technically possible *calculation* in an economic system that is actually applied."[3] The development of this formal or technical rationality is usually hindered by what Weber calls, "material rationality": the system of values which any society or organized group of people uses to rationalize its actions. There are an unlimited variety of such systems, among which Weber mentions the numerous ethical and egalitarian types of communism and socialism, hierarchies of feudal estates, political, utilitarian, and hedonistic doctrines.[4]

In both the paths from patrimonial to bureaucratic administration, one discerns the historical *Drang* of formal rationality as the catalytic agent. The common element is the pressure of technical economic needs in stimulating the metamorphosis of the patrimonial prince's administrative staff from a group of loyal dependents paid from the prince's household budget, without fixed areas of competence, and totally subject to the arbitrary will of their lord, into civil servants chosen by professional examinations, paid by the state, with a strict division of labor and with the duties of each man clearly prescribed by law.

---

* Weber does not explicitly use the terms "external" and "internal" in this chapter, but considering the fact that he frequently uses these terms to describe just the approach he uses here, I believe it is a legitimate inference that he is thinking in these terms. He does use "*Gesinnung*" in contrast to the "creation of technical means." *W.u.G.*, p. 826 (*E.S.*, p. 104).

In the one case, this evolution occurs without any involvement of the feudal aristocracy.[5] The patrimonial prince employs a "central official" to regulate his staff, and the increasing administrative complexities compel this official, in the interests of efficient administration of finances, to mold his staff in the direction of bureaucratic objectivity and to favor the rise of persons technically trained in bookkeeping.

In the other line of development, the patrimonial state acquires a bureaucracy with the aid of two closely related phenomena: the rise of the organized feudal estate as a political force and the evolution of a money economy. The chaos of relationships of individual feudal aristocrats to their patrimonial prince, who can turn to no other source than his vassals for any increase in his economic and military requirements, is a rigid one, fixed permanently by custom in each individual case. As long as economic and technical development stagnates, the prince's needs remain stable and all is well. But the rise of a money economy—a crucial advance in formal rationality—opens up a new source of power in times of war and a new opportunity for conspicuous consumption in times of peace. The continual struggle for pre-eminence between political entities gradually imposes the need for access to this new source of power on all who would remain in competition. But the old, rigid system of individual contracts between lord and vassal prevents any quick utilization of the feudality as a source of new revenues. To circumvent these individual contracts, the princes convened the noble estates as corporate bodies, to negotiate with them collectively either for new revenues or for the assumption on the part of the feudal estates of administrative obligations formerly fulfilled by the prince. The result was the *Ständestaat* (government by estates).

Superficially, the *Ständestaat* might appear to give new political life to the feudal nobles. Actually, it led to their political emasculation. In most cases the feudality, inspired by caste notions of honorable activity, was reluctant to become deeply involved in complex questions of fiscal ad-

ministration, and the same administrative needs which led
the princes to convene the estates also led them to develop
a centralized bureaucracy. And this bureaucracy quickly
became a tool of the patrimonial power against the power of
the *Ständestaat.* Even where the nobility, through the
Ständestaat, were themselves partly responsible for the development of royal bureaucracy, this bureaucracy was clearly
their mortal antagonist.[6] In his *Religionssoziologie* Weber
succinctly summarizes this mutual antagonism of patrimonial
prince and feudality when he writes:

> Everywhere we find the struggle of the lords against the
> holders or usurpers of lordly powers which have been
> appropriated by the estates. He attempts to expropriate
> them; they, him. To the extent that he succeeds in
> acquiring a staff of his own officials, dependent on him
> alone and bound to his interest, and to the extent that
> he acquires his own means of administration . . . so
> much the more is this struggle decided in his favor and
> against the gradually expropriated holders of estate
> privileges.[7]

In general, then, from the standpoint of Weber's "external" examination, the feudal aristocracy is historically
doomed to extinction because of its widespread inability to
accommodate itself to the demands of formal rationality, as
represented politically by the development of royal bureaucracies. Yet, apart from some rather esoteric comments about
the legal status of the aristocracy and some vague references
to standards of personal honor and dignity, Weber tells us, in
this "external" comparison of feudalism and patrimonialism,
virtually nothing of a positive nature about either. He focuses
overwhelmingly on their relationship to the mainstream of
technical progress—the evolution of formal rationality. And
in this context he defines the feudal aristocracy almost entirely
in negative terms.

A very different conception of the "free" nobility arises
when, in the last five pages of this chapter, he devotes himself to an "internal" examination of the kind of *"Gesinnung"*

produced by feudalism and by patriarchal patrimonialism, and compares their impact on the total way of life (*Gesamthabitus*) of the nations. In contrast to the clear if unwitting cooperation of the *Ständestaat* in the creation of the patrimonial bureaucracy, the difference in spirit between feudalism and patrimonialism is "extraordinarily strong."

> Feudal socialization leads . . . to a permeation of the most important life relationships with strictly personal bonds, which characteristically means that the chivalric feeling of dignity resides in precisely the cult of the personal. This feeling thus constitutes the most extreme antithesis of all objective-business relationships, which therefore must be, and always have been, valued by the feudal ethic as coarse and lacking in dignity. The opposition to commercial rationalism arises, however, from a number of other roots. First of all, from the specifically military character of the feudal system, which indeed is only transferred onto the structure of domination. The characteristically feudal army is an army of knights, and that means that the individual combat of heroes, not the discipline of the mass army, plays the decisive role. . . . Individual perfection in the personal art of weaponry was the goal of military education. Consequently, we always find in the system of education and the way of life a certain element which . . . belongs to the original capacities of both men and animals but is increasingly eliminated by every rationalization of life: *Play*. Under these social conditions, it is no more a mere "pastime" than in organic life, but is rather the naturally developed form in which the psychophysical powers of the organism are kept lively and supple. It is a form of "exercise" which, in its unforced and unbroken animality and instinctiveness, still stands beyond any division of "intellectual" and "material," of "spiritual" and "physical," no matter how much it may be sublimated through convention.[8]

Play, the foremost cultural activity of the feudal aristocrat, is the polar opposite and the barrier to technical, "formal" rationality.* The rejection of goal rationality in favor of immediately gratifying activity, a primary characteristic of play, epitomizes other aspects of aristocratic culture as well. A powerful aesthetic impulse, as a means to self-glorification, leads to the cultivation of music, art, and literature.[9] This aesthetic inclination combines with a naïve power impulse to create the need for ostentatious luxury—a blatant rejection of utilitarian criteria of consumption and thus "an eminent instrument of power for the assertion of mastery through mass suggestion." But, again, this use of luxury is utterly naïve, for functional thought in general and in particular, relating one's existence in any way to some kind of transcendent mission, is alien to aristocratic strata. "Their characteristic myth [*"Legende"*] is the value of their being."[10]

Much to the contrary, the code which dominates the official is that of the sober man of business:

> The patrimonial official receives his honor not from his "being," but from his "function." From his "performance" he expects rewards and advancement; in the context of his activity, the leisure, play, and commercial nonchalance of the knight must appear as wastefulness and incompetence. His characteristic caste ethic [*"Standesethik"*] leads, in this principal point, into the path of the bourgeois business morality.[11]

To be sure, the profit motive and the desire for economic independence of the bourgeois entrepreneur are antipathetic to the official.[12] But in most respects, the culture of the official is shaped by just that impulse of formal rationality which it shares with the bourgeois ethos and which is so clearly absent from the aristocratic. The educational systems associated with patrimonial or bureaucratic cultures testify eloquently to this. Weber distinguishes three such systems. One is the method, typified in China, of training a caste of literati in highly esoteric forms of communication. A second

---

* "Spiel . . . ein Gegenpol alles ökonomisch rationalen Handelns, der diesem den Weg verlegte." W.u.G., p. 828 (E.S., p. 1106).

is the clerical education, common to the Near East and the Latin Middle Ages, in methods of calculating and transcribing that were unknown to the feudal laity. The third is the specialized legal education which has its origin in the medieval university. It is also literary in character, but unlike the other two it leads directly, given the increasing rationalization of life, toward the highly specialized breed of modern man and toward that ideal concept of the modern bureaucrat, the "calling." This was, of course, the education Weber himself received. And there is no mistaking his rejection of his own background, when he writes:

> But it always lacks those traits of play and elective affinity with aesthetic culture, of heroic asceticism and heroic reverence, of heroic honor and heroic hostility to the "cold objectivity" of "business" which feudalism breeds and preserves.

Probably written between 1911 and 1914, this apparent championing of aristocratic values against *"Beruf"* and "objectivity" marks Weber's clearest antagonism to both the bureaucratic and the rational-ascetic modes of life, which by implication he seems to identify with each other. Much to the contrary, when the disasters of the later war years brought a resurgence of the tough-minded, ascetic aspect of his personality, he developed a totally different notion of the aristocratic code, in which cool objectivity, economic autonomy, and devotion to the "calling" of politics defined the potentialities for genuinely charismatic leadership *against* the vanity, lack of a sense of proportion, and economic dependence on their sinecures of the bureaucrats, the *"Berufspolitiker ohne Beruf,"* who had led imperial Germany to ruin.[13] But it took the shattering experience of defeat and the possibility and pressing urgency of "realistic" reform to return Weber to this posture. It really contradicts the general line of development—Weber's gradual revolt against his own heritage of ascetic rationalism—which first becomes visible in his discussion of mysticism in 1910 and which persists in the 1916 analysis of mysticism and eroticism and in the 1919 lecture, "Science as a Vocation." Certainly his comments on the authoritarianism of the patriarchal-patrimonial order give an additional note of bitterness and hostility to this revolt, which ultimately seems to be aimed as much against the German political character as against any abstract system of domination.

Precisely because the patriarchal-patrimonial order defines itself not in terms of its "being" but in terms of its function, it is capable of devising ideologies to mask and justify this function, which is really no more than naked domination. To better control the masses, and to undermine his most dangerous opponents in the aristocratic estates, the patrimonial prince legitimizes his power by presenting himself as the protector of his subjects' "welfare":

> The "welfare state" is the myth [*Legende*] of Patrimonialism, grown not from the free comradeship of pledged loyalty, but from the authoritarian relationship of father and children: the "father of his country" is the ideal of the patrimonial state.*

In family terms, Weber merely implies that he views the aristocracy as a band of free and equal brothers. But he leaves no doubt at all about his contempt for the authoritarian paternalism that is the mold of the bureaucratic state he lives in. In general, he strips the patrimonial prince of any genuine aristocratic virtue. Like the petty-bourgeois Junker he had excoriated in the '90's, the prince is usually a parvenu: "The abrupt rise from nothingness, from slavery and lowly service to a lord, into the precarious omnipotence of the

---

* W.u.G., p. 829 (E.S., p. 1107). Further: "In direct opposition to the minimizing of administrative functions in feudalism, which only concerns itself with the condition of its dependents to the extent that such concern is indispensable to its own economic existence, patriarchalism reveals a maximizing of administrative interests. For every new administrative function which the patrimonial prince appropriates to himself on the one hand signifies an elevation of his power position and psychological significance, and on the other, creates new sinecures for his officials."

Favorite, is typical for him." Other traits also echo Weber's great sensitivity to the power reflexes of his own departed *pater familias:*

> What he must combat in the interest of his power is both the economic independence of the bourgeoisie and the caste autonomy [*ständische Selbständigkeit*] of the feudal nobility, who are independent of the lord's favor. Because of their ultimate consequences, all feelings of intrinsic dignity on the part of the "subjects," simply because they exist, must be suspected of being hostile to authority.

Indeed, in this passage, probably written shortly before World War I, the sociologist presents his native land as one of the last, virtually impregnable fortresses of the patriarchal authoritarian ethos. Weber explains, briefly and brilliantly, how most of the other European states have managed to emancipate themselves from it, at least partially:

> In England, the minimizing of effective administration by the rule of local notables and the dependence of the lord's power on the voluntary cooperation of the stratum of notables, prevented . . . that internalized devotion to authority which in Germany has remained a virtually ineradicable inheritance of the untrammeled rule of the patrimonial prince and which appears to foreign observers as a lack of dignity. In France and the Latin countries, successful revolutions, and in Russia the lack of preconceptions of the social-revolutionary ethos [have similarly undermined traditional authority. But] from a political standpoint, the German was and is in fact, the characteristic obsequious "subject," in the most profound sense of the word. And consequently Lutheranism was the religion appropriate for him.

This contemptuous reference to Lutheranism as the German ideology of bureaucratic servility is by no means casual or isolated in *Wirtschaft und Gesellschaft.* He makes the same point in two other places, and in one of these—a comparison of German and Chinese bureaucracies—he explicitly points to "the role which is played by the piety of the child, as the foundation of all political virtues in the strictly patriarchal Lutheranism."[14]

Thus, we find three significant and related themes in Weber's comparison of feudal and patriarchal values. One is the equation of patrimonialism and its bureaucratic off-spring with the authoritarian dominance of the father over his children, and conversely, the implication that aristocracy is built on the freely given loyalty of brothers equal in dignity. The second is the juxtaposition of "Being," the core of the aristocratic code, vs. "Function," the basis of the bureaucratic, with all that this implies for the opposed values of the two ethics. A third is the harsh critique of Germany, as the land without a tradition of aristocratic autonomy to limit the arbitrary tyranny of the Prince and his officials.

The opposition of "Being" and "Function" is perhaps most significant. For one thing, it is a profoundly Nietzschean formulation. Indeed, where Weber discusses the social psychology of "privileged" vs. "nonprivileged" social groups in his sociology of religion, he follows closely on Nietzsche's heels, polemicizing with the philosopher primarily about the importance of *"Ressentiment"* as a key to the psychology of plebeian strata.[15] Nietzsche too had portrayed the ethos of the aristocrat in terms of an immense pride and joy in what he was—his "Being." But he saw the plebeian ethic only as the inversion of this aristocratic pride. Filled with hatred for his natural superior, but too weak to combat him openly, the commoner sublimated his hatred into *"Ressentiment,"* which assumed the ideological form of a simple reversal of all aristocratic values. Instead of the pride of the aristocrat, humility. Instead of the open hatred of the noble for his enemies, love. And in this way Nietzsche traced the genealogy of Christian morality.

But for Weber the plebeian's corollary of aristocratic "Being" is not *"Ressentiment,"* but rather the urge to become (*"sein werden"*) what he is not, i.e., to find relief from his suffering. In theological terms, this leads to a sense of ethical obligation (*"Sollen"*) to serve as a tool of the divine will in transforming the world. Both of these provide an ethical framework for increasingly rational efforts to work oneself out of the suffering which is the prevailing lot of the plebeian.

Thus Weber traces a line of continuity between the ethical rationalism of plebeian strata (a variety of material rationality) and formal rationality—a line which is clearly absent between the latter and the aristocratic code of "Being," just as it is between formal rationality and mystical religiosity. Indeed, Weber suggests a close correlation between mysticism and aristocracy. For one thing, he identifies mystical illumination as the characteristic religious tendency of privileged classes.[16] For another, *"Sein"*—"Being"—is not only emblematic of the aristocratic ethos but typifies the mystical experience as well.[17] But perhaps most significant of all is the psychological correlation of both the mystic and aristocratic ethics with exemplary prophecy, and of ascetic and plebeian with ethical prophecy. The ethical prophet, rooted in the ascetic-plebeian code of transcending a reality filled with pain, preaches a rational morality of subservience to the will of an all-powerful, transcendent deity, in whose service men are mere "instruments" for the realization of His commands. The exemplary prophet, like the mystic and the aristocrat, does not preach, but simply offers his own standard of "Being" (Weber uses the untranslatable word *"Zuständlichkeit"*), which is this kind of prophet's condition of contemplative possession of the Divine, as a model for those who would follow him.[18]

Interestingly, it is in the passage of the *Herrschaftssoziologie* cited above, where Nietzsche's name is not mentioned but aristocratic "Being" is, that Weber comes closest to the philosophy of the will to power. Although in the religious sociology he superficially molds his argument on Nietzsche (by juxtaposing the aristocrat's code of "Being" to the plebeian's antithetical morality), he is really con-

cerned more in that passage with the evolution of formal
rationality from the plebeian theology of suffering than he is
with the aristocratic viewpoint. But in the sociology of
domination, the direct opposite of the aristocrat is not the
suffering plebeian, but rather the ex-plebeian, the parvenu
prince, who has already risen to power by the strength of
his will and cunning. And although this prince reveals little
or no *Ressentiment*, he does live by precisely that will to
power which Nietzsche saw as the hidden motor of plebeian
Ressentiment. And like Nietzsche's plebeian, but unlike
the "nonprivileged strata" that Weber had discussed in the
Sociology of Religion, the parvenu prince stands against
the true aristocrat in a posture of struggle unto death.

But apart from the striking affinity with Nietzsche, the
polarity of "Being" and "Function" is even more significant
for its proximity to that other, better known antinomy of
Weber's work: charisma vs. rationalization. For when Weber
tells us that the patrimonial prince and his officials establish
themselves only by administrative efficiency, he puts them
clearly in the historical line of formal rationality. And just as
the aristocrat is defined by his "Being," it is surely a certain
higher type of "Being" which elevates the receiver of the
gift of grace (charisma) above his unredeemed contemporaries. Of course, in its narrow sense, charisma refers
primarily to religious grace.* But grace has a secular connotation, of physical and spiritual self-assurance without self-
consciousness, which though lacking in the German *Gnade*,
is the meaning of the word *Anmut;* and it is precisely *"Anmut
und Würde"* (grace and dignity) which Weber identifies as
the distinguishing characteristic of the aristocratic ethos.[19]
When we add to this the clear implication in *Wirtschaft und
Gesellschaft* of a link between the free feudal aristocracy
and some antecedent "following" of a charismatic warrior-

---

* It is only this religious connotation of charisma that Weber
has in mind when he juxtaposes the aristocratic ethos "through its
worldly orientation to the charismatic magical asceticism of prophets
and heroes"; *W.u.G.,* p. 828 (*E.S.,* p. 1106).

hero, the charismatic ingredient in the code of the feudal
aristocracy becomes unmistakable.*

In the chapter on the "Nature and Impact of Charisma,"[20]
Weber presents several more grounds for the notion that
aristocracy has the same relationship of affinity to charisma
that patriarchalism and bureaucracy have to rationalization:

> The patriarch is the "natural" leader of daily life
> (*"Alltag"*). The bureaucratic structure is only his
> rationally transposed counterpart . . . Charismatic rule
> is in all things, including its economic substructure, the
> precise opposite of the bureaucratic. If the latter is
> dependent on steady income, and consequently relies
> at least *a potiori* on a money economy and money taxes,
> charisma lives in and yet not of this world. . . . always
> —this is decisive—charisma rejects planful, rational
> earning, and in general all rational economics, as lacking
> in dignity. Herein also lies its harsh opposition against
> all patriarchal structures, which rest on the organized
> basis of the "household." . . . Genuine charismatic rule,
> therefore, recognizes no abstract legal propositions and
> regulations and no formal jurisprudence.[21]

All these attributes of charismatic authority are also
components of the aristocratic ethos, as Weber presents it.
Despite these affinities, however, it is impossible to make any
absolute identification of aristocratic feudalism as *the* historical embodiment of charisma. For Weber defines charisma
as specifically a-historical. In fact, it connotes more a psychological than either a sociological or an historical property. If it can be argued that a host of charismatic features

---

* "One can thus classify . . . feudal relationships in the following
way: . . . 3: 'free' feudalism: (a) the 'following' only by virtue of
personal ties of loyalty, without the bestowal of landlord rights (most
Japanese samurai, the Merovingian Trustis) . . . (c) 'vassalage': personal ties of loyalty and fief combined (Occident) . . ."; *W.u.G.*, p.
797 (*E.S.*, p. 1072). "The *administrative staff* of the charismatic lord
is no 'officialdom' . . . But it is selected by charismatic criteria. To the
prophet correspond his disciples, to the 'warrior prince' his 'following.'"
W.u.G., p. 180 (*E.S.*, p. 243). Also *W.u.G.*, pp. 838–9 (*E.S.*, pp.
1118–19).

appear in Weber's description of the free feudality, it is also evident that, from two antithetical perspectives, the aristocracy is sadly lacking in certain other traits which Weber elsewhere associates with charismatic leadership. These antithetical perspectives constitute the central ambivalence of Weber's late political philosophy. They are:

(1) The total freedom from any conventional framework, which is the underlying definition of charisma in *Wirtschaft und Gesellschaft*.[22]

(2) The total absorption of the "extraordinary" character of charisma into that process of institutionalization which Weber called the routinization of charisma; i.e., the understanding of charisma exclusively in terms of the ever more difficult but still feasible adaptation of the charismatic spirit to the increasingly rationalized and organized mass politics of the modern age.*

In terms of the first perspective, feudalism fails to qualify because, despite its hostility to rational economics, jurisprudence, or politics, it involves a fixed set of personal relationships—"stereotyped" is the word Weber uses[23]—which constitute an ongoing and potentially permanent social system. Thus, Weber says, "The charismatic hero derives his authority not from ordinances and regulations, as in the case of an official 'jurisdiction,' and not from traditional custom or *feudal pledges of loyalty* like the patrimonial power, but he wins and keeps it only through proof of his powers in life. If he wants to be a prophet, he must perform miracles; if he wants to be a warrior leader, heroic deeds."[24] "Feudal pledges of loyalty" as the basis of social position would seem to ex-

---

* Though Weber discusses the routinization of charisma at some length in *W.u.G.*, it appears there as the "slow death by suffocation" (p. 840; *E.S.*, p. 1120) of charisma in which "the essence of charisma is definitively surrendered and lost" (p. 842; *E.S.*, p. 1122). Only in his wartime and postwar writing do the formerly archaic forces of aristocracy and charisma appear as fully compatible with modernity.

clude not just the patrimonial prince, but the feudal aristocracy itself from the category of charisma.

But in terms of the second perspective, the feudal aristocracy must be dismissed from consideration as a contender for the modern variety of charismatic rule because it is too irrational, too incompatible in its ethic with the economically and politically indispensable advance of formal rationality. For indeed, in *Politik als Beruf*, Weber virtually identified genuine political leadership, even in a modern state, with charisma, and this certainly excluded from consideration the archaic irrationality of the feudal life style.

Weber gives us numerous hints to suggest that this capacity for genuine leadership has historically been found among aristocratic strata; but these strata are quite different from the Nietzschean aristocrats of *Wirtschaft und Gesellschaft*, who define themselves in absolute antithesis to the tradition of ascetic rationalism. In *Wahlrecht und Demokratie* (1917), for example, the emphasis is always on the coolness, distance, and reserve of the aristocratic statesmen of the eighteenth and nineteenth centuries—a posture of political wisdom which the author compares nostalgically to the egoistic sentimentality and arrogant subjectivity of the "plebeian" politicians of imperial Germany.[25]

In this more "realistic" perspective of Weber's, the key concept which binds together aristocracy, charisma, and political leadership is *Beruf* (calling)—i.e., precisely that concept from which, in *Wirtschaft und Gesellschaft*, Weber had clearly separated charisma.* The charismatic leader attracts his following because he appears to be "called" to his post by some kind of transcendent power. And indeed "the idea of the *calling* in its highest form" is at the root of the leader's charismatic power over his followers.[26] There are two ways

---

* See above, p. 245. See also *W.u.G.*, p. 834: "The bearers of charisma—the lord just as much as the disciples and followers—must stand outside of the bonds of this world if they are to carry out their mission, outside of the everyday callings ["*Alltagsberufe*"] and outside of everyday family obligations" (*E.S.*, p. 1113).

of finding one's calling in politics: living "for" or living "from" public service. Weber acknowledges that in a psychological sense almost everyone seriously engaged in it lives "from" politics: either in the sense of the sheer pleasure of possessing power or "from the consciousness of lending a *meaning* to his life through service in a cause." But in an economic sense, the distinction of living "for" and living "from" is absolute:

> He who strives to make politics a permanent source of *income* lives "off" politics as a vocation (*Beruf*), whereas he who does not do this lives "for" politics . . . In order for a person to be able to live "for" politics in this economic sense . . . he must, under normal conditions, be economically independent of the income which politics can bring him. That means, quite simply, he must have private means or must be in a personal position which yields a sufficient income.[27]

And elsewhere Weber defines as the chief requirement for a political aristocrat the ability to live *for* rather than *from* the state; i.e., "He must above all be economically free from the necessity of work, in order to stand ready, externally and above all internally too, for political ends."[28] Contrariwise, he who lives, materially, *from* politics finds his ideal type in the servile official.

Weber then writes something which sharply throws into relief his double standard for charismatic leadership. After repeating that this need for a private income is a feature of "normal conditions," he admits that the followers of a warrior prince—the very model of a charismatic situation in *Wirtschaft und Gesellschaft*—are totally unconcerned with normal economic conditions, but live from booty, confiscations, etc. But these, he says, are "extraordinary phenomena: in the economy of everyday life, only one's own fortune performs this service." So here is Weber, strenuously defining the everyday ("*Alltag*") conditions for charismatic leadership, dismissing as mere epiphenomena the "extraordinary" (*"ausseralltäglich"*) conditions in which the warlord and his band live outside of any ordered economy—and yet it was precisely such total antithesis to organized economic life (*"Alltag"*) which was a primary characteristic of charismatic rule in *Wirtschaft und Gesellschaft*.[29]

In the same place, however, that he dismisses the "extraordinary" existence of the warlord, Weber brings in another phenomenon which he views as its modern counterpart; through this reference we see at least a part of the basis for his return, in his public utterance of 1919, to the more ascetic, rational concept of politics he had apparently denigrated in the prewar analysis of charisma: as the contemporary example of "extraordinary" charisma, Weber names "the following of the revolutionary heroes of the street." Indeed, the revolutionary eruptions of postwar Germany seemed to have the markings of genuinely charismatic movements. But Weber was psychologically incapable of acknowledging any utopian possibilities of a socialist transformation at the end of the war. He considered the abortive German revolution only a "bloody carnival" which would have to give way before the demands of economic necessity. Still, in his search for a "realistic" political solution, he could not entirely surrender the notion of charisma to the devil. Instead he advanced what he had earlier discussed as the historical "routinization of charisma"[30] to the level of a "pure type" of charismatic leadership in all ages, and possible even in modern Germany in the form of a popularly elected president of the Reich.[31] Among the character traits necessary in such a political leader, Weber lists two which flow from the ascetic rationalism that is his dominant mood in *Politik als Beruf*—the feeling of responsibility and the sense of proportion—and one which reflects the demonic, charismatic core he wants to see preserved—"passion." But even the passion must be rational:

> Passion in the sense of *objectivity*: passionate devotion
> to a "cause," to the God or Demon which is its master.

. . . For the problem is precisely: How can burning passion and a cool sense of proportion be forced to coexist in the same soul? Politics is made with the head, not with other parts of the body or the soul. And yet devotion to it can only be born and nourished from passion, if it is not to be a frivolous intellectual game, but humanly genuine action. That powerful taming of the soul, however, which characterizes the passionate politician and distinguishes him from the mere "sterile excitement" of the political dilletante, is only possible through the cultivation of "distance" . . . The "strength" of a political "personality" signifies primarily the possession of these qualities.

There is no question but that in this passage and in others that he wrote during and after the war Weber sought to draw the line between the sobriety of the charismatic leadership he sought for Germany and the clumsy, nervous, and overheated prestige politics of Wilhelm II. Nor can there be any doubt that they also cast into the outer darkness of false charisma any kind of specifically irrational leadership movement such as National Socialism. Indeed, during the war Weber lambasted with devastating accuracy the ideological precursors of the corporate state.[32] Thus, the rational transformation of the concept of charisma in *Politik als Beruf* and the late political essays serves four important functions. It subjects the old regime of Imperial Germany to a devastating critique. It staunchly opposes any effort to abolish parliament in favor of some kind of corporate system of estates: parliaments are indispensable as an arena for the testing, through close political combat, of future leaders. It excludes from consideration as unrealistic and false the apparent rise of extraordinary charismatic leaders in the movements of revolutionary socialism. But it also keeps alive the possibility of charismatic leadership within the contemporary *Alltag*.

For the other side of Weber, his rejection of modernity and rationality, that great beast from the depths of the

Victorian subconscious, still confronts us. In the last decade of his life, it permeated his political as well as his religious sociology to such an extent that even in his severest critiques of the political folly he saw around him, charisma, this most Dionysian of concepts, though carefully surrounded by Socratic and Apollonian safeguards, dominates the scene. And when it emerges without these safeguards, when Weber writes of the affinity between mysticism and eroticism and of *Eros* as an escape from the cold "skeletal" hands of rationalization, as the only remaining breakthrough to the core of the truly living; when he describes the aristocratic ethos in terms of play, art, and "Being" and speaks of "its unintentional and unbroken animality and instinctiveness . . . beyond that division of 'intellectual' and 'material,' " . . . then we see the full extent to which this former incarnation of Puritan asceticism was questioning his own rationalist heritage and coming to terms with the "vitalist" breakthrough which dominated the intellectual culture of Europe in the years before World War I. Ernst Nolte partially comprehends this development when he writes: "That this descendant of the Puritans, this great representative and protagonist of European rationalism begins to lose confidence in his traditions, demonstrates more convincingly than the theses of Bergson or Klages the change in intellectual atmosphere that occurred around 1910."[33] But Nolte sees only the loss, not the breakthrough to all those underground regions of the self which Victorian culture had kept in chains and which were now, in a true return of the repressed, rising painfully to the surface of consciousness—through the Freudian revolution, through the growing impact of Nietzschean ideals, through the youth movement, through the *George-Kreis* and through German Expressionism.

Indeed, the very posing of the problem that Nolte uses —Weber's relationship to fascism—is a false one. For the visible danger in *fin de siècle* Europe was by no means a wildly destructive mass breakthrough of the irrational, but the contrary: the permanent victory over human spontaneity and autonomy of the machine, that harsh, material quintessence of the nineteenth century superego. That the reaction against this threat broke through with such violence in "the great . . . protagonist of European rationalism" was by no means a mere function of the changed intellectual climate, but evinced the intolerable psychic pressures which the Puritan code had imposed on this man of volcanic passions. For one can correlate the intellectual changes in Weber's last decade not only with the influence of this climate but also with a partial disintegration of the ascetic posture in the sociologist's personal life—what he himself, in describing the affinity of those intriguing mystical experiences with erotic intoxication, once called the "revenge of the animalic."[34]

Weber's Retreat from Ascetic Rationalism (1907-1920)

UNDERLYING WEBER'S development in the '90's toward an increasingly radical nationalism had been a certain fixed psychological and intellectual posture. It was basically the code of Puritan heroism that Weber tried to infuse into the politics of *fin de siècle* Germany, and it was certainly a very rigid form of Puritan asceticism, his mother's Calvinist heritage, that Weber embodied in his daily life in those years. The implication of this Puritanism for his relationship to his father, particularly the ambivalence inherent in his religious-psychological inheritance between the model of Calvinist work-slave and that of Calvinist tyrannicide, probably was the background of his total collapse after his father's death in 1897. But with this collapse, as Weber himself acknowledged, came relief from the "icy hand" of

unremitting, compulsive work. And in the years of his recovery after 1902, Weber invested a large part of his intellectual resources in unraveling the relation between Calvinist
theology and that ascetic impulse to unceasing labor which he
saw as the foundation of the spirit of capitalism.

Although Weber continued to present himself, particularly in his political writings during and just after the war,
as a champion of ascetic "modernity," his evolution after
his breakdown shows a powerful and highly significant
countertendency, away from the unqualified celebration of
ascetic rationalism he had himself embodied in his youth. If
the "God" of Weber's asceticism was Calvin, the "Gods"
that impelled him against his Puritan heritage were Nietzsche,
Tolstoi, and Dostoevsky.*

The chapters above have focused on the appearance of this
anti-ascetic current in Weber's scholarly work. In the years
between his first brief discussion of mysticism in 1910 and
World War I, this side of Weber appeared most prominently
in the political sociology of *Wirtschaft und Gesellschaft*,
especially in the material on aristocracy and charisma. The
political milieu of these years, which showed the increasingly
ruinous role of "professional politicians without a 'calling' "
in Germany's foreign policy, undoubtedly conditioned Weber's

---

* It is the principal merit of Wolfgang Mommsen's outstanding
essay on Weber's philosophy of history that he outlines the significance
of Nietzsche in this late theoretical evolution, just as it is Mommsen's
principal deficiency that he misses the significance of Weber's breakdown and hence categorizes even the Nietzschean component in Weber
primarily in terms of its compatibility with his Puritan presuppositions.
(See Wolfgang Mommsen: *"Universalgeschichtliches und Politisches
Denken bei Max Weber,"* Historische Zeitschrift, 1964, p. 574; future
references to this work will be cited as *Mommsen: "Universal."*)
Mommsen bases his argument primarily on Weber's marginal notes
in his copy of Simmel's *Schopenhauer und Nietzsche*, which do
show Weber's agreement with Simmel's interpretation of Nietzsche
in terms of strict intellectual self-discipline. But Weber probably made
these notes soon after the book was published in 1907 (he and Simmel
were close friends); they are almost certainly irrelevant to Weber's
analysis of aristocracy and charisma between 1911 and 1914, where
he seems to have in mind a very different side of Nietzsche.

growing feeling of hopelessness about the possibility of liberal reform, and it was, at least in part, this bleak outlook which underlay his perception of an absolute antagonism between rationalization (legal, bureaucratic, ascetic, and the wave of the future) and charisma (extraordinary, antinomian, aristocratic, and the glory of the past). Indeed, were the world of scholarship dealing with anyone else than the universally acknowledged protagonist of ascetic modernity, Weber's prewar view of charisma and aristocracy would long ago have been classified under the heading of "reactionary utopias."

During the war years, however, after an initial outburst of patriotic exuberance, Weber began soberly to reconsider the possibilities of fundamental liberal and democratic reforms in Germany, and this renewed contemplation of the opportunities offered by modernity for a more rational political existence re-ignited in him the spirit of ascetic rationalism. But only, it must be emphasized, in the sphere of immediate political reforms. For at about the same time that Weber was writing such a masterpiece of political analysis as *Wahlrecht und Demokratie in Deutschland*,[1] he was also working on his religious sociology, especially on that essay in which he came closest to a rejection of the whole ascetic ethos as antipathetic to the deepest needs of men. This simultaneity of a reawakened interest in the ascetic code as applied to politics and a highly skeptical stance toward it as it related to his personal philosophy characterized the two papers for which Weber is best known: "Science As a Vocation" and "Politics as a Vocation"—both delivered to students in Munich in the early months of 1919. Just as there could be no question, in the one essay, of Weber's emphatic endorsement of rational-ascetic standards for political behavior, so could there be none, in the other, of the author's frustration at finding himself the possessor of an albatross-concept of science, which, like the mariner's bird, left one with no opportunity for rest and, in an ultimate sense, had no rational meaning at all. The background of this unpleasant discovery was, as noted in Chapter 7, Weber's fascination with Eastern mysticism, particularly with the Tolstoian question of the meaning of death in a society which, unlike peasant *Gemeinschaft*, valued only beginnings and the process of accumulation, but not the life cycle as a whole.

[1]

THE INTELLECTUAL MILIEU: SOMBART, THE *GEORGE-KREIS*, LUKACS

WITH OUR UNDERSTANDING of this countertendency in Weber's work, toward the glorification of atavistic antitheses of modernity, we can begin to make sense of a great many features of his immediate intellectual milieu and his personal existence in these years. We can see the influence of his sociological colleagues—Tönnies, Michels, but above all Sombart—on his anti-modernism. We can also make more sense of Weber's strange mixture of intellectual companions in Heidelberg (the *"Weber-Kreis"*), which included Friedrich Gundolf, the disciple of Stefan George, and Georg Lukacs, before 1918 an aesthetician and a Tolstoian mystic and socialist. Most significantly, however, we can find traces of a revolt against the ascetic code in Weber's personal life, a revolt which had as its background the impact in prewar Germany of Freudian doctrine.

Tönnies and Michels both strengthened Weber's profound inclination, in the years after his collapse, to view Western civilization as a dead-end street. Of course, his attitude toward *Gemeinschaft* was ambivalent. But whether he viewed this concept in terms of paternal authoritarianism or brotherhood, he accepted completely Tönnies's conviction that the genuine *Gemeinschaft,* based on primitive ties of blood and religion, was a thing of the past. And this standpoint was crucial in his rejection of the notion that "organic" social ties might develop from the German war effort[2]—a notion that was essential to the postwar cult of heroism and militarism in which National Socialism was to be rooted. Indeed, like Tönnies (and perhaps partly under his influence), Weber associated modern socialism strictly with rational goal-oriented, *Gesellschaft,* and true communism exclusively with primitive forms of *Gemeinschaft,* which no amount of wishful thinking could resuscitate.[3] And if the net effect of Tönnies's influence was to strengthen Weber's skepticism toward the neo-romantic "corporate" theorists of his day, the impact of Michels strengthened Weber's longstanding refusal to take seriously the socialist appeal of revolutionary messianism.

Alongside this primarily negative influence of Tönnies and Michels, that of Sombart appears more positive as well as more complex and extensive. While Weber never developed any kind of editorial tie with Tönnies, and only worked with Michels on the *Archiv* for one year (1914), his association with Sombart as coeditor of that journal lasted from 1904 to his death. This is highly significant, for Sombart's outspoken anti-modernity and neo-romanticism, which was unambiguous from 1903 (*Die deutsche Volkswirtschaft*) onward, was surely no secret to Weber.

In all likelihood, the convalescing Heidelberg scholar was attracted to Sombart as a coeditor for three reasons: personality, scholarly direction, and acceptability to the old owner of the *Archiv.* Sombart's personality was a more flamboyant version of Weber's own. Although much more inclined than Weber, since his student days, to Bohemianism, Sombart similarly combined a capacity for hard work with a strong sense of intellectual independence, indeed defiance, toward accepted authority. It was a characteristic unwillingness to show even minimal respect, much less reverence, to his critics, which lost Sombart a major opportunity for advancement to Weber's own vacated position in Heidelberg in 1903, a move which Weber had strongly recommended to his colleagues.[4] And it was completely in harmony with Weber's own respect for his opponent's integrity that Sombart privately praised Rosa Luxemburg for her willingness to stand up publicly to the socialist party chiefs, after she had attempted to tear him to pieces polemically in *Die Neue Zeit*.[5]

More substantively, Sombart's scholarly interests after 1900, infused as they were with an anti-modernist critique that must have represented the temptation of Satan to Weber, clearly offered the latter a continual source of intellectual nourishment. Both men invested a major part of their intellectual energy between 1900 and 1914 in exploring the social psychology or "spirit" which underlay modern capitalism. Sombart broached the subject without adequately pursuing it in his *Moderne Kapitalismus* (1902), and Weber picked up the theme in his essays on Protestantism and capitalism, published two years later.

Weber's most noteworthy intellectual riposte to Sombart, however, appears between 1912 and 1918, in his changing response to Sombart's bifurcation of the capitalist spirit into an adventurous entrepreneurial component and a passive, calculating, commercial component.* Of course, there is a general similarity between the underlying historical presupposition of Sombart's dichotomy—the notion that the moving spirit of the past was an aggressive, adventurous personality bent on domination, while that of the present is an ever-calculating commercial rationalism—and Weber's polarity of charisma and rationalization. And this similarity does not change. But Sombart's notion of "heroic enterprise"

---

* Considering the intellectual proximity of these men in their work on the *Archiv*, it is hardly conceivable that Weber was not fully aware of Sombart's ideas on the capitalist spirit, which assumed a form very close to that of *Der Bourgeois* (1913) in his study *"Der Kapitalistische Unternehmer"* (*Archiv*, 1909).

lacked that emphasis on the hero's magnetic relationship to his following—a kind of democratic inversion of the Calvinist postulate of divine election—which permitted Weber, in the sobriety of his wartime essays, to transpose his notion of charismatic man into the conditions of modern mass society. For in his contemporary incarnation, the only charismatic trait that remained in Weber's concept of the political leader was precisely his personal ability to attract the support of significant groups of people. Otherwise he functioned, according to Weber, entirely within the framework of rationalization and disenchantment. This reversal of values from his prewar anti-modernist posture, which had been very close to Sombart's, to his wartime tough-mindedness, emerges unmistakably from a comparison of two passages, one written before and one during the war.

In both of these, the first in his discussion of charisma in *Wirtschaft und Gesellschaft* and the second in *Wahlrecht und Demokratie* (1917), Weber distinguishes between "booty capitalism"—which depends largely on the spectacular opportunities for profit that are offered by war, piracy, or imperialism—and rational, everyday capitalism.[6] But these two sides of the capitalist spirit receive quite different evaluations in the two works.

In the prewar analysis, Weber finds even in the sphere of capitalist economics "the antagonism of charisma and everyday life." On the one hand, there is "the modern 'professional' bureaucratized [N.B.] everyday capitalism"; on the other, the timeless phenomenon of booty capitalism, organized through the power of a charismatic leader to attract financial and personal support, and similar to the great enterprises established through the ages for purposes of colonial exploitation. Although less clear than in the rest of his discussion of charisma at this time, there is at least a hint of contempt for the representative of ascetic rationalism, characteristically shown to be totally enmeshed in that bureaucratization Weber so profoundly detests; and there is certainly a trace of admiration for the charismatic hero-organizer of booty capitalism.*

In the polemic of 1917, directed against those who opposed equal suffrage and a stronger parliament in the name of some kind of corporate state, Weber's attitude toward the two forms of the capitalist spirit is completely reversed. Faced with the practical question of which form of capitalism would be most favorable for Germany's economic and cultural future, Weber's reversion to his earlier ascetic tough-mindedness is unmistakable.

A part of the national ecstasy over the *Volksgemeinschaft,* it would seem, was the belief, widespread among the stratum Weber sarcastically called "our literati," that capitalism, an arch-enemy of the German spirit, could be eliminated by a continuation of the existing state-controlled war economy. In Weber's eyes, this war economy was of course only another form of capitalism—the one which he had earlier juxtaposed to rational everyday capitalism as charismatic. But in 1917 there is not even a nostalgic whiff of the charismatic about it. Not that rational capitalism is glorified: far from it. With its vocational ethic of duty and its vocational sense of honor, it has created "that iron cage . . . through which economic labor receives its present form and destiny. . . . a *system* which *inescapably* rules the economy and through it the everyday destiny of man."[7] But the alternative to this rational private capitalism would not be less bureaucratic domination and rigidity, but more. The workers under the proposed form of state socialism would be more oppressed

---

* Weber's protestation, at the outset of his chapter on charisma, that he was using the concept of charisma in a completely value-free sense, should be taken in the same sense as the protestations of Lady Macbeth. His repeated expressions of despair at the bureaucratization of the world, his repeated identification of bureaucracy with the fateful process of rationalization, left only charisma as the waning source of human creativity, at least in the prewar years, when he had not yet conceived of that accommodation of ascetic rationalism to charisma which appears in the political essays of 1917 to 1919. On the charismatic bias in Weber's thought, see *Mommsen: Max Weber,* p. 287.

than before by the unification of state and private bureaucracies and would be deprived of the chance of maneuvering
one against the other in their own interest. And the notion
that this kind of war socialism undercut the iniquitous profit
motive aroused all of Weber's polemical scorn. A close look
at the real motives behind the war economy revealed

> A wild dance around the golden calf, a gambler's snatch-
> ing at those accidental opportunities which bubble
> through all the pores of this bureaucratic system, a loss
> of every standard for any sense of distinction or re-
> straint in business ethics—and an iron compulsion for
> every businessman to join the howling and go along
> with the hyenas of this unparalleled Golgotha of all
> economic ethics—just as much, or rather in much greater
> degree than has usually been the case when capitalist
> profits were stuck to the footprints of the God of War
> —or of Saint Bürocratius.[8]

That the stigma of "Saint Bürocratius" has been trans-
ferred from rational, everyday capitalism to its wartime
counterpart and that the notion of charisma seems to have
vanished altogether from the field of economic activity, is
a measure both of Weber's departure from his anti-modernist
position before World War I and of his considerable differences with the chauvinist wartime polemics of Sombart, from
whom, after all, he had probably adapted the idea of
the "double nature" of the capitalist spirit in his earlier
work.

But Sombart, who remained at least nominally a social
scientist, represented only the outer edge of the neo-romanticism that swept through German culture in the years before
the war. Within his own circle in Heidelberg, Weber exchanged thoughts regularly with men who reflected the
forces at the very center of Germany's new anti-modernist
wave: Friedrich Gundolf, a leading disciple of Stefan George;
and the Hungarian, Georg Lukacs, whose beliefs in these
years epitomized the powerful hold of Slavic culture over

many German intellectuals.* And it was through Gundolf
that Weber met George, the charismatic "master" of a tightly
knit *Kreis* (circle) of anti-modernist poets and social critics.

Stefan George (b. 1868) was himself, with Rainer
Maria Rilke and the Austrian Hugo von Hoffmannsthal, one
of the most important poets of the Wilhelmian era. Unlike his
peers, however, he early adopted a quasi-mystical ideology
that was antagonistic to his age, and institutionalized himself
within a cult of worshipful admirers. Spending a good part
of each year with his disciples in Munich, Berlin, and from
1910 on, Heidelberg, George seems to have needed the circle
as a buffer between the harsh, bustling reality of Imperial
Germany and his own reserved, sensitive, and thoroughly
anachronistic character. Together with such disciples as
Gundolf and Karl Wolfskehl, he published the *Blätter für
die Kunst* (12 volumes, 1892–1919) and the *Jahrbuch für die
Geistige Bewegung* (3 volumes, 1910–12). As the titles suggest, the *Blätter*, consisting largely of verse—with brief,
esoteric essays mixed in—were intended primarily for those
already close to George, while the *Jahrbuch*, undertaken at a
time when George could hope to profit by a widespread neo-
romanticism in literary and scholarly circles, contained much
longer prose essays and appeared to have had a larger audience in mind. But in both journals, and in George's own
slim volumes of poetry, striking innovations in spelling,
grammar, and typography, made the works of the *Kreis* difficult for the lay reader.

Nonetheless, if we examine the "constituency" of the
Kreis—the narrower circle of George's disciples and
the broader one of those personally friendly either with George
or his closest followers—we find a remarkable number of the
liveliest minds of early-twentieth-century Germany. Gundolf was, with George, the principal German translator of

---

* Marianne writes that Gundolf and Lukacs were two of the few
guests in Weber's salon who were bright and forceful enough to serve
as independent centers of discussion when Weber was around; *Lebensb.*,
p. 511.

Shakespeare and the author of major studies of Shakespeare and Goethe. Hofmannsthal was himself very close to George for a while, though he never became an adherent of the *Kreis*.[9] Heinrich Rickert, the philosopher, was an ardent admirer of George and tried, unsuccessfully, to interest Weber in him before Weber's breakdown.[10] Georg Simmel, very close to the Berlin circle, received the master in his home frequently,[11] and his articles of 1901 and 1909 on George may have influenced Weber (after the breakdown) in his interest in the poet.[12] The graphologist and metaphysician Ludwig Klages, a rediscoverer of Bachofen's matriarchal theories, was an adherent of the Munich *Kreis* before his excommunication in 1904. At least one prominent economist, Edgar Salin, became part of the Heidelberg *Kreis* in his student days (around 1912), and another one, Arthur Salz, was personally sympathetic to it. (Salz, a close friend both of Gundolf and Erich Kahler, then a moving spirit of the *Kreis* in Munich, was married to the sister of Ernst Kantorowicz, another adherent of the *Kreis* and the author of a classic study of the Hohenstaufen Frederick II. At the same time Salz, like Gundolf, was also a close friend of Max Weber.) Another friend of Gundolf, and of the *Kreis*, was E. R. Curtius, the historian of literature.* In Heidelberg, although Max Weber was on the best of terms with Gundolf, most of George's adherents found a more congenial milieu in the home of Max's brother, the sociologist Alfred Weber.[13]

What was the doctrinal core that exercised such influence over so many independent spirits? Ernst Troeltsch, in an outstanding essay on the intellectual mood of Germany after World War I, describes it in these terms:

> Here, everything is prophetic seriousness and most sacred endeavor. The value system which he [George]

---

* Curtius almost joined the *Kreis* in 1914, during a passing fit of abject devotion to the "Master." See Friedrich Gundolf: *Briefwechsel mit Herbert Steiner und Ernst Robert Curtius* (Amsterdam, 1963), p. 236.

embodies is modeled in large measure on Plato, Dante and Nietzsche, is based on modern historicism, and not . . . on nationalism. Rather he excises everything liberal, democratic, socialist, nationalist, and individualist, with merciless severity. In the manner of aristocratic, Spartan Hellenism, he wants to create a strict aristocracy, with body and spirit in complete harmony; he wants to ally it with Roman-German ideas of discipledom and heroism and with Catholic ideas of the mystical bond of communion. 'Hellenic-Catholic,' Gundolf has called it, whereby 'Catholic' means the mystical, actually anti-Christian element in Catholicism. The spirit of the whole is religious, but thoroughly pagan and harshly aristocratic. . . . completely opposed to any sort of Protestantism. That this value system stands against all modern practices, above all against the contemporary mass character of the human race, with its consequences of industrial labor, capitalism, and socialism, naturally, all this he knows best himself. He scorns this world with a monumental loathing and recognizes as medicine against it only the 'holy war' and the 'holy pestilence.'[14]

Gundolf (b. 1880), one of George's closest disciples until the master cut him off for marrying against his advice in 1926,[15] met George through Karl Wolfskehl while still a student in 1899.[16] Gundolf studied German literature and history in Heidelberg (as well as Munich and Berlin) around the turn of the century, and, as is often the case, the student experience dominated the next decade of his life. Heidelberg, he wrote in 1907, despite all English spinsters, honeymooners, instructors, and fraternity men, was an imperishably romantic place, where "the shadows of Arnim and Brentano and Hölderlin . . . still maintain their twilight existence around the gigantic, fateful castle." Two years later, he still saw it "like a landscape out of Jean Paul, a dream of the past and of paradise."[17] It was with this notion of the significance of Heidelberg that, in 1909, Gundolf made the acquaintance of Max Weber,[18] whose own fermenting dissatisfactions with modernity had at that time hardly become apparent even to himself and who was known principally for his work on Protestantism and capitalism, a seeming apotheosis of both. A year later, in 1910, two events occurred which were to have a marked impact both on the cultural life of Heidelberg and on the development of Weber's thought: Gundolf, supported by Eberhard Gothein, the art historian, and Alfred Weber, received an academic position at the university, and Max Weber, through Gundolf's mediation, met Stefan George and began, in August 1910, a series of personal discussions with him which were to continue until June 1912.[19]

Weber's encounter with George occurred at just the right moment in his life. Before the breakdown, he had been cold to Rickert's effort to interest him in George; and in the period of initial recovery (about 1902–1908) he was still too close to the Puritan asceticism he was analyzing in his essays on Protestantism and capitalism for discourse with the diametrically opposed views of George to be fruitful. But around 1910, as part of a general relaxation of his inherited asceticism, Weber began to take a much greater interest in the arts, particularly literature and music.[20] And George, with Rilke, was one of the poets who most intrigued him.

In May 1910, a few months before he met George, Weber wrote a letter to a friend, in which admiration for George's poetry went side by side with a marked ambivalence toward the *Kreis* and its message. Comparing George himself to Dante (to whom the poet in fact liked to compare himself), and identifying the *George-Kreis* as a charismatic sect, he found the cult of Maximin, a handsome fifteen-year-old youth whom George had worshipped and then mourned after his sudden death in 1904, to be "absolutely absurd."[21] Furthermore, Weber was, then and later, extremely hostile to the leadership cult around George. And he consistently viewed the attempt of the *Kreis* to serve as the catalyst of a new *Gemeinschaft* of high culture—an aesthetic Reich that would offer an alternative to, perhaps even a replacement for, the degrading commercialism and vulgar modernity of Bismarck's creation—as doomed to "disintegrate on the iron rock of real social and economic relations."[22] Nonetheless, in Weber's description of the turn taken by the George-Kreis about 1910, away from art for art's sake, toward this cosmic goal of historical renewal, there is an implication of profound respect: "George, an ascetic with aesthetic characteristics, like so many other ascetics, is stepping out of the cloister in order to rejuvenate and to rule the world from which he first fled." Half a decade earlier, he had used very similar terms to describe the emergence of Christian asceticism from the monastery and its attempt to control all aspects of human behavior during the Reformation. And the imagery of that earlier passage—striding into the market place of life, slamming the door of the monastery behind, penetrating the daily routine of life with methodicalness[23]—had decidedly autobiographical overtones. Perhaps here lay the basis of Weber's considerable respect for the poet. The impossibility of George's heroic attempt to infuse the world with the magic of a lost age may have recalled to Weber the seemingly inevitable doom that had awaited his own atavistic enthusiasm for the magic of freedom—a form of naïve Puritan heroism—a decade earlier.

In the actual conversations with George, Weber, according to Marianne, exercised much tact and self-control to retain and develop the relationship.[24] George was hostile to the world of scholarship, finding in scientific conceptual formulations an enemy of his own creativity and desire for spiritual experience. Of course, Weber (not to mention Gundolf and Simmel, George's only other friends within the academy) was anything but an orthodox scholar. Nonetheless, whenever the discussion turned to questions of ultimate values, Weber was careful not to overwhelm the poet "dialectically."[25] For the most part the discussion remained at a level of "the simply-human," on which understanding between the two was complete. Indeed, Marianne writes that her husband preferred to discuss with Gundolf his theoretical differences with the Kreis.[26] But when conceptual matters did arise in the conversations with George, "Weber understands, in oral exchange, how to embody his knowledge in vivid shape, and no inner experience is alien to him."[27] Apparently two such substantive conversations concerned the status of women in modern society, which George seemed to think was too emancipated and the Webers, not enough, and the meaning of heroism, which George considered insufficiently physical in the modern age and Weber, insufficiently intellectual. On this latter difference, Marianne wrote at the time:

> When we spoke of the significance of the steadily increasing intellectual struggles of modern man, which perhaps produce spiritual heroism instead of physical, he said to me, "Miscreant, miscreant! You want to make everything even more to spirit, and thus you destroy the body." That precisely *he* needs highly refined men as a sounding board, and not the heroic killers of earlier times, he is apparently unaware. But what are "viewpoints." There came warmth, humanity and vigor from him, which we had to love—there is more to him than his Zarathustra-convictions.[28]

Yet, the clear differences between these men tended to center primarily—apart from the cult around George's person, which Weber found contemptible—not around questions of ultimate value, but rather around the possibility of implementing these values in the twentieth century. Disenchantment, rationalization, and mass society—although he became steadily more apprehensive of their cultural effects—were "inexorable destiny" to Weber; to the poet, they constituted a sham culture which his new aesthetic Reich would replace. Weber also maintained an undertone of scorn for the fact that most of George's adherents were men of independent means: they could dissociate themselves spiritually from mass society, but only because they could live from the labor of others. Without the goods of industrial society, they would be just as lost as everyone else, an accusation which George and his disciples adamantly denied.[29]

On certain more fundamental questions of value, however, there was a broad similarity of spirit; indeed it is entirely possible that the encounter with George may have catalyzed into conscious thought certain subcurrents in Weber's developing outlook which were profoundly antagonistic to the ascetic modernity of which he was the reputed champion. For there can be no doubt that Weber sympathized both with George's aristocratic code and with his criticism of the modern metropolis.

Shortly after Weber's initial encounter with George occurred that initial meeting of the German sociological society, at which Weber for the first time made the systematic distinction between mysticism and asceticism. It is, of course, impossible to say whether George influenced the apparently sudden flowering of Weber's interest in *Gemeinschaft* and Slavic mysticism, but in other sessions of that meeting, Weber twice mentioned George's name: once rather neutrally, in a comparison of religious and aesthetic sects,[30] but the other, in an ambivalent but decidedly impassioned description of the impact of the modern metropolis on cultural life.[31] In this latter discussion, a commentary on Sombart's paper, "Technology and Culture," Weber raised the question of whether modern technology was related in some way to formal aesthetic values. He argued that it was, in that the construction of a world of formal aesthetics was in many cases a reaction against "the whole savage dance of sounds and colors, the impressions which arouse sexual fantasy, and the experiences of varieties of spiritual constitutions, which affect the hungry rabble through all kinds of apparently inexhaustible possibilities for ways of life and happiness." Much of modern art, Weber argued, was either a protest against this world, a means of flight from it, or a celebration of it. George's highly formalized lyricism was a rather desperate defense:

> Such a degree of concentration on the last bastions of purely aesthetic forms, unassailable by the tumult produced through the technology of our life, could not be attained unless the lyricist has been thoroughly permeated

by the impressions of the modern metropolis, which threaten to drown him and shatter and parcel out his soul—even though he may damn them to the abyss.

It was only a year before that Weber vehemently condemned such "parceling out of the soul" through the omnipotence of the bureaucratic ethos. It is unlikely that he felt any greater tolerance for it when he saw the metropolis as its source.

But there is more than indirect evidence for Weber's conservative distaste of the metropolis in these years. Apparently he attributed much of his family's misfortune to his childhood move from Erfurt (a town of 45,000 in 1875) to Berlin. A letter to his mother of 1914 makes this clear:

> How well it would have been had we always stayed in the old town. For very many of all the problems and all the difficulties that came later were the consequence of the transplantation to the Berlin atmosphere, particularly after the old friends of the first period departed. . . . For this sunken and forgotten generation of the bourgeoisie, whose history will never be written, was worth knowing and brought a spirit into the house which formed a counterweight to the metropolitan atmosphere of estrangement—which indeed had a strong impact on the relation of the children, at least the sons, to the parents.[32]

That Weber—like Nietzsche, Sorel, and George—valued highly the aristocratic life style, cannot be denied by any one who has read his work carefully. But his conception of it—paralleling his conception of charisma—varied considerably from his prewar discussion of the feudal way of life in *Wirtschaft und Gesellschaft* to his wartime polemic in *Wahlrecht und Demokratie*. The neo-romantic accents of the earlier description, where Weber defined the significance of "play" for the feudal aristocracy in terms of unbroken animal instincts and as "a form of exercise which . . . stands beyond any division of 'intellectual' and 'material,' of 'spiritual' and 'physical,'" paralleled much of the Nietzschean rhetoric of his day, but it is entirely plausible that his closeness in these years to George and Gundolf (whose definition of aristocracy was in this respect almost identical to Weber's)* was the major factor in his anti-modernist understanding of both aristocracy and charisma.

Nostalgic fondness for Gundolf and George after the intimate discussions ceased in 1912 appears occasionally in the mass of published Weberiana: in 1915, a letter from Heidelberg, where Weber was supervising a military hospital, complains that "Since Weihen-Stefan and Gundelchen [George and Gundolf] have gone, I am totally alone, see no one . . . of any meaning for me."[33] And Helmuth Plessner recalls that in the revolutionary days of 1919 in Munich, Weber ironically addressed one overflowing student audience with a sentence frequently used by George to anathematize mass society: "Your very number is a crime."[34]

George in turn had great respect for Weber, despite his hostility to Weber's "scientific" neutrality, and it was undoubtedly increased by Weber's public defense of the *Kreis* (in 1910) against what he considered an unfair lampoon in the *Süddeutsche Monatshefte*.† Thus, George, in what may have been his only public endorsement of a work of scholarship, mentioned Weber's work on the connection between Protestantism and capitalism as "the classical book of Max Weber."[35] Indeed, in Friedrich Wolter's history of the *Kreis*, written with George's authorization in 1930, Weber com-

---

* According to Troeltsch, Gundolf viewed "the complete absorption of the spirit in the body, the complete physicalizing of the spirit," as "the essence of all truly aristocratic culture . . .*"; *Lebensb.*, p. 75.

† Weber wrote: "Stephan [*sic*] George and his disciples serve, in decisive points I suppose, 'other Gods' than I, much as I esteem their art and intentions. That does not alter the circumstance that I am internally compelled to bring the most unconditional purely *human affirmation* to the simple genuine seriousness with which George personally approaches his mission and to the simplicity and genuine devotion with which Gundolf remains loyal to his cause and his Master." *Lebensb.*, p. 501

pletely dominates the chapter on "The Poet and the Forces of the Age."

In this presentation of Weber, Wolters, though he mistakenly sees in the sociologist a union of Prussianism and Puritanism, makes one very profound observation when he calls Weber "A man who always defended the opposite of what was natural to him, who most preferred to represent the opinion that was most difficult for him, as if the test of moral behavior rested in never choosing what corresponded to his own nature and could be accomplished without inner resistance." This strikes, of course, at the root of Weber's tortured asceticism, but ignores the considerable evidence that in the last decade of his life, perhaps partially through the stimulus of George himself, Weber was shaking loose from it.

The relation to Georg Lukacs, falling as it did in the same years as Weber's encounter with the poet, may also have been significant in Weber's development away from asceticism. A Hungarian who had studied under Simmel in Berlin, Lukacs, during the half-decade from 1910 to 1915, managed to add to his initial training as philosopher and literary critic a powerful involvement in Tolstoian mysticism and a passion for social revolution. Shortly after the publication in Germany of his first book, *Die Seele und die Formen* (1911),* he settled in Heidelberg, where he quickly became a regular participant in Weber's Sunday-afternoon discussion group and remained there until 1915. Lukacs appears to have influenced three aspects of Weber's late evolution: his interest in formal aesthetics, his interest in Slavic culture as an anti-modernist challenge to his earlier values, and his curiosity —personal as well as sociological—about erotic phenomena.

It was of course as an aesthetician that Lukacs first became known, and it was as an aesthetician that Weber praised him highly. The sociologist wrote to him that he found in his early work a comprehension and analysis of the formal side of literature which had hitherto been neglected for studies

---

* A Hungarian edition appeared in 1910.

of the writer or his audience. Focusing on the works themselves was to Weber "the definitively correct posing of the
problem," and he was most curious to see how Lukacs's concept of form would emerge—a problem somewhat analogous
to the one Weber was encountering in those years in his
methodological concern with "ideal types."

But Lukacs's significance in Weber's development extends
far beyond the realm of formal aesthetics. Lukacs quickly
became a representative—probably the most articulate one—
of the Slavic mysticism which a rather large contingent of
Russian students (and some teachers) in Heidelberg had
already brought to Weber's attention. Indeed, Weber stated
explicitly in 1905 that his knowledge of "Soloview's belief in
the ethical-religious characteristic of the political task of
Russiandom" came from a representative of that position
(almost certainly one of the Russian students then in Heidelberg).*

The brief mention at that time of Soloview's viewpoint as
totally opposed to the Western "success-ethic," and as leading
directly to the absolutist Tolstoian ethic of nonresistance to
evil, was pejorative in tone, suggesting Weber's earlier aversion
to the unceasing moralizing of his aunt, mother, and—perhaps
—cousin. But by 1910, as we have seen, Weber was more
sympathetic to Slavic culture, viewing it as a meaningful
alternative to the worldly asceticism of which he was beginning to weary. In fact, the first speaking engagement that
Weber accepted after his breakdown was to celebrate with
Russian students the fiftieth anniversary of Heidelberg's Russian reading room (1912).[36] Furthermore, Weber was so impressed by the pluck of the Eastern European students
before the war—and so depressed by the conformity of the
German ones—that he told his young friend Paul Honigsheim
that if he ever held a seminar again he would accept only
Russians, Poles, and Jews.[37]

In these years, the presence of Lukacs and his friend Ernst

---

* Cf. P.S., p. 36. The representative was probably Fedor Stepun,
author of a book on Soloview. See Honigsheim in M.W.z.G., p. 240.

Bloch must have offered repeated stimulus for Weber's interest in Eastern mysticism. According to Honigsheim, Russian religion and literature were prominent in Lukacs's arguments, and Bloch (who like Lukacs became an important Marxist philosopher after World War I) used to summarize his hoped-for "religious-collectivist realm of justice" in the phrase, "a life in the Dostoevskian sense."[38] Honigsheim, in fact, could, in his memoir, recall no Sunday afternoon at which Dostoevsky was not mentioned,[39] and Marianne wrote that Max planned to write a book on Tolstoy.[40] Certainly the Tolstoian position of absolute, uncompromising dissociation from the entire worldly culture of violence and exploitation was one which Weber respected, even at the height of his martial enthusiasm in early 1916, as the consistent antithesis to his own ethic of "responsibility" and worldly struggle.[41] And it was this kind of rejection which Weber found, in chiliastic form, in Lukacs and Bloch.*

In 1912, Lukacs wrote a short story, *"Von der Armut am Geiste,"* which probably reveals the kind of discussions occurring in the *Weber-Kreis* at that time. It certainly reflects Weber's own ambivalence between the values of mystical anti-intellectualism and formal philosophical analysis.

The story is a dialogue which reveals the thoughts of a young man who, after the suicide of the girl he loved, has decided to kill himself. His reflections concern primarily his lack of true "goodness" (*"Güte"*) and his consequent failure to understand that his love was on the verge of suicide and that he might have prevented it. Lukacs's "goodness" appears

---

* *Cf. Lebensb.*, p. 509: "Eschatological hopes of a new emissary of the transcendent God moved these young philosophers, and they saw in a socialist order founded on brotherhood the basis of salvation. For Lukacs, the splendor of worldly culture, especially its aesthetic side, meant the Antichrist, the 'Luciferian' competition against God's effectiveness. But full development of this realm *was* to occur, for the choice of the individual between it and the transcendent could not be alleviated. The final struggle between God and Lucifer is still to come, and depends on the decision of mankind. Ultimate goal is salvation *from* the world, not, as for George and his circle, fulfillment in it."

to be similar to Weber's notions both of charisma (in its broadest sense, as a "gift of grace") and of mystical, acosmic love. It also suggests a rather interesting connection between these Weberian concepts and the German historicist notion of *Verstehen*, or "intuitional understanding." "Please do not tell me," says the tormented young man, "that I could not have known. . . ."

> Her silence would have sounded far over the land that lay between us, had I been graced with goodness. . . . Knowledge of men is an interpretation of expressions and symbols, and who knows if they are true or false. . . . But goodness is grace. Do you recall how the secret thoughts of others become obvious to Francis of Assisi. He doesn't figure them out. No. They are obvious to him. His knowledge lies beyond symbol and interpretation. He is good. In such moments, he is the other. . . . The good man no longer interprets the soul of the other, he reads in it as in his own, he has become the other. Therefore goodness is miracle, grace, and redemption. The descent of heaven to earth.[42]

This goodness, this divine power to merge one's identity with the Other, is fully antinomian. Public duties, ethical obligations, all formal relationships which are intended to mediate between men have become, for Lukacs's hero, in reality a barrier between them. Like charisma, Lukacs's "goodness" means "being graced with the power to break through the forms."[43] At one point, it also reveals the Dionysian side of charisma:

> Goodness is possession, it is not mild, not refined and not quietist; it is savage, cruel, blind, and adventurous. The soul of the good man is emptied of any psychological content, of reasons and consequences; it has become a pure white leaf on which destiny writes its absurd command, and this command is carried out blindly, rashly, and cruelly. That this impossibility becomes the deed; this blindness, clairvoyance; and this cruelty, goodness—that is the miracle and grace.

The antipathy to "goal-oriented," "responsible," or "useful" action, which characterized both mystical and feudal-aristocratic ethoi for Weber, is also evident in Lukacs's "goodness" and, moreover, replete with Slavic references:

> What does goodness care for consequences. . . . Goodness is without use as it is without reason. For all consequences lie in the external world of mechanical forces, unconcerned with us, and the motives for our deeds come from the merely symbolic world of the psychological, from the periphery of the soul. But goodness is divine, metapsychological. When goodness appears in us, paradise has become reality and the divinity is awakened in us. . . . Do you recall Sonya, Prince Myschkin, Alexei Karamasoff in Dostoevsky? You have asked me whether there are any good men: here they are. And you see, their good too is fruitless, confusing, and without consequence. It stands out incomprehensibly and uncomprehending from life, like a lonely great work of art. Whom did Prince Myschkin help? And did he not sow tragedies everywhere?[44]

Yet at the close of this dialogue, the young man emerges with a highly formal notion of ethical obligation, quite compatible with Weber's idea of finding one's *Daemon* and obeying it, which seems to have its source in an idea interjected about halfway through the story. Lukacs refers to an ancient legend about the construction of the temple, according to which the Devil destroyed every night what was built in the day, until the men resolved to sacrifice the wife of the work master. The sacrifice was meaningful in terms of finishing the work, but surely not in terms of the work master or his wife. Then follows a reformulation of Simmel's paradox of the tragedy of culture, which, as we have seen, was adapted by Weber in his sociology of religion: "The work grew out of life, but has grown away from it. It originated in man, but is inhuman, indeed antihuman."[45] Gradually, Lukacs makes a connection between the need for utter devotion to one's "work" in loving someone and the same kind of devotion to art or any other task (such as the "inhuman" one of building the temple). "Poverty of the spirit," a sundering of the self from all other interests, prepares one for a quasi-mystic sense of being "possessed" by one's work, which is true virtue.[46] By the end of the story, Lukacs is speaking of the fulfillment of duty and the observance of formal rules in specific castes of men, which alone lead one to God. The protagonist of the story feels condemned to death by this metaphysical order, because his love for the girl and desire to help her were transgressions of his own caste; he simply lacked the grace that would have been necessary to do the "work": to love her, and, through his love, save her.

Weber thought so highly of this story that he proposed showing it to the lover of one of Marianne's friends, together with *The Brothers Karamazov*, to dissuade him from the idea that moral behavior should be judged by its results rather than its inherent worth.[47] Indeed, the highly problematic relationship between erotic behavior and the ascetic code which dominated his earlier years was of considerable concern to Weber in his last decade. Well before his brilliant discussion of eroticism in 1916, he was asking Lukacs how he proposed to deal with it in the context of his aesthetic theory.[48] And shortly before the outbreak of the war, in one of his periodic convalescences in northern Italy, he read carefully *Marie Donadieu*, a novel by Charles-Louis Philippe which deals subtly with a rather complicated *menage à trois*, and asked Marianne to send him Lukacs's *Die Formen der Seele* (the book contained thirty pages on Philippe).[49] But this concern cuts much more profoundly into Weber's life than at the level of merely scholarly interest. For the Oedipal situation of his younger years seems to have left Weber with a bitter heritage which indeed must have been a significant factor in his breakdown and his slow recovery: he never consummated his marriage.[*]

---

[*] Interview with Eduard Baumgarten in Freiburg, July 13, 1968. Professor Baumgarten, the son of Max Weber's cousin Fritz, was an intimate of the Weber family from his student days during World War

[2]

THE PERSONAL EVOLUTION

IT IS UNLIKELY that we shall ever know the complete history of Weber's tormented personal life. Although he wrote a detailed chronicle of his illness for a psychiatrist, Marianne destroyed it in the last months of World War II for fear that it would fall into the Nazis' hands and be used to discredit him.[50] Nonetheless, from published materials and from material available to Eduard Baumgarten, the holder of most of Weber's remaining personal papers, it becomes clear that Weber gradually came to terms with his own sexual impulses, which he had for decades attempted to repress, during precisely those years when his theoretical defense of the ascetic code began to crumble. Between 1911 and 1914, Weber did have an extramarital relationship with a young woman in Heidelberg, who, for personal considerations, shall remain unnamed.* Although little of any significance is known about this relationship, we can understand much of its origin in

---

I until Marianne's death in 1954. He has also been a confidant of close friends of Max and Marianne, such as Karl and Gertrud Jaspers, Else Jaffé, and Mina Tobler, and has in his possession several bundles of Weber's correspondence, including most of the remaining letters to members of his family and those to the woman identified below as "X." In addition, a letter of 1900 that Frieda Weekly wrote, shortly before the birth of her first child, to her sister, the later Else Jaffé, refers to Max and Marianne's sexual problems: "Woman, have a child, and you are happy! I am so sorry for your Marianna Weber . . . " It is of course possible that what Else had told her sister was only in the context of Weber's breakdown.

* Interview with Eduard Baumgarten in Freiburg (Ebnet), July 13, 1968. Weber had an extensive correspondence with this person, but the most intimate letters were burned. The remainder—over a hundred—are in Professor Baumgarten's possession and bear the following salutations: *"Liebes Kind," "Liebes——chen"* (diminutive of the lady's last name), and *"Liebe Judith"*—not her real first name but that of a character in Gottfried Keller's *Der Grüne Heinrich*, to whom Weber liked to compare her.

terms of the interaction between Weber's gradual release from the "icy hand" of ascetic compulsiveness and the revolution in morals that began to break out in Central Europe before the First World War. The youth movement, the feminist movement, avant-garde currents in the arts, and the intellectuals' overwhelming sense of boredom and restlessness with bourgeois culture were certainly major components of this revolution, but among a few of Weber's friends the immediate stimulus was a somewhat distorted version of the ideas of Freud.

When the proto-Freudian evangel, with its sharp impact on those closest to Max and Marianne, reached Heidelberg in 1907, the educated circles there were already involved in a wave of Bohemianism which, probably for a year or two, had been threatening to engulf the town.* Unconventional mores, which previously had been known only in the artist and student quarter of Munich, began to challenge the accepted morality of the older generation. Gundolf was not the only one at this time to see the shades of Hölderlin, Arnim, and Brentano along the banks of the Neckar. Marianne also saw the new romanticism, but seems to have been reminded as well of the antinomian *Sturm und Drang*:

> New types, spiritually related to the Romantics, again placed in question the "bourgeois" order of thought and life. In the name of personal freedom, they fought for old and new ideals of conduct. The validity of generally binding norms of behavior was doubted; one either sought an "individual law" or denied every "law" so as to let feeling alone prevail over the ever-changing stream of life. Above all, this attack on the received tables of value strove to liberate the ascent of Eros.

---

* *Lebensb.*, pp. 408–12. As usual, Marianne gives few dates. The Freudian clearly arrives on the scene in 1907, and Marianne says the Bohemian culture was there already when he arrived. After a very general description of the Webers' Heidelberg friends between about 1905 and 1910, she starts her discussion of the new subculture with the phrase "about this time."

For it was from him that "law" and "obligation" demanded the most palpable sacrifice. What value could
norms have which so often extinguish the splendor of
blood-warm life, repress natural impulses, and above
all prevent the blossoming and fertility of so many
women? Indeed, law, duty, asceticism, all these notions
stem from the bedevilment of sexuality by a Christianity which one has outgrown. It is better to shape
one's destiny from one's own nature, to let the hot
currents of life storm through and then bear the consequences, than to crawl prudently through the arid
path of the staircase of morality.[51]

Weber's reaction to all this was characteristically ambivalent. Before 1910, he was in general prepared to support
opponents of the authoritarian patriarchalism that had dominated his own home and which he identified with the bureaucratic arrogance and irresponsibility of German politics. He
particularly supported the feminist movement, in which
Marianne played a significant role. But in this period, he
still accepted, with only moderate changes, the ascetic code
of his mother, justified philosophically by the Neo-Kantianism
of the day. Feminism was not, for the Webers, a vehicle to
emancipate women altogether from the bonds of matrimony,
but only from its authoritarian side, which subjugated wives
to their husbands, and from that middle-class Puritanism
which equated morality exclusively with sexual ethics (or,
more precisely, an ethic of sexual unhappiness).[52] Beyond
this they refused to go: "Sensual pleasure could not . . . be
an end in itself, even in the form of an aesthetically sublimated eroticism."[53] Thus, when one of the feminist organizations, popular among the students and supported by
Weber, gave a sympathetic hearing to arguments for a right
to free love and to children out of wedlock, Weber denounced
it: "Crude hedonism and an ethic which would only benefit
the man as goal of the woman! . . . it is simply nonsense."
    Into this already overcharged situation strode, in 1907,
a disciple of Freud, with apparently charismatic powers,

proclaiming sexual communism. As long as marriage continued to exist as a means of caring for the needs of women
and children, he argued, Eros should avoid any contamination
with it. To the contrary, husband and wife should maintain
their independent sexual lives, without jealousy and with as
much freedom and lack of exclusiveness as prevails in their
nonsexual friendships. The impermanence of love relationships and the need for a variety of them should be accepted
as facts of life. As Marianne sums up his argument: "The
sexuality underlying [love] requires many-sided satisfaction.
Its limitation through monogamy "represses" natural instincts
and endangers psychological health. Therefore: away with
the chains which hinder men from experiencing ever new
stimuli; free-love alliances will redeem the world."

The Webers (who obviously had their own sexual problems) were not such bluestockings as to condemn out-of-hand
extramarital relationships, particularly where they were a
kind of desperate refuge from the ruins of a failed marriage,
one continued only for the children's sake: such was the
experience of some of their intimate friends.[54] But such a
principled denial of marital sexuality appeared blasphemous
to them; insofar as people they knew and liked adhered to
the message of the "Freudian," they looked on it as a danger
to civilized morality.

When the gentleman submitted a manuscript to the
Archiv, Weber wrote a detailed, highly emotional letter
rejecting it. He was appalled by what he viewed as a cowardly
surrender of ethical character to impulse, advocated in the
name of a supposedly higher ethic, the ethic of healthy,
unstrained nerves. In the psychoanalytic terms of the later
Freud, Weber was defending the primacy of superego over
id.*

---

* Weber by no means identified the master with his pupil. He
had no doubt "that Freud's ideas can become an interpretive resource
of great significance for whole series of cultural phenomena, especially
in the history of religion and morals. . . . The precondition would be an
exact casuistry [*sic*] of an extent and security which today, contrary to

Following several pages of extremely elaborate invective, frequently centering around some variant of the word "Philistine," Weber reached the core of his argument:

> We can separate all ethics, whatever their material content, into two large groups. One makes principled demands on a man, which he is generally not capable of meeting, except in great high points of his existence, and which direct his *striving* into the infinite: the hero-ethic. The other is modest enough to accept one's everyday "nature" as the maximum demand: "average ethic." It seems to me that only the first category, the "hero-ethic" can call itself idealism, and under this category belong both the ethic of the *old* unbroken Christianity and the Kantian ethic. . . . —But insofar as the "psychiatric ethic" only makes the demand: admit what you "are," what you have desired, it really makes no new demands of an ethical nature. The father confessor and the old-style ministry had in fact no other task . . . than just this, and in Freudian therapy it is precisely a question of the rejuvenation of the confession—with somewhat different technique. Only the goal here is *still* less ethical than was the case with the old indulgence of Tetzel.

This is undoubtedly the kind of thing Wolters meant when he said that for Weber "the test of moral behavior rested in never choosing what corresponded to his own nature and could be accomplished without inner resistance." At the end of the letter, Weber reinforced his point with a reference to Nietzsche. The Freudian appeared to him as a follower

---

all assertions does not exist (though it may in two or three decades): one need only follow all that Freud has altered in a decade, and how frighteningly small, despite everything, his material still is, which is very understandable and *no reproach at all*. But instead of this necessarily specialized work, we now see Freud's adherents, especially Herr Dr. X, turn partly to metaphysical speculation and, what is worse, partly to the question (childish from the standpoint of strict science) . . . can one not construct a *Weltanschauung* of a practical nature from that?" *Baumg.*, pp. 644–5.

of the weakest part of Nietzsche, the "biological embroidery" which that thinker wove around the edge of "his thoroughly moral doctrine"—"the 'morality of excellence.'" Surprisingly, in a letter which was sent not to the author, but "for the instruction of the coeditor, Dr. Edgar Jaffé,"[55] Weber veered sharply in this last paragraph from the furious sarcasm of his earlier criticisms and spoke of the "nobility" of the author's "personal charisma" and of his "acosmic love, which I profoundly respect," urging only that he abandon his professional jargon and bias and dare to be himself: i.e., something better than a follower of the worst side of Nietzsche.[56]

In fact, the letter was sent to Else Jaffé, Edgar's wife,[57] and the sugar at the end was probably inserted to keep a small, but for Weber very important, segment of Heidelberg society from exploding into warring camps. Frieda Gross, the wife of the Dr. Gross who wrote the article, was a close and old friend both of Marianne and of Else; indeed, she introduced the two in 1894 or 1895 when Else was a girl of twenty and Marianne a young bride in Freiburg.* And the relationships between and around these three women— Weber's wife and two of her closest friends—reveal in microcosm the tensions and conflicts which preceded and finally led into Weber's own retreat from asceticism.

We know somewhat more about Else Jaffé than about Frieda Gross, partly because her sister (also named Frieda) married D. H. Lawrence and a fair amount of information about her may be gleaned from his and his wife's published letters and from works on them. Born Else von Richthofen in 1874, the eldest daughter of an impoverished branch of that aristocratic clan (the celebrated flying ace was a distant cousin), she had the kind of cosmopolitan background frequently enjoyed by the more enlightened members of the

---

* Interview with Else Jaffé in Heidelberg, July 15, 1968, concerning her friendship with Max and Marianne Weber. A note from Frau Jaffé to Eduard Baumgarten (*Baumg.*, p. 474, fn. 1) refers to a visit to the Webers in those years.

European aristocracy. Her mother was of French descent, her father's mother, Polish, and she attended a teacher's college in Metz (a French city until 1870). Just before her years there, she attended a finishing school in Freiburg, and it may have been at that time that, perhaps simply out of independence of spirit, she decided to obtain a university education. At any rate, she talked of her plans with her friend, the later Frieda Gross, who was the adopted daughter of Aloys Riehl, a professor of Philosophy at Freiburg. Because of the unusualness of this intellectual drive—there were virtually no women in the German university system at that time—Frieda introduced Else to *her* friend, Marianne Weber, who, because of her husband's academic status, presumably could give inside advice and perhaps persuade him to help.

Through Marianne, with whom Else soon developed what was to be a lifelong friendship, Else did meet Max, and indeed, some years later, in 1898 began working on her doctorate with him in Heidelberg. The topic, suggested by Weber, was "the historical change in the position of the authoritarian parties [in Germany] to labor legislation and the motives for this change."[58] But her mentor's collapse at that time forced Else to transfer to the University of Berlin, where she did most of her work on the thesis. She published it in 1901 and, in 1902, married Edgar Jaffé, an economist with private means who appears to have been a *Privat-Dozent* in Heidelburg. A year later, it was he who purchased the *Archiv* from Heinrich Braun and began, with Weber and Sombart, the new editorial regime of the journal.*

---

* *Lebensb.*, p. 313, and Julie Braun-Vogelstein: *Heinrich Braun, ein Leben für den Sozialismus* (Stuttgart, 1967), pp. 143–4. In its first fifteen years under Braun, the *Archiv* had served as a forum for leftist social scientists like Sombart, who worked within the predominantly conservative *Verein für Sozialpolitik*. Under the new editors, it developed a tone and approach which separated it ever more sharply from the older, more state-oriented German social science and which ultimately led to the establishment of sociology as a discipline completely separate from "political economy." The change in title when the

Until 1909, Weber, who could have related to Else either as a friend of his wife or as the wife of a colleague, never departed from the rather constrained framework of the professor-student relationship.[59] Yet the seeds of what later developed into an uncommonly close friendship were almost certainly planted long before.* It is in this context that we should understand the overheated polemic against Gross, for not only was he the husband of Marianne's old friend, but both Else, who even then was surely more than a star pupil to Weber, and her sister Frieda, whom she introduced to Gross, were markedly influenced by his theories. Indeed the sister, then married to Ernest Weekly, an English academician, was influenced enough to have a brief affair in Munich at this time, which she immortalized in her memoirs.† It may have been this case—it was certainly this *kind* of case —which led Weber to write an angry letter to Marianne, exclaiming:

> These people, who build their relationships on dishonesty, want to campaign against the hypocrisy of convention! But you, I think, may not stand by silently. In my opinion you must risk your friendship to the N's [*sic*] to say to them how you stand, and you cannot stand other than I, even if milder in form.[60]

It would be easy, considering Weber's own sexual problems, to shrug off his acerbic hostility to Gross as sour grapes

---

new editors assumed control in 1904 indicated the direction: the *Archiv für Soziale Gesetzgebung und Statistik* (archive for social legislation and statistics) became the *Archiv für Sozialwissenschaft und Sozialpolitik* (archive for social science and social policy).

* This is Professor Baumgarten's view of the situation, and I cannot find fault with it.

† Frieda Lawrence: *Memoirs and Correspondence* (London, 1961), pp. 89 *ff.*; also p. 160 for Frieda's letter to Edgar Jaffé about the affair. Through Frieda, Gross's Freudianism was later to have a major impact on the history of English literature. D. H. Lawrence, Frieda's second husband from 1912 until his death, probably received his first significant knowledge of Freud through her; Harry T. Moore: *The Intelligent Heart* (New York, 1962), pp. 176–7.

—but that would lose sight of the main problem, which was Weber's rootedness in an ascetic code of self-transcendence, which stood, ethically and psychologically, in absolute opposition to any ideal of harmony between character and instinct. For despite the intellectual exploration of his Calvinist superego in the essays on Protestantism and capitalism, Weber continued in this period to view any concession to his tormentingly rebellious "animality," in his behavior or conscience, as a surrender of his humanity. Indeed, one of the few facts that seems to have been preserved from Weber's written description of his symptoms is that his intermittent sleeplessness from 1898 until his death was based at least partly on a terror of uncontrolled nocturnal ejaculations.* So that a major cause of his breakdown and the painful years of recovery was probably the compounding of his guilt over his father's death by a parallel guilt over his inability to control his sexual impulses.

Nonetheless, Weber was faced with one challenge after another to the ethic he so strenuously defended. In the summer of 1907, his brother Alfred moved from Prague to Heidelberg, where he had an appointment at the university.[61] Instead of settling down close to Max and Marianne, he chose a residence at the other end of the city and did not conceal from them the reason: he had freed himself (in Prague) from

---

* Interview with Eduard Baumgarten, July 20, 1968. Professor Baumgarten obtained his information about the manuscript from Jaspers (*Baumg.*, p. 641; it was left to Karl Jaspers after Weber's death, but was returned to Marianne after 1933 and destroyed by her in 1945). Jaspers, according to a written statement by Baumgarten (in a letter to the author of December 15, 1968) viewed Weber's autopathography as "a *classic* of its kind beyond any comparison in the whole literature known to him, a classic not only because of its ethos of absolute truthfulness (hiding *nothing*) but also as to all its details, which were reported on a level of extreme minuteness and drastic concreteness. He (Jaspers) would not dare to replace this priceless literary loss by a cut-and-dried attempt of recapitulating a a number of points that he could particularly remember.—Questioned, however, on a few details that B. [Baumgarten] himself remembered from other sources, particularly Marianne Weber herself, Prof. J. confirmed the point of that 'terror of uncontrolled nocturnal ejaculations.'"

Helene Weber's influence. They had not. He thus had different convictions, and he and they would be better off living separate lives.[62] About 1911 Alfred and Else Jaffé became close friends, and soon thereafter, intimate.*

In the *Lebensbild*, Marianne quotes from four letters in which her husband defends his views on sexual ethics (among them the one cited, where he urges Marianne to make her opposition clear at the risk of destroying a friendship[63]). But gradually, Weber's hostility to an ethic of sensual pleasure weakened. One of the first signs was a quite romantic appreciation of the Pisan *Camposanto:* "How childlike and joyful it all is and how innocent and unaffected in all its artful balance."[64] Another was a gradual modification of his attitude toward sexual liberty. Because so many of their friends were involved in one kind of sexual problem or another, he came to understand that "It can happen that externally imposed renunciations cripple the spirits of [some] men . . . that they thereby become small, pharisaic, and bitter. In such cases it is better for them to sin."

Perhaps both of these factors—the sensuous appreciation of the southern landscape and a more sympathetic interest in the problems of others—merged during a trip into Italy that he and Marianne undertook with the Jaffés in 1910.[65] Between Trieste and Venice, Marianne had to return to Germany to speak before a women's organization; Max continued with the Jaffés and, for the first time, allowed his professorial manner to drop with Else. Also for the first time, these two, who rose considerably earlier than Edgar, were

---

* The relationship was widely known; a reference to it appeared after Jaffé's death in D. H. Lawrence's letters. The earliest suggestion of it that I am aware of is in a letter from Gundolf to Curtius dated November 1910: "I had splendid conversations with Alfred Weber and Frau Jaffé—you also must become acquainted with these two noble human beings." (Gundolf: *Briefwechsel mit Herbert Steiner und Ernst Robert Curtius*, p. 177.) A second indication appeared in 1912, when Else was able to obtain the use of Alfred Weber's flat near Munich for her sister and D. H. Lawrence after their honeymoon. (Moore: *The Intelligent Heart*, p. 168.)

able to spend some time alone with each other. (Previously Marianne, herself much closer to Else than Max, had sat in on all their discussions.) A friendship developed between them which, though interrupted by the Jaffés' move to Munich in 1911, was to be of great value to Weber in the last two years of his life, spent largely in that city. In fact, Baumgarten views the Venetian experience itself as crucial for some of the most significant aspects of Weber's thought in his last decade.*

But most significant of all was the gradual change in Weber's theory of the relationship between asceticism and Christian morality. As remarked above, crucial to the formation of the concept of charisma in Weber's mature work was the separation of a Christian ethic of compassion from his mother's Calvinist asceticism. In 1907, in the letter on Gross, Weber still saw "the ethic of the *old* unbroken Christianity" in terms of the Kantian ethic of ascetic heroism. The only alternative was some form of self-indulgent hedonism, which he condemned out of hand. By 1910, a dramatic change had occurred in Weber's view of the moral alternatives. Weber then presented ancient Christianity as specifically mystical and saw its tradition as continued in Greek and Russian Orthodoxy. To this mysticism Calvinist asceticism was opposed in the same way that *Gesellschaft* was to *Gemeinschaft*. The hubris of transcendent, Faustian man, dominating his own nature and the world's, had given way to a serious consideration of Christian mysticism as an alternate mode of existence.

In the following year, 1911, began Weber's relationship to the young lady we shall call "X." It lasted in full intensity until 1914, and on a less passionate level until his death in 1920. During the prewar period, as has been shown, his movement away from asceticism and toward admiration for aristocratic and mystical modes of charisma benefitted

---

* *Baumg.*, p. 667: "In Venice, a revolution occurred in him equivalent in extent to that of Albrecht Dürer."

from his intellectual companionship with Sombart, Gundolf, George, and Lukacs. But in 1913 and 1914, an additional personal experience enhanced Weber's understanding of the anti-Victorian currents then transforming European culture. On spring vacations near the North Italian lakes, he encountered colonies of outcast Bohemians which, though more political, were similar, in their rejection of the received morality, to those advocates of free love in Heidelberg whom Weber had fought in 1907. Anarchists, communists, and vegetarians, as well as utopian adherents of Freud, sought refuge in the area and tried to live openly according to their ideals. Though poverty and all sorts of pressures and conflicts beset them, they experienced an adventure of the spirit which Marianne characterizes by the same word Max used to describe charisma: *"ausseralltägliches"* ("extraordinary," or, when delatinized, "out of the everyday routine"). Almost certainly as a result of his loosening up in the intervening years, Weber's response to these people was far from the severity of his earlier Kantianism. He immersed himself in their problems, and, particularly when it came to old acquaintances, gave all the personal and legal support he could muster.*

One such acquaintance, whose son Weber reluctantly tried to free from German military duty by changing his citizenship, was probably Franziska Gräfin zu Reventlow, a legendary figure of the Munich Bohème.† Another ac-

---

* "Brotherly readiness to help and the joy of combat are his motives—his reward: thankful friendship and the enriching insight into the singular world of people with quite different perspectives than his own and into the consequences of their acts"; *Lebensb.*, p. 532.

† In Weber's letters quoted in the *Lebensbild*, he refers to her only as "the Gräfin." But he mentions that she is the author of a novel on the Munich *George-Kreis* in which Graf Andrian and herself are prominent characters. Franziska Gräfin zu Reventlow was close to the *George-Kreis* during the time Leopold Andrian was active in it (roughly 1895–1900) and did write a novel about it. (See Bernard Zeller, Werner Volke, and Gerhard Hay, eds.: *Stefan George 1868–1968, der Dichter und Sein Kreis* (Stuttgart, 1968), pp. 176–7.) She also had a male child out of wedlock and in 1909 moved to Ascona, a Swiss town five miles

quaintance to whom Weber volunteered his legal talents, and with whom he developed a friendship that lasted at least into the war years, was that same old friend of Marianne's whose husband had caused so much trouble in 1907: Frieda Gross.*

Given her husband's views on sexual matters, which he appears to have carried into practice,† it is understandable that Frieda developed an affair of her own. Her lover was a Swiss anarchist named Karl, and her legal troubles arose when, because of her cohabitation with a man who, when he was not in prison, was unemployed, a suit was instituted to prevent her from living with her children. Weber fought in the courts for over a year for Frieda's right to these children, all the time arguing with her that her case had little chance unless she and Karl established separate residences.[66]

Karl, the anarchist lover, however, seems to have stimulated not only Weber's human sympathy but his intellectual curiosity as well, in a way that would probably have been impossible half a dozen years earlier. In 1907, Weber had paired the ethic of ancient Christianity with the Kantian one, in the sense that both demanded heroic transcendence (and, where necessary, repression) of one's animality. In 1910, he had associated ancient Christianity with acosmic love and a sense of meaningfulness based on such love— the mystical antithesis of all-mastering asceticism. By 1914 he was perceiving hitherto unsuspected connections between that same fundamentally Christian mysticism of Tolstoy

---

from Italy, on the Lago Maggiore, most of which is in Northern Italy. It was she who coined the ironical term *"Weihen-Stephan"* for George, which Weber used in 1915. For these and other details of this remarkable woman's life, see *Süddeutsche Zeitung*, July 27, 1968, p. 17, and H. E. Schröder: *Klages, die Jugend* (Bonn, 1966), pp. 254–304.

* *Baumg.*, p. 491, reveals that the woman to whom Marianne gave the pseudonym "Dora" was in reality Frieda Gross.

† The reference in one of Weber's letters, excerpted in the *Lebensbild* (pp. 422–3), to "K's girl friend," whose "action is an assertion of her self-respect in view of the freedom which her husband took for himself," probably signifies Frieda and her lover Karl.

and eroticism. Frieda's lover wavered between the mystical and the erotic view of life, just as a side of Weber himself did in these years. Possessed by a "religious belief" in the future liberation of Eros (Weber wrote to Marianne), Karl "keeps waiting for the moment of great inner illumination, when he will do something quite great and prophetic. . . . Furthermore, he would like to bring about complete goodness and neighborly love through acosmism of eroticism. I had already told [Frieda] why that wouldn't work, and she admits that the logical consequence would be Tolstoian asceticism, to which he has always tended."*

The "interchangeability" of eroticism and mysticism, and the function of eroticism as an escape from the skeletal coldness of reified ascetic rationality into "the core of the truly living," was one of Weber's most fascinating insights in his essay of 1916. Weber may or may not have been aware of how his changing ideas on the relationship between Christian ethics and asceticism mirrored the profound changes in his ultimate value code that accompanied his friendship with Else Jaffé, his affair with "X," and his insights into Karl's ambivalence between eroticism and mysticism. But that the mirror, the changes, and the personal involvements were there, is not subject to question.

This is far from saying that Weber completely abandoned his ascetic code after the experience in Venice. Indeed, after his first effort, in 1910, at an organized Sunday-afternoon discussion with friends in his new house did not produce the desired intellectual fireworks, he revealed his still pow-

---

* *Lebensb.*, pp. 534–5. The phrase "Tolstoian asceticism" is misleading, except in the sense that Weber is emphasizing the renunciation of fleshly desires which is, for Tolstoy as for most mystics, a physical precondition for the acquisition of mystical grace or illumination. Weber makes clear in his sociology of religion that, for the mystic, this kind of asceticism is ethically neutral, indifferent in the eyes of the deity, whereas for the true ascetic, worldly or otherworldly, it is a spiritual obligation (in Christianity, a part of the punishment for original sin), and with this ethical force behind it, it much more readily becomes an end in itself. *W.u.G.*, pp. 424–7.

erful Calvinism when he burst out to Marianne: "Never again—unbearable and immoral (*sic!*) to have to talk for the sake of talking."[67] But he was certainly more receptive than previously to anti-modernist, erotic, mystical, and aristocratic views that were incompatible both with this inherited asceticism and often with each other.

In general, he tried to keep these conflicting values in separate compartments of his life. Thus, he never breathed a word of his affair with "X" to Marianne, and wherever his passion went, he never seems to have stopped treating her with a tender chivalric consideration. In fact, his unconsummated love for Marianne at times appears similar to the acosmic mystical love he mentioned in 1910 and analyzed at length in his sociology of religion. In 1908, he speaks of such love (in a letter to Marianne) in terms of Tolstoy, and shortly before the end of his life, of Quakerism.*

But at least twice in his later work he seems to be making oblique reference to his affair and how it related to his feeling for Marianne. In the 1916 discussion of eroticism and mysticism, he wrote:

> As the knowing love of the mature man relates to the passionate sentimentality of the youth, so does the mortal seriousness of this intellectualized eroticism relate to the chivalric troubadour; compared with the latter it affirms precisely and consciously the naturalness of the sexual sphere, as the creative power incarnate.[68]

And it was probably again a reflection on his own experience when he wrote in *Politik als Beruf* (1919):

> We will rarely find that a man whose love turns from one woman to another does not feel the need to legiti-

---

* *Lebensb.*, p. 428. *R.S.I*, p. 563. The dedication of *R.S.I* to Marianne is a quote from this presentation of the Quaker ethic: *"bis ins Pianissimo des höchsten Alters."* It suggests that in Quakerism Weber found a meeting point between, on the one side, the mystic sense of acosmic love and of a meaningful life cycle, and on the other, the sense of mutual responsibility demanded by the ethical rationalism that he drew from his ascetic heritage and Kantian training.

mize this for himself by saying: she was unworthy of my love, or she has disappointed me or something of the sort. This is an attitude that, with a profound lack of chivalry, adds a fancied "legitimacy" to the plain fact that he no longer loves her and that the woman has to bear it. By virtue of this legitimation, the man claims a right for himself and besides causing the misfortune seeks to put her in the wrong.*[69]

This *Motiv* of chivalry and compassion appears elsewhere in Weber's last decade than in his more intimate friendships. In 1915, Ernst Troeltsch, the theologian and old friend of Weber, who from 1910 shared with him the old Fallenstein house on the Neckar, was the administrator of a military hospital in Heidelberg, and Weber, in charge of a number of such hospitals, was his superior. Weber's policy was to permit Germans to visit wounded French prisoners of war. But public opinion was opposed. Troeltsch gave in to this pressure and forbade such visits, whereupon Weber openly denounced the prohibition as a "wretched case of chauvinism," "un-German," "dishonorable," "bourgeois cowardice" (*"Bürgerfeigheit"*), and broke off relations with his neighbor.[70]

Though the courage, independence, and passion of this kind of stand were rooted in fundamentally conservative, aristocratic values, Weber's defiance of constituted authority and his willingness to help almost any underdog were frequently misconstrued by young radicals who hoped to use his charisma to transform the rather stodgy social-democratic left. Shortly before World War I, when Lukacs, with his friend Ernst Bloch, was turning increasingly toward an apocalyptic revolutionary socialism, he looked to Weber "to rescue socialism from this wretched relativism in which it has been buried by this Franck and his group [South Ger-

---

* Unlike *Wissenschaft als Beruf*, which Weber allowed to be published from a stenographic copy of his lecture, *Politik als Beruf* was thoroughly revised and expanded by Weber before publication.

man revisionists]."[71] Weber's conversion to militant patriotism on the outbreak of war was a profound disappointment to these men, but his renewed hostility after a year or so to the mindless chauvinism of his contemporaries gradually restored his reputation among student socialists and adherents of the youth movement, then looking for leadership in their opposition to bourgeois society and the war. When Weber finally poured out his hostility to the incompetence and irresponsibility of the imperial regime at the Burg Lauenstein conference in 1917, a youth movement rally addressed by a host of maverick intellectuals,* he struck unexpected chords of response. For Theodor Heuss, the later President of the Federal Republic of Germany,

> These few days in the picturesque old castle received their significance from the force of the accusations which Max Weber cast against the Kaiser and his milieu. He openly challenged the latter to indict him for *lèse-majesté* so that he could then invite people [leading civilian and military members of the imperial regime] to testify as witnesses under oath.—It was a genuine explosion, which frightened some of the audience. (Ernst Krieck, the later leading "pedagogue" of National Socialism, as diligent as he was tedious, implored me to calm Weber down; the whole meeting might be broken up by the police. I answered only: "Can you put out a volcano with a glass of water.")[72]

The magnificent naïveté of the incident inspired Heuss to wonder if Weber was not actually a "secret Romantic," despite his public contempt for such types in German politics.[73] Actually, Weber's eruption had its source in an aristocratic contempt for the characterless "plebeian" politicians of the imperial regime.[74] As we have seen, before the war Weber saw aristocratic charisma in anti-modernist terms, as a glorious anachronism, the political equivalent of what

---

* Meinecke, Jaffé, Sombart, and Tönnies were among them; *Lebensb.*, p. 642.

mystical charisma meant in the religious sphere. After 1916, Weber retained this anti-modernist stance only in his sociology of religion and his personal philosophy: he had adapted his notion of aristocratic charisma to the limitations and potentialities of modern politics and ascetic rationalism. But the youth tended to respond as Heuss did, more to the man than to his message or conscious intent.

Drawing on his memories of Weber before and during the war, the economist Edgar Salin (then an adherent of George) has written:

> The impact was exculsively the impact of his person. Weber would surely have viewed it as a complete misunderstanding of his theory of the forms of rule if anyone had described him as a "charismatic leader"—he didn't want to be that and he wasn't. But he did possess a charisma completely his own, and it radiated from him whether he had gathered colleagues and friends of his own age around him, or was speaking with Gundolf and his young friends, or was discussing with the rising generation of revolutionary socialists: with Ernst Bloch—their prophet; Georg von Lukacs—their philosopher; and Emil Lederer—their economist.[75]

In 1917–18, partly in response to his appearance at the Burg Lauenstein, a new generation of socialist and pacifist students in Heidelberg began gathering around Weber. Their most prominent representative was the poet Ernst Toller, who was to be the military commander, in 1919, of the short-lived Bavarian Council Republic and one of the most important playwrights of the Weimar period. Toller, whose touching faith at this time in a pacifist revolution later emerged in his play *Masse-Mensch*, argued that the war could and should be stopped by demonstrations and propaganda urging the troops to refuse to fight—he was probably inspired by the Bolshevik Revolution of a few months earlier, which had been preceded by mass desertions from the Russian army. Weber opposed him: Toller's plan, if successful, would only break the nation's will to exist. As we have seen, Weber had no faith in the possibility of a meaningful social revolution.* His great fear was that a socialist experiment would only further weaken the German economy and that after its failure, foreign capital would dominate the nation. The ultimate result of such a disaster would be an unprecedented growth of chauvinism, a resurgence of the witless Right.[76]

Thus he argued against Toller that the best hope for the peace movement would be for the war to devour itself by a military standoff, for no nation to gain from the war. Nonetheless, Toller's group continued to look for leadership from Weber and asked him to agree to an appeal which demanded, according to Marianne, "among other things the rule of Eros in the world and the abolition of poverty."[77] Weber refused, finding a frightening lack of realism in the program; his offer to debate the issue with the group was rejected. But when Toller and his group were arrested for advocating a general strike, Weber requested a hearing before the court and obtained Toller's release.[78] Later, when Toller was arrested for his part in the Bavarian Council Republic, Weber again defended him in court, describing his naïve unrealism as an ethic of convictions (the opposite in Weber's theory to an ethic of responsibility) which unintentionally enmeshed him in the hysteria of the masses; the scholar pleaded in the poet's defense that "God made him a politician in a fit of anger."†

Political courage, a high sense of personal honor, and

---

* For the psychological background of his skepticism see above, pp. 223–6.

† *Lebensb.*, p. 711. Other examples of youth groups looking to Weber for leadership include a discussion with representatives of the youth movement at Burg Lauenstein (*Lebensb.*, pp. 644–5) and a pacifist group in Frankfurt shortly before the war's end (p. 648). A group of radicals around the poet Paul Ernst and the Socialist Otto Neurath, who wanted to establish rural communes, seem to have obtained Weber's most serious consideration, though Marianne does not say they sought his leadership. It was characteristic that Weber accepted as meaningful a radical perspective based on the cultivation of communal ties within small groups. *Lebensb.*, pp. 726–7.

the charismatic attraction that Weber's passionate brilliance exerted on those near him had characterized him even before his breakdown. But what repeatedly led young radicals such as Lukacs and Toller to mistake him for a potential revolutionary leader was the break in Weber's rational asceticism around 1910, that sharp split in his values which the nightmare vision of the "iron cage" had anticipated as early as 1905. Though Weber's political perspective never swerved from the line of ascetic modernity and its plagues, and thus clearly excluded the option of revolutionary socialism, the changed personal morality and intellectual passions of his last decade threw increasingly into question that ethic of transcendence, self-renunciation, and mastery which had for over a century served Europe as the moral backbone of bourgeois society and which had earlier been the core of his personality and work. It was probably this self-questioning and the attendant interest in new gods— Tolstoy, Nietzsche, and George: in short, the gods of charisma—which induced in Toller the misconception that Weber might actually come out for the universal rule of the god of love.

Max Weber never had an opportunity to work out unambiguously the final direction of his thought. Nineteen months after the war's end, while revising his *Religionssoziologie* for publication, he was stricken with a severe lung infection. In Munich, on the fourteenth of June, 1920, after several days of delirium and in the midst of a thunderstorm, he died.

CONCLUSION

Weber and German History

Weber's intellectual development, based though it was on his personal background, problems, and experiences, nonetheless merged at certain crucial points with the history of his epoch: in his plea for a liberal imperialism in 1895, in his anti-modernist interests before World War I, and in his impassioned defense of political sobriety against the apocalyptic hopes of German youth during the turmoil at the end of the war. But the most fundamental link between Weber and his age—and ours—lay not in these specific connections but rather in the underlying challenge which the ethical assumptions of bourgeois civilization began to experience during his lifetime. In large measure, Weber's stubborn demand for value neutrality was a device to conceal this challenge, which his breakdown had forced him to take up and which was the precondition both for his recovery and for the breakthroughs of his last decade.

There are of course points at which any scholar must use a scalpel to keep his own passions from prejudicing the results of an investigation. But Weber, like most latter-day celebrants of Weberian value-neutrality, seems to have been frequently unaware of how profoundly a "scientific" view of a problem may be shaped by basic psychological predispositions about what is possible and what, desirable. His rejection of Gross's, admittedly distorted, Freudianism, for example, was based, on the one hand, on a contemptuously hostile rejection of the man's sexual ethic as "hedonistic" and "Philistine," and on the other, on Gross's lack of value-neutrality. Would value-neutrality have been an issue if Gross had accepted Weber's own ascetic ethic of heroic transcendence?

In fact, most of Weber's important work is infused with his values, and in his last decade there is a rather desperate effort, in the purely personal sphere, to reach that harmony between libidinal drives and rational ethics which he had earlier seen as weakness and which, haunted by the experience of his breakdown, he still saw as impossible in the sphere of public life. The development of Weber's thought thus appears to be intelligible only in terms of the history of values and of the epochal psychological types which give rise to such values.

A model of virility to those who encountered him personally, Weber behaved in his formal functions—as husband, professor, and politician—as a cripple for most of his mature life. In his functioning outside of these formalized areas of life, however, he revealed a potency that was often uncontrollable, both in his tormented sexual life and in his explosions of personal and political wrath. Like Sombart, the organized routines of life appeared so arid, so reified to him that he could come to terms with them neither on the marriage bed nor in his professional life. Unlike Sombart, the force of his will and character enabled him to avoid any total immersion in the neo-romantic, irrational currents that National Socialism was later to exploit.

To be sure, Weber did hold official positions subsequent to his breakdown: as a hospital administrator during the war and then, for about a year before his death, as a professor in Vienna and Munich. But his hostility to the rules of institutionalized structures made his political talents, which were great, permanently inaccessible to his nation. Even after his brilliant wartime polemics against the imperial system had brought him national prominence, Weber's refusal to work with or flatter professional politicians led the German Democratic Party, which he had helped found in November 1918 and which sorely needed his kind of leadership, to place him so low on their list of Reichstag candidates that he withdrew his name in disgust.[1] And it was a doctor who had worked under Weber during the war who compared him to the Greek god Dionysos.

We should not dismiss this comparison lightly. For the notion of charisma, as Weber defines it in *Wirtschaft und Gesellschaft* is indeed Dionysian. In fact, in its most extreme formulation,[2] charisma stands opposed to ascetic rationalization similarly to the way Dionysos stands opposed to Zarathustra in the work of Nietzsche; certainly, in Weber's sociology of religion, Dionysos epitomizes orgiastic cults of self-intoxication, primitive anticipations of the mystical belief in divine possession, while Zarathustra is the bearer of a "struggle against the magical cult of intoxication and for belief in his own divine mission"—a step toward ethical prophecy and ascetic rationalism.[3] But if Dionysos is a mythic metaphor for charisma, a most illuminating side of this metaphor is this god's significance for women. Weber recognized that Dionysian and other orgiastic cults usually promoted the emancipation of women and he also recognized the importance of women in "pneumatic" sects. Nietzsche, too, posited a relationship between Dionysos and women, and where he did so he emphatically associated the god with symbols which suggest Weber's notion of mystical charisma:

> Apollo stands before me as the transfiguring genius of the *principii individuationis*, through which only the appearance of redemption is attainable, while under the mystic joyful cry of Dionysos the spell of individuation is exploded and the path to the mothers of Being, to the innermost core of things lies open. . . . In Dionysian art and its tragic symbolism the same nature addresses us . . . "Be as I am!" Under the ceaseless change of phenomena, the eternally creative primal mother, eternally compelling to existence, eternally satisfying herself in this change of phenomena.[4]

This book is not the place to investigate at any length the significance of masculine and feminine symbolism in the culture of Imperial Germany. But we have repeatedly encountered the problem of personal rebellion in that authoritarian, bureaucratic, overstructured society, and on the basis of our knowledge of Weber some preliminary speculation on the subject seems appropriate. For there has been a widespread tendency among intellectual historians to try to deal with the anti-modernist currents of pre-Nazi Germany from the standpoint of an anti-ideological liberalism, i.e., to see them as evidence of a nationwide pathological propensity for false metaphysics and primitive nationalism, to which certain high-minded pragmatic types, like Weber, were fortunately immune. That this assumption requires radical revision should by now be evident. An examination of the broader implications of Weber's case may clarify the direction such a revision might take.

The most striking part of Weber's work after 1910 on politics and religion is the significance of charisma, simply because it seems to defy any logical classification as to origin or historical relationship to the dominant "progress" toward rationalization. To be sure, Weber's concretization of the anti-modernist form of charisma in atavistic feudal aristocratic and mystical life styles frees him from any accusation that his idea could be used to justify fascism. But certainly these embodiments are not identical with charisma per se, which seems so protean in Weber's original definition as to elude classification: berserk warriors, shamans, prophets, leaders of great expeditions, they all share the power to attract others to their cause and to break through existing structures of authority. But what is the source of this power?

Nietzsche's association of Dionysos with the primal mother is an interesting starting point. For if we examine carefully the ideas Weber associates with charisma, we find a number of rather archaic feminine characteristics among them. Weber presents charisma as synonymous with *pneuma*, the "breath" of the Holy Spirit.* And the common quality linking charisma and the Holy Spirit is the feminine, indeed, maternal, quality of divine grace. Furthermore, the secular notion of grace (*Anmut*) is integral to Weber's notion of aristocratic charisma even in his more ascetic, post-1914 understanding of aristocracy.[5] Another noteworthy relationship is the one Weber perceives in his comments of 1910, between Slavic mysticism and Tönnies's concept of *Gemeinschaft*. Though in Weber's presentation, *Gemeinschaft* signifies the bonds of brotherhood, Tönnies saw the mother-child relationship as its basis. It is also notable that the beginning of Weber's ethical hegira was Calvinism, of all the Protestant churches the one most closed to the feminine breath of the Holy Spirit, the one in which grace was hardest to come by and charisma the least present. The end was Quakerism, a religion in which infusion by the Holy Spirit regularly induced spontaneous discourse by church members and grace and charisma were abundant. What does all this add up to?

Before his breakdown, Weber was, as the son of his Calvinist mother, pledged to contradictory tasks that ended in his self-destruction. He was to defend his mother, which not only meant rebelling against his father but also, in the sublimated sphere of politics, imposed on him a radical nationalist revolt against the larger authoritarian structure which his father epitomized: the rigidly bureaucratized German Empire. But he was also to be so much the master of his baser emotions and drives that he could, like the Puritans he was later to analyze, demonstrate his purity by his unremitting ascetic activity, by his capacities as a Calvinist work-slave. Thus would he win the grace of Helene Weber, who in this respect was no more feminine than

---

* *R.S.III*, pp. 429–30: "Pneuma, as charisma and indicator of the proof of an exemplary state of grace . . ." *R.S.I*, p. 550: "the actual mystical or pneumatic, religiously charismatic quest for salvation of the religious virtuoso . . ."

Jehovah. Between the too-successful revolt against the father and the Pyrrhic victory over his libido, Weber mastered himself into a sanatorium.

But his discovery that his inherited ethic led to collapse coincided with a similar discovery by his generation and the one following. With the prospects of the political sublimation of repressed instinct brought to an end by the victories of European liberalism between 1860 and 1870, the mortal hostility of the bourgeois superego for libidinal impulse—the psychological underpinning of the Victorian ethic of transcendence—would have to cease or all Europe would become a madhouse. This perception was the mainspring of the revolution in morals before World War I, which took shape in the German youth movement, the feminist movements, *Lebensphilosophie,* and the rapid spread of Bohemianism among artists and intellectuals.

As we have seen, around 1910, Weber personally participated in this liberation of Eros; indeed, he may have been spared a repetition of his earlier collapse by it (Marianne mentions relapses in the early months of 1908 and 1909[6]). In point of fact, his extended celebration of charisma as an "emotional life-force" antagonistic to the dreary construction of the "iron cage" coincided with his coming to terms with his own emotional life-force: his erotic faculties. Through this surrender to "animality" Weber was at last able to obtain from a woman he loved the grace of sexual release. What charisma represented then, in Weber as in German culture, was the resurrection of the long-suppressed deities of the libido, of femininity, Eros, and community, of blind passion as well as compassion. The gift of grace was the grace that comes from accepting, rather than mutilating, one's nature.

The absolute antagonism between charisma and *Alltag* was a reflection of the total inability of the organized structure of German society to accommodate to these forces. Parsons's theory of the connection between this overformalized structure and the complete irrationalism of the neo-romantic currents around it,[7] points to the basic flaw in the German Empire: it was dominated by the Prussian ruling class—a bureaucratic military caste with aristocratic pretensions. Because this caste had created a modern rationalized state before industrialization and before the Bismarckian unification, and had no intention of giving up its control, there was neither the need nor the possibility of any serious bourgeois initiative in political or social matters after 1870. But precisely because its aristocratic pretensions were fake, it totally lacked that charisma and grace which Weber correctly saw in the genuine feudal aristocracy.* In France, for example, as Jesse Pitts has pointed out, the aristocratic notion of "prowess," similar in some ways to charisma, spread a leaven of aesthetic individualism through bourgeois culture, which both slowed the onset of economic rationalism and provided a generally accepted code by which the rebels, Bohemians, even anarcho-syndicalists of the prewar period could link up to the oldest cultural traditions of the land.† The paternalistic, bureaucratic ethos of the German feudal caste, however, was incapable of serving as any such model for the libidinally rebellious generation of 1910.

---

* Ernst Nolte sees the problem in a similar light in *Three Faces of Fascism* (New York, Chicago, San Francisco, 1966), p. 299.

† "Prowess depends upon an opportunity and a capacity which cannot be predicted. It depends upon a gift of grace (*sic!*) which can be withheld . . . In French prowess there is little of the Protestant "calling" with its rationalization, systematization and reliability of individual behavior.

. . . In a relatively stable society the best fields for prowess must be those where unpredictability of performance can be high without endangering social order—for example, limited warfare (preferably in colonial lands); conspiracies that never succeed; contemplative religion; missionary activities; gratuitous personal relationships (love, friendship, *politesse*); craftsmanship; and elegant selection and use of consumer goods. . . . prowess is intuitive, intensely individual, and unpredictable . . . The French do not have the cult of the tragic surmounting of self that is characteristic of the Germans. Prowess is above all the discovery of the predetermined harmony, rather than the imposition of the individual will.

Jesse R. Pitts: "Change in Bourgeois France," in Stanley Hoffmann, ed.: *In Search of France* (Cambridge, Mass., 1963), pp. 242, 244.

Early novels of both Thomas Mann and his brother Heinrich—*Buddenbrooks, Death in Venice,* and *Professor Unrat*—all substantiate this point. There is simply no meeting place between the instinctual needs of the academic and commercial bourgeoisie and their everyday reality. Thomas Buddenbrooks turns his back on his early love, devotes himself to the family grain trade, and is ultimately devoured by it. His musically gifted son, Hanno, who understands Thomas's plight and is totally estranged from his business and society, dies of typhoid before reaching maturity. In *Death in Venice,* Aschenbach, his moral will destroyed by his secret passion for a fourteen-year-old boy, can only die of cholera. Raat, through his love for the Blue Angel, becomes Unrat, the fool, the child. The absolute antithesis in these novels between inner harmony and the empty striving of everyday life may have been derived from Schopenhauer, but it reflects the opposition between the clattering dullness of their society and the sudden outpouring of instinct before the war. It was in reaction to such a division that Weber, who confronted the problem in his own person, wrote of the "unforced and unbroken animality and instinctiveness" of aristocratic play, which stood "beyond any division of 'intellectual' and 'material,' of 'spiritual' and 'physical.'" Such was the grace of "charisma."

A SKETCH OF
THE PERTINENT
BIBLIOGRAPHY
ON MAX WEBER

In 1927, FRIEDRICH MEINECKE wrote that Marianne Weber's biography of her husband "necessarily broadened into a family history, because Max Weber can only be completely understood on the basis of his family." Somewhat twisting the framework of Goethe's *Iphigenie auf Tauris*, Meinecke cast Weber's mother in the role of an Iphigenia and added that ". . . in Max Weber himself, we can see an Orestes, when we learn how, out of love for his mother, he intervened ruthlessly against his own father and then shortly afterward was shattered by his sudden death." Not content to leave the significance of such classical conflict at the purely personal level, Meinecke then went on to briefly describe the antagonism of Max Weber toward his father as representing "the historical opposition of two generations."*

In view of Weber's own acknowledgment that "the evaluative ideas which dominate the investigator and his age" determine "the object of investigation," it would seem

---

* Meinecke's review of the *Lebensbild* first appeared in the *Historische Zeitschrift*, Vol. 135 (1927), and has been reprinted in René König and Johannes Winckelmann, eds.: *Max Weber zum Gedächtnis* (Köln, Opladen, 1963) (*Sonderheft 7* of *Kölner Zeitschrift für Soziologie und Sozialpsychologie*), pp. 143–7.

to be only logical to ask further what relation these personal and historically bound frameworks have to his theoretical work as a whole, and whether, indeed, that sociologist's values stop short, as he would like us to believe, of molding the allegedly value-free parts of his work as well: his scientific methodology, and the results of his inquiries into the universal *Drang* of rationalization in politics, economics, and religion. Thus, Meinecke's line of thought suggests that Weber's theoretical work requires, for a proper understanding of it, a threefold relativization: first, it implies that Weber's theoretical work is based significantly, perhaps more than he would himself admit, on the man's own values; second, that these values are derived from Max Weber's historical position in a particular generation of German society; and third, that both the values which direct the theoretical work and the historical situation of Max Weber are intimately related to certain classical familial antagonisms.

There are excellent reasons why, until less than a decade ago, the vast literature on Max Weber had largely ignored the approach suggested by Meinecke's seminal comments. To be sure, during the Weimar republic, a few extremely insightful studies were made of the underlying value assumptions which informed Weber's sociology. In particular, Weber's Munich lecture, "Science as a Profession," inspired a brilliant spate of attacks and defenses by Erich Kahler, Arthur Salz, Ernst Troeltsch, and Max Scheler.[*] And Albert Salomon in 1925, and Karl Löwith and Christoph Steding in the early '30's published important studies of Weber which related his values to some of the crucial themes of

---

[*] Erich von Kahler: *Der Beruf der Wissenschaft* (Berlin, 1920); Arthur Salz: *Für die Wissenschaft gegen die Gebildeten unter ihren Verächtern* (Munich, 1921); Ernst Troeltsch: *"Die Revolution in der Wissenschaft," Schmollers Jahrbuch,* XLV (1921), pp. 1001–30; Max Scheler: *"Weltanschauungslehre, Soziologie und Weltanschauungssetzung," Kölner Vierteljahreshefte für Soziologie und Sozialwissenschaften,* Jahrg. 2, No. 1, reprinted in Scheler: *Gesammelte Werke* (Bern, 1963), Vol. 6.

Western history.* But the kind of approach that would have taken up Meinecke's suggestion of Weber as Orestes and examined the theoretical work from this perspective was excluded by several considerations: the fact that many members of his family were alive and professionally active (e.g., his wife and his brother Alfred); that Weber's *Nachlass*, without which it would be impossible to check on and supplement the voluminous biography that Marianne Weber wrote of her husband,† was her property, and that she was

---

* Albert Salomon: "*Max Weber,*" *Die Gesellschaft,* 1925, pp. 131–53; Karl Löwith: "*Max Weber und Karl Marx,*" *Archiv für Sozialwissenschaft und Sozialpolitik,* Vol. 67, 1932, Nos. 1 and 2, reprinted in Löwith: *Gesammelte Abhandlungen* (Stuttgart, 1963), pp. 1–67; Christoph Steding: *Politik und Wissenschaft bei Max Weber* (Breslau, 1932). The first two works are a world apart from the third both as to style and content. Salomon's and Löwith's essays are well reasoned and focus on the themes of charisma and rationalization as Weber's framework for viewing western history. Steding's is loose and in spots given to absurd generalizations, but includes some magnificent insights into Weber's identification with charismatic Old Testament prophets and seventeenth-century Puritans, and a brief but fascinating comparison of *The Protestant Ethic and the Spirit of Capitalism* with Mann's *Buddenbrooks* (Steding, pp. 18–19).

† Marianne Weber: *Max Weber, ein Lebensbild* (1926). I have used the 1950 reprint, published in Heidelberg. Wolfgang Mommsen, in the course of examining the *Nachlass,* discovered a number of factual inaccuracies in such things as the dating of letters and sometimes in Marianne Weber's quotations from letters and other unpublished documents. (See his *Max Weber und die deutsche Politik* [Tübingen, 1959], p. viii. Certainly Marianne's presentation of her husband's attitude to Stefan George is much more beneficent than Edgar Salin's in *Um Stefan George* (München, 1954), pp. 107–10. *Cf.* with the *Lebensbild,* pp. 498–507 *passim.* Indeed, according to Eduard Baumgarten, one contemporary critic of the *Lebensbild,* apparently on the basis of its sentimentality, said that it was historically valuable because "it put in a more favorable light the old and much-underestimated legal practice of immolating widows." But the publication of Weber's early letters (*Jugendbriefe* [Tübingen, 1936]), of various documents from the *Nachlass* in Eduard Baumgarten's *Max Weber, Werk und Person* (Tübingen, 1964), of a collection of *Nekrologe,* reviews of the *Lebensbild* and personal memoirs by those who knew Weber well, in *Max Weber zum Gedächtnis* (René König and Johannes Winckel-

unlikely to provide access to it to those who, from the academic standards of the age, she could only view as scandalmongers; finally that the application of psychoanalytic categories to intellectual biographies, which would seem to be the most fruitful way to proceed from Meinecke's insight, was unheard of in the 1920's.* In any case, German sociologists before the Nazi era were primarily concerned with unraveling and evaluating the theoretical corpus of Weber's work in methodology and the sociology of religion.† His principal introduction to American sociologists, apart from the international debate over his thesis on the Calvinist origins of the capitalist spirit, came via the heavy methodological work of Talcott Parsons (*The Structure of Social Action* [New York, 1937]), a formidable barrier to involvement in anything so profane as the master's own values and emotions;** and the single significant breach in that barrier, the biographical introduction of Gerth and Mills to their Weber anthology of 1948, did no more than superficially relate Weber's political writings to his "inordinately strong Oedipus situation."†† In postwar Germany, Weber's work,

---

mann, eds. [Köln, Opladen, 1963]), and finally the reliance of Mommsen himself on the *Lebensbild* at certain points (e.g., *Max Weber und die deutsche Politik*, pp. 2, 3, 19) all suggest the substantial, if not absolute, accuracy of the *Lebensbild*. In the lack, then, of any opportunity for immersion in the *Nachlass*, such as Dr. Mommsen's, this author has relied for biographical details primarily on Marianne Weber's work and on the *Jugendbriefe*, secondarily on the corroborating and supplementary material just mentioned.

* Meinecke (p. 143) felt it necessary to defend even Marianne Weber's delicate, and in many cases quite Victorian, treatment of her husband's relationships with his parents from "the reproach that she unveiled too much of the purely personal, most intimate experiences of Max Weber and his family." Meinecke warned that "Some will find the book indiscreet."

† The classical study of this sort is Alexander Schelting's *Max Webers Wissenschaftslehre* (Tübingen, 1934).

** See Günther Roth and Reinhard Bendix: *"Max Webers Einfluss auf die Amerikanische Soziologie," Kölner Zeitschrift für Soziologie und Sozialpsychologie,* Jahrg. 11, 1959, pp. 41–2.

†† Hans Gerth and C. Wright Mills: *From Max Weber, Essays in Sociology* (London, 1952), p. 29. Gerth and Mills's synoptic presenta-

largely buried and ignored under the Nazis,* was resurrected and almost universally celebrated for over a decade as the theoretical source of value-free sociology†—a not unreasonable position in the light of the values which had overwhelmed German scholarship in the preceding twelve years. But this celebration ended abruptly in 1959, with the publication by Wolfgang Mommsen of a penetrating study of Max Weber, based on exhaustive examination of unpublished materials, as a prime mover in German liberalism's embracement of imperialism in the mid-'90's and a ruthless advocate for most of his career of nationalist *Realpolitik.**
The fact that this indictment was couched in the framework of an extremely balanced and carefully researched presentation of Weber's political thought, which gave full credit to Weber's most brilliant insights into the politics of his age, gave Mommsen's work an impact on German scholarship, particularly the younger generation, which the earlier, much briefer and somewhat one-sided study of J. P. Mayer†† was never able to attain. As a result of Mommsen's book, an academic feud developed between the younger scholar and Johannes Winckelmann, the principal postwar editor of Weber's works and until then the most important German commentator on Weber's work. The antagonism engendered by Mommsen's work flared again at the 1964 meeting of

---

tion of Weber's breakdown and the family tensions preceding it neatly summarized the most relevant passages of the *Lebensbild,* but the only clear suggestion that this emotional constellation may have affected his work is in the last paragraph, where the authors write, "Surely Weber's life illustrates the manner in which a man's relation to political authority may be modeled upon his relation to family disciplines."

* See, for example, K. H. Pfeffer's *Die deutsche Schule der Soziologie* (Leipzig, 1939), where Weber is dismissed in two lines as a purveyor of empty ideal types and Nietzsche is discussed for ten pages.

† Ralf Dahrendorf: *"Betrachtungen zu einigen Aspekten der deutschen Soziologie," Kölner Zeitschrift für Soziologie und Sozialpsychologie,* Jahrg. 11, 1959, p. 144.

** Mommsen: *Max Weber und die deutsche Politik.*

†† J. P. Mayer: *Max Weber and German Politics* (London, 1944).

the *Deutsche Gesellschaft für Soziologie* in Heidelberg, commemorating the one hundredth anniversary of Weber's birth, when Herbert Marcuse launched a new attack on Weber. The principal accomplishment of Weber's insistence on separating values from science, according to Marcuse, was the subjection of sociology to nonscientific—i.e., irrational—values, which eluded altogether any rational questioning or testing. Thus, Weber's inaugural address at Freiburg "subjects value-free political economy with ruthless openness to the demands of imperialist power politics,"* and, "In Max Weber's analysis of industrial capitalism, philosophical, sociological-historical and political motives are fundamentally tied together." Though both Mommsen and Marcuse agreed that Weber's values shaped his theoretical work, Marcuse was broadening Mommsen's critique from an approach which linked Weber's values to the power ethos of Imperial Germany, to one which related his very concept of reason to a certain ethos of domination found both in technical science and advanced capitalism. Mommsen, in effect, was reaching back to an aspect of Weber which most contemporary German sociologists willfully ignored because it sullied their notion of Weberian, value-free sociology as a form of liberal scientism—a proud heirloom of German liberal thought and therefore a bulwark against both totalitarian ideology and against any possible tie between German liberalism and Nazism. One implication of Mommsen was that Weber's work was not value-free enough. Marcuse, however, went further than Mommsen and seemed to be arguing that it was ultimately not possible to exclude values from the very core of one's work as a social scientist, and that Weber's *and contemporary sociology's* insistence on such exclusion only laid open the social sciences to uncritical acceptance of the prevailing ethos of domination. That Mar-

---

* Herbert Marcuse: *"Industrialisierung und Kapitalismus,"* in *Max Weber und die Soziologie Heute, Verhandlungen des fünfzehnten deutschen Soziologentages,* p. 161. An English translation of this paper was published in *New Left Review* in 1965.

cuse's critique was directed as much at the norms of contemporary American social science as at those of Max Weber
was made evident at Heidelberg in the acid commentaries
on his paper by his American colleagues Benjamin Nelson
and Reinhard Bendix.*

Though Mommsen promptly dissociated himself from
the notion that he was a "public prosecutor against Max
Weber," and criticized, as "his defender," a detail in Marcuse's argument, it may have been the stimulus of Marcuse's
paper which in the following year led Mommsen to publish what is probably the most important analysis of the
relationship between Weber's values and his theoretical
oeuvre yet to appear, a beautifully organized fifty-six page
treatise called *"Universalgeschichtliches und politisches
Denken bei Max Weber."*† This work, when placed alongside Mommsen's book of 1959 and the earlier work of Salomon, Löwith and Steding, completes the integration of
Weber's work into its historical context: the book of 1959
carefully related the values and ideas expressed in Weber's
political sociology to his political and social environment;
the essay of 1965 relates the values in Weber's political
sociology to an implicit philosophy of history, which Mommsen sees as informing Weber's sociology as a whole and
which, if not directly influenced by Nietzsche, surely reveals
striking similarities between Weber and that philosopher.

To date, then, Mommsen, Marcuse, and their precursors
have produced a remarkable body of analysis relating Weber's values, on the one hand, to his theoretical work, and
on the other, to his historical position. But so far as I am
aware, no one has yet dealt with the problem implicit in
Meinecke's review of the *Lebensbild*: that of locating the

---

* Ibid., pp. 184–200.

† *Historische Zeitschrift*, Vol. 201, Dec. 1965, pp. 557–612. On p.
609, though questioning one of Marcuse's conclusions, Mommsen agrees
with Marcuse's view of Weber as "the classical representative of bourgeois individualist capitalism" and refers to *"das grosse Referat Mar-
cuses."*

source of Max Weber's values and politico-historical consciousness in the intimate tragedy of a modern Orestes. My own study of Max Weber has been devoted to the relationship between that tragedy and the values which permeated the sociologists's political, religious, and historical theory.

This work, then, makes no pretense of providing an overview or a synopsis of Weber's entire corpus—for such a survey the reader is directed to the recent books by Julien Freund and Reinhard Bendix,* or to the more compressed study in Lewis A. Coser's forthcoming history of sociological thought. Indeed, the first half of my work concerns only the entwining of biography and intellectual perception in Weber's career before his breakdown, focusing primarily on the personal and theoretical ramifications of his writings of 1890–5 on the agrarian and political crisis of the German East. The second half of the book, though not so well grounded as the first in biographical detail, deals with Weber's better-known and more intellectually mature writings in the period after his breakdown: the sociology of religion, the wartime political writings, and the massive but uncompleted *Wirtschaft und Gesellschaft*. In this section I have elaborated, on the basis of my analysis of the earlier work, a theoretical framework for a comprehension of the later, centering on Weber's perception of an historical antagonism between charisma and rationalization, and linking this dichotomy to his relationship to Nietzsche. I must acknowledge in this connection my debt to Wolfgang Mommsen's study of Weber and Nietzsche in the *Historische Zeitschrift* (mentioned above), which provided an invaluable starting point for my reflections.

---

* Julien Freund: *The Sociology of Max Weber*, trans. Mary Ilford (New York, 1968); Reinhard Bendix: *Max Weber, An Intellectual Portrait* (New York, 1962).

ABBREVIATIONS
USED IN FOOTNOTES
AND NOTES

Archiv   From 1904: *Archiv für Sozialwissenschaft und Sozial-politik.* Before 1904: *Archiv für Soziale Gesetzgebung und Statistik.*

Baumg.   Baumgarten, Eduard: *Max Weber, Werk und Person.* Tübingen, 1964.

E.S.   Weber, Max: *Economy and Society,* 3 vols., ed. Guenther Roth and Claus Wittich. Totowa, N.J., 1968.

G & M   Gerth, Hans, and C. Wright Mills: *From Max Weber, Essays in Sociology.* London, 1952.

Jb.   Weber, Max: *Jugendbriefe.* Tübingen, 1936.

Lebensb.   Weber, Marianne: *Max Weber, ein Lebensbild.* Heidelberg, 1950.

Mommsen: Max Weber   Mommsen, Wolfgang: *Max Weber und die deutsche Politik.* Tübingen, 1959.

Mommsen: "Universal."   Mommsen, Wolfgang: *"Universalgeschichtliches und Politisches Denken bei Max Weber," Historische Zeitschrift,* 1965, pp. 556–612.

M.W.z.G.   König, René, and Johannes Winckelmann, eds.: *Max Weber zum Gedächtnis.* Köln, Opladen, 1963 (*Sonderheft 7* of *Kölner Zeitschrift für Soziologie und Sozialpsychologie*).

Protestant Ethic   Weber, Max: *The Protestant Ethic and the Spirit of Capitalism,* trans. Talcott Parsons. New York, 1948.

P.S.   Weber, Max: *Gesammelte Politische Schriften.* Tübingen, 1958.

R.S.I Weber, Max: *Gesammelte Aufsätze zur Religionssoziologie*, Vol. 1. Tübingen, 1922. (Also *R.S.III* for Vol. 3.)

S.R. Weber, Max: *The Sociology of Religion*. Boston, 1967.

S.S.P. Weber, Max: *Gesammelte Aufsätze zur Soziologie und Sozialpolitik*. Tübingen, 1924.

S.W.G. Weber, Max: *Gesammelte Aufsätze zur Sozial und Wirtschaftsgeschichte*. Tübingen, 1924.

W.L. Weber, Max: *Gesammelte Aufsätze zur Wissenschaftslehre*. Tübingen, 1951.

W.u.G. Weber, Max: *Wirtschaft und Gesellschaft*. Köln, Berlin, 1964.

NOTES

Introduction

1. In his *Essays in Sociological Theory* (Glencoe, Ill., 1949; rev. ed. 1954).
2. Paul Honigsheim: *"Der Max-Weber-Kreis in Heidelberg," Kölner Vierteljahreshefte zur Soziologie,* Vol. 4 (1925), pp. 271–2.
3. Albert Salomon: *"Max Weber," Die Gesellschaft,* Vol. 2 (1925), pp. 131–53.
4. Ibid., p. 146.
5. Carl Schorske: "Politics and the Psyche in fin de siècle Vienna: Schnitzler and Hofmannsthal," *American Historical Review,* Vol. 66, July 1961, pp. 930–46.
6. Harry Pross: *Jugend, Eros, Politik* (Bern, München, Wien, 1964), pp. 31–7. See also Parsons: *Essays in Sociological Theory,* p. 318.
7. On the utility of nationalism as a "realistic" outlet for latent aggression, see Parsons: *Essays in Sociological Theory.*
8. Christian Graf von Krockow: *Die Entscheidung, eine Untersuchung über Ernst Jünger, Carl Schmitt, Martin Heidegger* (Stuttgart, 1958), p. 28.
9. For an interesting analysis of the negative integration of the German socialists into their society, see Guenther Roth: *The Social Democrats in Imperial Germany* (Totowa, N.J., 1964).

Chapter 1

1. Marianne Weber: *Max Weber, ein Lebensbild* (Heidelberg, 1950) (hereafter cited as *Lebensb.*), p. 198.
2. Ibid., 35.
3. Otto Döhner: *Das Hugenottengeschlecht Souchay de la Duboissière und seine Nachkommen* (Neustadt, 1961).
4. *Lebensb.,* pp. 45, 72.
5. Ibid., pp. 4–5.
6. Ibid., p. 20.
7. Ibid., p. 23.
8. Ibid., pp. 15–16.
9. Ibid., p. 33.
10. Ibid., p. 47.
11. Ibid., p. 54.
12. Ibid., pp. 44–5.

13. Ibid., p. 72.
14. Ibid., pp. 72–3.
15. Eduard Baumgarten: "Bemerkungen zu den Jugendbriefen," in Max Weber, Werk und Person (Tübingen, 1964) (hereafter cited as Baumg.), p. 308.
16. Lebensb., p. 69.
17. Ibid., p. 69; also p. 60.
18. Ibid., p. 73; Baumg., p. 308.
19. Lebensb., p. 80.
20. Quoted in Andreas Dorpalen: Heinrich von Treitschke (New Haven, 1957), p. 261.
21. For his critique of Kuno Fisher's Theatricalism, see Max Weber: Jugendbriefe (Tübingen, 1936), letter to Helene Weber, June 17, 1882, p. 53. Future references to this work will be designated by Jb. followed by the initials of the recipient (Max Weber, Sr.; Helene Weber; Hermann Baumgarten; Emmy Baumgarten; Klara Weber; Alfred Weber; Fritz Baumgarten), the date, and the page.
22. Jb., M.W.S., May 5, 1883, p. 74.
23. Jb., H.W., Dec. 15, 1882, p. 64.
24. Dorpalen: Heinrich von Treitschke, p. 178.
25. Lebensb., pp. 93–4.
26. Ibid., p. 94.
27. Jb., M.W.S., Feb. 23, 1884, p. 103.
28. Lebensb., p. 70.
29. Ibid., p. 93; my italics. Weber's own testimony to this appears, significantly, in a letter to his father; see Jb., M.W.S., March 15, 1885, p. 150.
30. Jb., M.W.S., Feb. 23, 1884, p. 103.
31. Lebensb., p. 190.
32. Ibid., p. 95.
33. Ibid., p. 96.
34. Ibid., p. 97.
35. Jb., H.W., July 8, 1894, p. 121; Baumg., pp. 29–30.
36. Lebensb., p. 101.
37. Ibid.
38. Jb., H.W., Dec. 6, 1885, p. 191; Baumg., pp. 36–7.
39. Lebensb., p. 98.
40. Ibid., p. 99.
41. Ibid., p. 98.
42. Ibid., p. 104.
43. Ibid., p. 105.
44. Ibid., p. 109.
45. Ibid., p. 139; Baumg., p. 54.
46. Ibid.
47. Lebensb., p. 129; Baumg., pp. 32, 311.
48. Jb., H.W., June 16, 1885, pp. 159–62; Baumg., pp. 32–3 (excerpt only).

CHAPTER 2

1. Baumg., p. 629; my italics.
2. Lebensb., p. 169.
3. Ibid., p. 189; Jb., H.B., Jan. 3, 1891, p. 326.
4. Max Weber: Gesammelte Aufsätze zur Sozial und Wirtschaftsgeschichte (Tübingen, 1924) (hereafter cited as S.W.G.), pp. 312–443.
5. See Schriften des Vereins für Sozialpolitik, Vol. 55, 1892.
6. Lebensb., p. 171.

7. Ibid.

8. *Jb.*, E.B., April 22, 1893, p. 367.

9. See Weber's complaints in *Baumg.*, p. 61.

10. Max Weber's letter to his siblings in 1918; *Baumg.*, p. 629. For a less drastic definition of Weber Sr.'s attitude, see *Lebensb.*, p. 114.

11. *Lebensb.*, p. 165.

12. *Baumg.*, p. 629; *Lebensb.*, p. 164.

13. *Jb.*, E.B., July 5, 1887, pp. 252–3.

14. *Lebensb.*, p. 167; letter to E.B. in *Baumg.*, pp. 47, 629; *Jb.*, E.B., Easter Sunday, 1887, p. 225.

15. *Lebensb.*, p. 167.

16. *Baumg.*, p. 629.

17. Quote in *Baumg.*, p. 631, from *Nachlass* material in his possession (E.A. II, 111).

18. *Lebensb.*, p. 111.

19. Ibid., p. 122.

20. Ibid., pp. 170, 192, 225–6.

21. Ibid., p. 122.

22. Ibid., p. 226.

23. Ibid., p. 271.

24. *Jb.*, H.W., March 16, 1887, pp. 217 ff.

25. *Jb.*, E.B., Feb. 17, 1888, p. 287.

26. Ernest Jones: *Hamlet and Oedipus* (New York, 1954), p. 87.

27. *Jb.*, E.B., May 8, 1887, p. 238.

28. *Jb.*, E.B., July 5, 1887, p. 253.

29. *Baumg.*, p. 627.

30. *Jb.*, E.B., July 5, 1887, p. 255.

31. Reference to Weber's parents in Heidelberg; *Jb.*, E.B., Oct. 21, 1887, p. 275.

32. *Jb.*, E.B., Oct. 21, 1887, p. 274.

33. *Jb.*, E.B., July 5, 1887, p. 255.

34. *Jb.*, E.B., Aug. 20, 1887, p. 269.

35. See pp. 274–7 of the *Jugendbriefe*.

36. *Jb.*, E.B., Oct. 21, 1887, p. 276.

37. *Lebensb.*, p. 206.

38. *Jb.*, E.B., Oct. 21, 1887, p. 278.

39. *Jb.*, E.B., Feb. 17, 1888, p. 286.

40. *Jb.*, E.B., Oct. 21, 1887, p. 280–1.

41. *Lebensb.*, pp. 214–15. See also *Jb.*, H.B., Jan 3, 1891, pp. 326–7; *Baumg.*, p. 75.

42. *Jb.*, H.B., April 30, 1888, p. 297.

43. *Jb.*, H.B., June 29, 1887, p. 248.

44. *Jb.*, H.B., April 25, 1887, p. 234.

45. Quoted in Erich Marck's biographical introduction to Baumgarten's *Historische und Politische Aufsätze und Reden* (Strassburg, 1894), pp. cix, cx.

46. *Jb.*, H.B., Nov. 8, 1884, p. 146.

47. *Jb.*, H.W., Aug. 15, 1888, pp. 305–6.

CHAPTER 3

1. The four summaries are: (1) the *"Ausblick"* of Weber's *Die*   *Verhältnisse der Landarbeiter im ostelbischen Deutsch-*

land (*Schriften des Vereins für Socialpolitik*, Vol. 55, 1892, pp. 774–804, partly reprinted in *Baumg.*, pp. 88–101); (2) *"Die ländliche Arbeitsverfassung"* (*Schriften des Vereins für Socialpolitik*, Vol. 58, 1893, reprinted in *S.W.G.*, pp. 444–69); (3) *"Entwicklungstendenzen in der Lage der ostelbischen Landarbeiter,"* *Archiv für Soziale Gesetzgebung und Statistik* (hereafter cited as *Archiv*), Vol. 7, 1894, pp. 1–41 (revised version in *Preussische Jahrbücher*, Sept. 1894, reprinted in *S.W.G.*, pp. 470–507); (4) *"Der Nationalstaat und die Volkswirtschaftspolitik,"* 1895, in Max Weber: *Gesammelte Politische Schriften* (Tübingen, 1958) (hereafter designated as *P.S.*), pp. 1–25. These will be referred to below by year of publication.

2. 1892: *Baumg.*, pp. 779, 790.
3. 1893: *S.W.G.*, p. 449.
4. 1894: *S.W.G.*, p. 472.
5. 1892: *Baumg.*, p. 93.
6. 1894: *S.W.G.*, p. 472.
7. Ibid., p. 450.
8. 1892: *Baumg.*, p. 97.
9. See Robert Pöhlmann's review of Weber's *Die römische Agrargeschichte* in the *Historische Zeitschrift* of 1893.
10. See Weber's first major work, *Zur Geschichte der Handelsgesellschaften im Mittelalter* (Stuttgart, 1889), published in *S.W.G.*, especially Part III, *"Die Familien und Arbeitsgemeinschaften,"* pp. 344–86. Lujo Brentano, in his obituary on Weber, said of this work: *"Es wurde darin*

der Nachweis geführt, wie sich die Handelsgesellschaften aus der alten Familiengemeinschaft bei Ausscheiden der einzelnen Mitglieder entwickalt hatten"; René König and Johannes Winckelmann, eds.: *Max Weber zum Gedächtnis* (Köln, Opladen, 1963) (*Sonderheft 7* of *Kölner Zeitschrift für Soziologie und Sozialpsychologie*) (hereafter cited as *M.W.z.G.*), pp. 40–1. It is noteworthy that the title of Weber's inaugural dissertation, of which the history of medieval trade just mentioned was an expansion, was *"Entwicklung des Solidarhaftprinzips und des Sondervermögens der offenen Handelsgesellschaften aus den Haushalts - und Gewerbegemeinschaften in den italienischen Städten,"* which strongly suggests that the original focus of the work was that same evolution from patriarchal to capitalist society (or from *Gemeinschaft* to *Gesellschaft*) which was Weber's framework between 1892 and 1895. (On title of thesis, see Winckelmann, *"Webers Dissertation,"* *M.W.z.G.*, p. 10.)

11. 1892: *Baumg.*, p. 94.
12. 1893: *S.W.G.*, pp. 450–1.
13. See Ferdinand Tönnies: *Community and Society* (New York, 1963), with valuable commentaries by Sorokin, Heberle, Loomis, and McKinney. Weber generally refers to the earlier system as *Patriarchalisch.* 1892: p. 790 (*Baumg.*, p. 91); 1893: *S.W.G.*, p. 450; 1894: *S.W.G.*, p. 488; 1895: *P.S.*, pp. 7–8.

He does, however, mention at one point *"ein festes gemeinschaftliches Interessenband um Herrn und Arbeiter";* 1894: *S.W.G.,* p. 488.

14. 1893: *S.W.G.,* p. 453.
15. 1895: *P.S.,* p. 16.
16. Ibid., pp. 19–20; also 1893: *S.W.G.,* p. 445.
17. 1895: *P.S.,* p. 23.
18. *Schriften des Vereins für Sozialpolitik,* Vol. 58, 1893, pp. 1, 220.
19. *Jb.,* H.B., April 18, 1892, p. 343; *Lebensb.,* p. 191.
20. Ibid.
21. *Lebensb.,* p. 154.
22. *Baumg.,* p. 689; *Lebensb.,* p. 191; *Jb.,* H.B., April 18, 1892, p. 343.
23. *Lebensb.,* p. 190.
24. *Baumg.,* p. 85; *Jb.,* E.B., April 22, 1893, p. 367.
25. *Jb.,* K.W., Jan. 9, 1893, p. 359, par. 1.
26. *Lebensb.,* p. 204.
27. *Baumg.,* p. 82; *Jb.,* H.W., Sept. 14, 1892, p. 350.
28. *Lebensb.,* p. 207.
29. Ibid.
30. Ibid., pp. 209–10.
31. *Jb.,* H.W., May 3, 1884, p. 115.
32. *Jb.,* E.B., Sept. 2, 1893, p. 374.
33. *Jb.,* E.B., April 22, 1893, p. 368.
34. *Jb.,* Lujo Brentano, Feb. 20, 1893, pp. 363–5.
35. 1892: *Baumg.,* p. 93.
36. Ibid., p. 95.
37. 1892: *Baumg.,* pp. 90–1.
38. Ibid., p. 96.
39. 1895: *P.S.,* p. 21.
40. 1893: *S.W.G.,* p. 445.
41. Ibid., p. 450.
42. S. R. Tirrell: *German Agrarian Politics After Bismarck's*

Fall (New York, 1951), p. 237, discusses Bennigsen's support for the Farmer's League in the tariff debates of 1893.

43. Wolfgang Mommsen: *Max Weber und die deutsche Politik* (Tübingen, 1959) (hereafter cited as *Mommsen: Max Weber*), p. 109: *"Ich selbst trage meinen Namen von Westfalischer Leinwand . . ."*
44. 1893: *S.W.G.,* pp. 454–5.
45. 1893: *S.W.G.,* pp. 455–6.
46. 1893: *S.W.G.,* p. 456.
47. Ibid., p. 465.
48. *Jb.,* E.B., April 22, 1893, p. 368.
49. 1893: *S.W.G.,* p. 469.
50. Arnold Sachse: *Althoff und sein Werk* (Berlin, 1928), pp. 112–13.
51. *Lebensb.,* p. 229.
52. Ibid., pp. 215 ff., 219; *Jb.,* K.W., July 15, 1893, p. 371, and H.W., July 26, 1893 (probably should be dated July 29), p. 373.
53. *Lebensb.,* p. 230.
54. *Mommsen: Max Weber,* fn. p. 3, refers to three separate publications of Weber's memories of Althoff in October and November, 1911.
55. Sachse: *Althoff und sein Werk,* p. 114.
56. See Döhner: *Das Hugenottengeschlecht . . . ,* p. 317 (*"Magenlähmung"*); *Lebensb.,* p. 267 (*"Magenblutung"*).
57. *Lebensb.,* p. 267.
58. *Jb.,* K.W., April 28, 1893, p. 369.
59. *Jb.,* H.W., July 26, 1893, p. 372.
60. *Lebensb.,* p. 220.
61. Vol. 7, 1894, pp. 1–41.
62. Max Weber: *"Entwicklungs-*

tendenzen in der Lage der ostelbischen Landarbeiter," *Preussische Jahrbücher,* Vol. 77, Sept. 1894, pp. 437–73. The reprint in Weber's *S.W.G.,* pp. 470–507, is of this slightly altered version, to which I shall refer except where it differs more than trivially from the *Archiv* version. For the sake of simplicity, I shall in general refer to the reprint in the *Gesammelte Aufsätze* (1894: *S.W.G.,* pp. 470–507) as though it were the reprint of the *Archiv* article. (It was listed as such in *S.W.G.* and was long thought to be such a reprint; the error was only revealed in Johannes Winckelmann's *"Verzeichnis der Schriften Max Webers,"* in his edition of *Max Weber, Soziologie, Weltgeschichtliche Analysen, Politik* (Stuttgart, 1956), p. 491.)

63. *S.W.G.,* p. 445.
64. Ibid., p. 471.
65. *P.S.,* p. 20.
66. *S.W.G.,* p. 472.
67. Ibid., p. 473.
68. Ibid., p. 472.
69. Ibid., p. 476.
70. Ibid.
71. *S.W.G.,* p. 479.
72. Ibid., p. 474.
73. Ibid., pp. 472–3, 489.
74. I refer here to *S.W.G.,* pp. 450–6, taken from *Schriften des Vereins für Socialpolitik,* Vol. 58, 1893, pp. 69–75.
75. I shall refer in this section only to those parts of the *Archiv* study that are taken over whole into *S.W.G.*
76. Ibid., pp. 477 *ff.*
77. Ibid., p. 488.
78. Ibid.
79. Ibid., pp. 489–90.
80. Ibid., pp. 490–504; *Archiv,* Vol. 7, 1894, pp. 20–38.
81. *S.W.G.,* p. 493.
82. Sombart, letter dated Oct. 5, 1893, in the *International Institute for Social History,* Amsterdam.
83. See Sombart's letter to Lang dated *"Pfingsten, 1894"* in the *International Institute for Social History,* Amsterdam.
84. *Schriften des Vereins für Socialpolitik,* Vol. 58, p. 113.
85. *Archiv,* Vol. 7, 1894, p. 38 (*S.W.G.,* p. 504).
86. *Schriften des Vereins für Socialpolitik,* Vol. 58, p. 88.
87. *Archiv,* Vol. 7, 1894, p. 38.
88. *S.W.G.,* p. 507.
89. *Archiv,* Vol. 7, 1894, p. 36.
90. See *S.W.G.,* pp. 492, 496, 498, 502 *ff.*
91. *S.W.G.,* p. 503.
92. *Baumg.,* p. 96.
93. *Mommsen: Max Weber,* pp. 78–80.
94. In *Germany and World Politics in the Twentieth Century* (New York, 1960), pp. 72–109. For a detailed discussion of the various representatives of liberal imperialism, see Friedrich C. Sell: *Die Tragödie des deutschen Liberalismus* (Stuttgart, 1953), pp. 275–98.

Chapter 4

1. *Lebensb.*, p. 260.
2. Ibid., pp. 232, 260.
3. The letter, dated Oct. 15, 1896, is quoted in *Mommsen: Max Weber*, p. 142.
4. *Lebensb.*, pp. 264–5.
5. Ibid., p. 267.
6. Ibid., p. 274.
7. Ibid., p. 276.
8. Ibid.
9. Ibid., p. 299.
10. Ibid., pp. 278–300.
11. Ibid., pp. 280, 277, 297.
12. Ibid., p. 287.
13. Sigmund Freud: "Mourning and Melancholia," in *Collected Papers* (London, 1953), Vol. IV, pp. 155–6.
14. Ibid., p. 158.
15. Max Lerner, ed.: *Essential Works of John Stuart Mill* (New York, 1961), Preface of Max Lerner, pp. 3–4.
16. Ibid., p. 83.
17. Ibid., p. 87.
18. Ibid., p. 85.
19. *Jb.*, H.B., Dec. 31, 1889, p. 324, H.B., Jan. 3, 1891, p. 330.
20. *Lebensb.*, p. 38.

Chapter 5

1. Wolfgang Mommsen: *"Universalgeschichtliches und Politisches Denken bei Max Weber,"* Historische Zeitschrift, 1965, pp. 565–75; further references to this work will be cited as *Mommsen: "Universal."*
2. Max Weber: *Gesammelte Aufsätze zur Soziologie und Sozialpolitik* (Tübingen, 1924), p. 402; future references to this work will be cited as *S.S.P.*
3. For a similar interpretation, see E. Baumgarten's *"Einleitung"* to Winckelmann: *Max Weber, Soziologie, Weltgeschichtliche Analysen, Politik*, p. xvii.
4. See *Mommsen: "Universal.,"* p. 573: Christoph Steding: *Politik und Wissenschaft bei Max Weber* (Breslau, 1932), pp. 88–9; Gerhard Masur: *Prophets of Yesterday* (London, 1963), pp. 192, 202; Max Scheler: *Schriften zur Soziologie und Weltanschauungslehre* (Bern, 1963), p. 14; Ernst Nolte: *Three Faces of Fascism* (New York, 1965), p. 449.
5. *Lebensb.*, p. 236.
6. *Mommsen: Max Weber*, p. 598. Hans Gerth and C. Wright Mills: *From Max Weber, Essays in Sociology* (London, 1952), p. 166; hereafter cited as *G & M*.
7. *S.S.P.*, p. 414.

CHAPTER 6

1. *Baumg.*, pp. 554–5.
2. For the best example of this early use of Marx, see Weber's review of Friedrich Naumann's *"Was heisst Christlich-Sozial"* in *Christliche Welt*, Vol. 8, 1894, p. 475.
3. On Marx and Weber, see *Baumg.*, pp. 571–80; Karl Löwith: *"Max Weber und Karl Marx,"* *Archiv*, Vol. 67, 1932, Nos. 1 and 2, reprinted in Löwith: *Gesammelte Abhandlungen* (Stuttgart, 1960), pp. 1–67; *G & M*, pp. 46–50; Talcott Parsons: *The Structure of Social Action* (Glencoe, Ill., 1949), pp. 503–13; H. Stuart Hughes: *Consciousness and Society* (New York, 1958), pp. 316–23; Theodor Schieder: *The State and Society in Our Time* (New York, 1962), p. 66; Judith Janeska-Bendl: *Methodologische Aspekte des Idealtypus* (Berlin, 1965), pp. 89–114; Eugene Fleischmann: *"De Weber à Nietzsche,"* *Archives Européennes de Sociologie*, 1964, pp. 193–8. Fleischmann's emphasis on an *early* influence of Marx on Weber does not appear well founded to me.
4. Max Weber: *The Protestant Ethic and the Spirit of Capitalism*, trans. Talcott Parsons, (New York, 1948), pp. 72, 90; hereafter cited as *Protestant Ethic*.
5. *Baumg.*, p. 603.
6. Max Weber: *Gesammelte Aufsätze zur Wissenschaftslehre* (Tübingen, 1951), pp. 166–7; hereafter cited as *W.L.*
7. *Cf.* Schieder: *The State and Society in Our Time*, p. 66; R. Aron: *"Max Weber und die Machtpolitik"* in *Max Weber und die Soziologie Heute, Verhandlungen des fünfzehnten deutschen Soziologentages* (Tübingen, 1965), p. 114.
8. *P.S.*, p. 309; also pp. 520, 527, 535.
9. *Ibid.*, p. 320; *S.S.P.*, p. 498.
10. *P.S.*, p. 499.
11. *S.S.P.*, p. 499.
12. *Ibid.*, pp. 505–11.
13. *Ibid.*, p. 495.
14. Max Weber: *Wirtschaft und Gesellschaft* (Köln, Berlin, 1964) (hereafter cited as *W.u.G.*), pp. 164, 723, 727. Also see the new English translation of this work, edited by Guenther Roth and Claus Wittich: *Economy and Society*, 3 vols. (Totowa, N.J., 1968), pp. 223, 983, 988; this work will hereafter be cited as *E.S.* All quotes from this work, however, are my translations from the German edition—the English edition was not available at the time of writing.
15. *P.S.*, pp. 244, 251, 315, 318.
16. *W.u.G.*, p. 218 (*E.S.*, p. 293).
17. *S.S.P.*, p. 508.
18. *Cf. Mommsen: "Universal.,"* p. 601.
19. Friedrich Nietzsche: *The*

Genealogy of Morals, trans. Francis Golffing (New York, 1956), Third Essay, Chapters XXIV–XXVII, pp. 286–98.

20. *S.S.P.,* p. 414.
21. E.g., in his letter to Harnack of 1906, cited in *Mommsen: "Universal.,"* p. 574, fn. 48.

CHAPTER 7

1. *Protestant Ethic,* pp. 23–7.
2. Ibid., pp. 113–14; *Archiv,* Vol. 21, 1905, p. 22.
3. *S.S.P.,* pp. 462–70.
4. Ernst Troeltsch: *Aufsätze zur Geistesgeschichte und Religionssoziologie* (Tübingen, 1925), pp. 168–74.
5. *Cf.* Max Weber: *The Sociology of Religion* (Boston, 1967) (hereafter cited as *S.R.*), p. 222, and Sigmund Freud: *Civilization and Its Discontents* (London, 1949), p. 69.
6. Freud: *Civilization and Its Discontents,* p. 80.
7. *W.u.G.,* pp. 415, 917 (*E.S.,* pp. 531, 1204–5).
8. *"Antikritisches Schlusswort"* (1910), reprinted in *Baumg.,* p. 176.
9. *S.R.,* p. 176.
10. *W.u.G.,* p. 871 (*E.S.,* p. 1153).
11. *S.R.,* p. 56.
12. Max Weber: *Gesammelte Aufsätze zur Religionssoziologie* (Tübingen, 1922), Vol. 1 (hereafter cited as *R.S.I;* also *R.S.III* will be referred to: Vol. 3), p. 257.
13. See *S.R.,* Chapter V, "The Religious Congregation, Preaching and Pastoral Care"; *W.u.G.,* pp. 355–60 (*E.S.,* pp. 452–7).
14. *S.R.,* Chapters VI, VII, and VIII; *W.u.G.,* pp. 368–405 (*E.S.,* pp. 468–518).

15. *W.u.G.,* pp. 422–33, 447–71 (*E.S.,* pp. 541–3, 576–610; *S.R.,* pp. 164–83, 207–45); *Archiv,* Vol. 41, 1916, pp. 387–421, revised version in *R.S.I,* pp. 536–73 (*G & M,* pp. 322–59).
16. *W.u.G.,* p. 423 (*E.S.,* pp. 542–3).
17. See letter to Harnack, cited in *Mommsen: "Universal.,"* p. 574, fn. 48.
18. *W.u.G.,* pp. 735, 737 (*E.S.,* pp. 998–9, 1002). See also Albert Salomon: *"Max Weber,"* *Die Gesellschaft,* 1926, No. 1, pp. 139–40.
19. Letter to Harnack of 1906, quoted in *Mommsen: "Universal.,"* p. 574.
20. *W.u.G.,* p. 424 (*E.S.,* p. 544).
21. Ibid., pp. 425–6 (*E.S.,* p. 545); *S.R.,* p. 171.
22. *W.u.G.,* p. 426 (*E.S.,* pp. 546–7).
23. Ibid.
24. Ibid.
25. Ibid., p. 427 (*E.S.,* p. 548); *S.R.,* p. 173.
26. Ibid.
27. *S.R.,* p. 174; *W.u.G.,* p. 427 (*E.S.,* p. 549).
28. *W.u.G.,* pp. 428–9 (*E.S.,* p. 550).
29. See above, fn. 15.
30. *R.S.I,* pp. 544–5.
31. *Cf. W.u.G.,* pp. 456–64 (*E.S.,* pp. 590–601).

32. *R.S.I*, p. 549.
33. *"Zweckrationale Handeln,"* *R.S.I*, p. 553.
34. *R.S.I*, pp. 563–4.
35. Ibid., p. 556.
36. Baumgarten, who reprints both passages, also remarks on the development from one to the other. See *Baumg.*, pp. 472 ff.
37. *R.S.I*, pp. 561, 563.
38. See *Baumg.*, pp. 472–80.
39. *R.S.I*, p. 563.
40. *Baumg.*, p. 677.

41. *W.u.G.*, p. 396 (*E.S.*, p. 506).
42. *S.S.P.*, pp. 466, 470.
43. *R.S.I*, p. 564.
44. Ibid., pp. 569–70.
45. Ibid., p. 571.
46. *Baumg.*, p. 491.
47. Ibid., p. 493.
48. Ibid., p. 495, fn. 1.
49. Ibid., p. 496.
50. Ibid., p. 498.
51. *W.L.*, p. 593; *G & M*, p. 152.
52. *P.S.*, p. 495; *G & M*, p. 79.
53. *W.L.*, p. 596.
54. Ibid., p. 592.

CHAPTER 8

1. *Cf. W.u.G.*, p. 725 (*E.S.*, pp. 985–6).
2. *W.u.G.*, p. 702 (*E.S.*, p. 954).
3. Ibid., p. 60 (*E.S.*, p. 85).
4. Ibid.
5. Ibid., pp. 811–12 (*E.S.*, pp. 1088–9).
6. Ibid., p. 810 (*E.S.*, p. 1086).
7. *R.S.I*, p. 271.
8. *W.u.G.*, pp. 826, 827 (*E.S.*, pp. 1104, 1105).
9. Ibid., pp. 813, 828 (*E.S.*, pp. 1090, 1106).
10. Ibid., p. 828 (*E.S.*, p. 1106).
11. Ibid., p. 830 (*E.S.*, p. 1108).
12. Ibid., pp. 829–30 (*E.S.*, pp. 1107–8).
13. *P.S.*, p. 532, and below, pp. 247 ff.
14. *W.u.G.*, p. 778 (*E.S.*, p. 1050). See also *W.u.G.*, p. 859 (*E.S.*, p. 1141), and *Baumg.*, p. 449.
15. *R.S.I*, pp. 241 ff.
16. *W.u.G.*, p. 395 (*E.S.*, p. 505).
17. Ibid., p. 430 (*E.S.*, pp. 552–3).

18. *R.S.I*, pp. 257–8.
19. *P.S.*, p. 270.
20. *W.u.G.*, pp. 832–40 (*E.S.*, pp. 1111–20).
21. Ibid., pp. 832, 833–4, 835 (*E.S.*, pp. 1111, 1112–13, 1115).
22. Ibid., pp. 832–40 (*E.S.*, pp. 1111–20).
23. Ibid., p. 810 (*E.S.*, p. 1086).
24. Ibid., p. 835 (*E.S.*, p. 1114); my italics.
25. *P.S.*, pp. 258–74 and *passim*.
26. Ibid., p. 496.
27. *G & M*, pp. 84–5; *P.S.*, p. 501.
28. *P.S.*, p. 260.
29. *W.u.G.*, pp. 834, 841 (*E.S.*, pp. 1113, 1121).
30. Ibid., pp. 841–2 (*E.S.*, pp. 1121–2).
31. *P.S.*, p. 532.
32. Ibid., pp. 244–58.
33. Ernst Nolte: *"Max Weber vor dem Fascismus,"* Der Staat, Vol. 2, 1963, No. 1, p. 17.
34. *R.S.I*, p. 561.

CHAPTER 9

1. *P.S.*, pp. 232–79.
2. Ibid., p. 243.
3. *W.u.G.*, p. 839 (*E.S.*, p. 1119).
4. Honigsheim: "*Der Max-Weber-Kreis in Heidelberg*," pp. 167–8; *Lebensb.*, p. 277.
5. Letter from Sombart to Otto Lang, Dec. 22, 1900, *International Institute for Social History*, Amsterdam.
6. *W.u.G.*, pp. 838–9 (*E.S.*, p. 1119); *P.S.*, pp. 241–3. See also *W.u.G.*, p. 377 (*E.S.*, pp. 479–80).
7. *P.S.*, p. 242.
8. Ibid., p. 252.
9. R. Boehringer: *Mein Bild von Stefan George* (Düsseldorf, München, 1968), pp. 44 ff.
10. *Lebensb.*, p. 496.
11. Boehringer: *Mein Bild von Stefan George*, p. 85.
12. Georg Simmel: *Zur Philosophie der Kunst* (Potsdam, 1922), pp. 29–46, 74–9.
13. Edgar Salin: *Um Stefan George* (München, 1954), p. 107.
14. Ernst Troeltsch: "*Die Revolution in der Wissenschaft*," *Schmollers Jahrbuch*, Vol. XLV, 1921, No. 4, p. 72.
15. Victor A. Schmitz: *Gundolf* (Düsseldorf, 1965), p. 44.
16. Friedrich Gundolf: *Briefe* (Amsterdam, 1965), p. 11.
17. Ibid., pp. 37, 48.
18. Salin: *Um Stefan George*, p. 338.
19. Kurt Hildebrandt: *Erinnerungen an Stefan George und Seine Kreis* (Bonn, 1965), pp. 179–81; Honigsheim, in *M.W.z.G.*, p. 239; *Lebensb.*, pp. 502–7; Friedrich Wolters: *Stefan George und die Blätter für die Kunst* (Berlin, 1930), p. 471.
20. Honigsheim, in *M.W.z.G.*, pp. 234–49; *Lebensb.*, pp. 496 ff., 542–3; Schmitz: *Gundolf*, p. 174.
21. *Lebensb.*, p. 500.
22. Wolters: *Stefan George und die Blätter für die Kunst*, p. 475.
23. *Protestant Ethic*, p. 154.
24. *Lebensb.*, p. 503.
25. Ibid.
26. Ibid.
27. Ibid.
28. Ibid., p. 506.
29. Wolters: *Stefan George und die Blätter für die Kunst*, p. 476.
30. *S.S.P.*, p. 446.
31. Ibid., p. 453.
32. *Lebensb.*, p. 562.
33. *Baumg.*, p. 494.
34. *M.W.z.G.*, p. 34.
35. Hildebrandt: *Erinnerungen an Stefan George und Seine Kreis*, p. 180. George referred to Weber's study in the third volume of the *Jahrbuch für die geistige Bewegung* (1912).
36. *Lebensb.*, pp. 509–10.
37. Honigsheim in *M.W.z.G.*, p. 172.
38. Ibid., p. 240.
39. Ibid., p. 241.
40. *Lebensb.*, p. 509.
41. See "*Zwischen zwei Gesetzen*" (an anti-pacifist polemic) in *P.S.*, pp. 141 ff.

42. Georg Lukacs: *"Von der Armut am Geiste,"* *Neue Blätter*, 1912, No. 5–6, pp. 70, 74.
43. Ibid., p. 72.
44. Ibid., pp. 73–4.
45. Ibid., p. 82.
46. Ibid., pp. 88–9.
47. *Lebensb.*, p. 536.
48. Ibid., pp. 508–9.
49. Ibid., p. 532; Georg Lukacs: *Die Formen der Seele* (Berlin, 1911), pp. 197–227.
50. *Baumg.*, pp. 641–2.
51. *Lebensb.*, p. 409.
52. Ibid., p. 412.
53. Ibid., p. 410.
54. Ibid., p. 414.
55. *Baumg.*, p. 644.
56. Ibid., p. 648.
57. Interview with Eduard Baumgarten, July 13, 1968.
58. Robert Michels cites this work in his study of Schmoller: *Bedeutende Männer* (Leipzig, 1927), p. 105.
59. Interview with Else Jaffé, July 15, 1968.
60. *Lebensb.*, p. 422.
61. Ibid., p. 404.
62. Letter to the author from Eduard Baumgarten, July 28, 1968.
63. *Lebensb.*, pp. 421–3.
64. Ibid., p. 428 (a letter of 1908).
65. Interview with Else Jaffé, July 15, 1968, and *Baumg.*, p. 667.
66. *Lebensb.*, pp. 532–8.
67. Ibid., p. 511.
68. *R.S.I*, p. 561.
69. *P.S.*, p. 536; *G & M*, p. 117. (The last two sentences are Gerth's translation.)
70. *Baumg.*, p. 624.
71. Lukacs's words as recalled by Honigsheim, *M.W.z.G.*, p. 186.
72. Quoted in *Baumg.*, pp. 498–9.
73. *Baumg.*, p. 499.
74. *P.S.*, pp. 272, 299.
75. Edgar Salin: *"Max Weber une seine Freunde,"* in *Die Zeit* (Hamburg), April 24, 1964.
76. *Lebensb.*, pp. 690–1.
77. Ibid., p. 648.
78. Ibid.

CONCLUSION

1. See *Mommsen: Max Weber*, pp. 299–304.
2. *W.u.G.*, pp. 832–40.
3. Ibid., pp. 348, 349, 467.
4. Friedrich Nietzsche: *Werke in Drei Bände* (München, 1954–6), Schlechta edn., Vol. 1, pp. 88, 93.
5. *P.S.*, p. 270.
6. *Lebensb.*, pp. 426, 456.
7. See above, p. 144 *ff*.

INDEX

A Note About the Author

Arthur B. Mitzman was born in Newark, New Jersey, in 1931 and did his undergraduate work at Syracuse University and Columbia University. He received an M.A. in history from Columbia in 1959 and a Ph.D. in the History of Ideas from Brandeis University in 1963. He taught at Brooklyn College and Goddard College and was an assistant professor of history at the University of Rochester from 1965 to 1969. He is now Associate Professor in Social Theory at Simon Fraser University in Vancouver, British Columbia. Mr. Mitzman is married and the father of two children.

A NOTE ON THE TYPE

The text of this book was set in Caledonia, a Linotype face designed by W. A. Dwiggins. It belongs to the family of printing types called "modern face" by printers—a term used to mark the change in style of type letters that occurred about 1800. Caledonia borders on the general design of Scotch Modern, but is more freely drawn than that letter.

The book was composed, printed and bound by The Haddon Craftsmen, Inc., Scranton, Pennsylvania. The typography and binding design are by Anita Karl.